The Univ

what was already poi- $\overline{\text{Li}}$
about TWWOO
    - half-humans
    - cyborgs (Tin Man)
    - utopia

The Universe of Oz

Essays on Baum's Series and Its Progeny

Edited by KEVIN K. DURAND
and MARY K. LEIGH

McFarland & Company, Inc., Publishers
Jefferson, North Carolina, and London

ALSO OF INTEREST: *Buffy Meets the Academy: Essays on the Episodes and Scripts as Texts.* Edited by Kevin K. Durand (McFarland 2009)

LIBRARY OF CONGRESS CATALOGUING-IN-PUBLICATION DATA

The uviverse of Oz : essays on Baum's series and its progeny /
   edited by Kevin K. Durand and Mary K. Leigh.
     p.   cm.
   Includes bibliographical references and index.

   ISBN 978-0-7864-4628-5
   softcover : 50# alkaline paper ∞

   1. Baum, L. Frank (Lyman Frank), 1856–1919 — Criticism and
interpretation.   2. Baum, L. Frank (Lyman Frank), 1856–1919. Wizard
of Oz.   3. Baum, L. Frank (Lyman Frank), 1856–1919 — Adaptations.
4. Baum, L. Frank (Lyman Frank), 1856–1919 — Stories, plots, etc.
5. Baum, L. Frank (Lyman Frank), 1856–1919 — Film and video
adaptations.   6. Fantasy fiction, American — Film and video adaptations.
7. Children's stories, American — History and criticism.   8. Fantasy
fiction, American — History and criticism.   9. Fantasy films — History
and criticism.   10. Oz (Imaginary place) I. Durand, Kevin K. J.
(Kevin Karl Jones), 1967– II. Leigh, Mary K. III. Title: Baum's
series and its progeny.
PS3503.A923Z89   2010
813'.4 — dc22   2009051575

British Library cataloguing data are available

Cover images ©2010 Shutterstock

Manufactured in the United States of America

McFarland & Company, Inc., Publishers
  Box 611, Jefferson, North Carolina 28640
   www.mcfarlandpub.com

Contents

Preface; or, Scholars Walk the Yellow Brick Road

The turn of the last century brought with it a book that so radically changed the face of children's literature, and indeed, of popular literature, that even commercials in the Super Bowl of 2009 featured its characters. L. Frank Baum's vision in *The Wonderful Wizard of Oz* is one that so readily resonated with generations of readers, young and old alike, that Hollywood waded into the Land of Oz, and in 1939, one of the most beloved movies of all time splashed across the silver screen. However, just because the movie, with its sepia-toned Kansas and Technicolor Oz, and the books before it, with their intricate alternative universes, have captivated audiences — both movie-going and reading ones — does not mean that either is necessarily worthy of the scholarly study that has preceded this volume, to say nothing of this volume itself. But, the universe of *The Wizard of Oz* has piqued far more than passing interest as entertainment. The world of Oz has been among the most fertile grounds for discussions of everything from imperialism to friendship, from economics to urban planning, from psychology to philosophy to religion to literature. The spin-offs and tie-ins that Baum's world has inspired have been far from pale imitations. Gregory Maguire's *Wicked* trilogy (which looks set to become longer still) has taken up the baton admirably, refocusing the discussions to matters of good and evil, objectivism and perspective, race, gender and sex, among others. In the intervening years, *The Wiz* provided an invaluable source for discussions of race in America (and in Oz). This is to say little about the vast reach into the cultural psyche of one generation after another, from literature to commercials.

Simply put, Oz is that rare world that entertains and challenges. It is a place where scholars find rich levels of meaning, intriguing insights into the human condition, and, at times, perplexing riddles that tax imagination and creativity. But, of course, a fan of the universe would hold such views. Any-

1

time one comes to popular culture, one is faced with the question of popular culture scholarship — to what extent is popular culture scholarship merely an academic playground in which self-important folks read far more into a work than it contains? Or, perhaps, the question is even more fundamental: Is popular culture scholarship worthwhile scholarship at all?

To those who might dismiss such things as *The Wizard of Oz* as a passing fancy, I shan't point out its enduring legacy, its far-reaching influence on the language of culture, or its firm grip on the imagination of countless people. Instead, I shall point beyond *The Wizard* in its many incarnations to the practice of scholarship itself, whether of Oz or of any popular culture text, literary or visual or both. Indeed, I shall point to the (arguably) greatest of the philosophers, Plato.

Plato began the discipline that has come to be known as literary criticism in the context of pondering such questions of moment as Truth, Knowledge, and Virtue. While he could not have anticipated Foucault, Adorno, Lacan, Kristeva, or hooks, all literary critics owe the founding of our art to Plato. Whatever his reaction to the theatre and literature of his day (e.g., Aristophanes's *The Clouds*, Homer's *Iliad*) as works of art and entertainment, one thing is clear — he took them seriously. In fact, Plato took them so seriously that in one of his greatest works, *Republic*, when constructing the "ideal city," he has Socrates and his interlocutors cast out the writers because their work was so potentially ensnaring of the mind. A brief reflection on Plato's own work would leave a scholar to wonder whether or not he would have had those interlocutors consign him to banishment as well. In other words, Plato was a far spinner of words and yarns himself. Whatever the case, both Plato and his student, Aristotle, took seriously the popular culture of their day, and would, should they be dropped into the twenty-first century, take seriously many of the works of popular culture in this new era.

This should not be taken to suggest that all pop culture is created equal. No, much like the pigs in *1984*, some is much more equal than others. By some accounts, no more than ten percent of that which finds its way to today's satellite streams is worthy of the bandwidth it consumes. Even if we suppose that that number is high, we are left with the following analogy. Something on the order of less than ten percent of all of the works of the ancient playwrights and poets have survived, and much of that which has survived was not considered the ultimate example of its form even then. Take, for example, Aristophanes's play *The Clouds*. In the competition in which it was first performed, it finished third in its category (comedy), behind two works that have not survived the ravages of time. And that was only for the year 432 BCE. Thus, the work was not even considered the best of its year, much less its era, although, it must also be noted that Plato also argued in *Apology* that the play was instrumental in the ultimate conviction and execution of philosophy's first martyr, Socrates.

As a matter of importance and meaning, there is no question that popular culture vehicles are among the most effective for exploring topics of critical importance. Plato used Homer to discuss the nature of the good life, of becoming a good human being. So, too, Gregory Maguire provides a template for much of the same conversation. In Homer, we find notions of heroic virtue; in *Wicked,* we are reminded how influential the perceptions of the masses are when ascribing words like "good" and "bad" to actions or people. In Aristotle, we see an argument about the nature of possible friendship illustrated with examples drawn from the popular opinion of Athens. For Aristotle, friendship must be between equals — never could a Lion, a Scarecrow, a Tin Man, and a little girl be considered as even potential friends. In Baum, we see friendship among those very different beings, and thus, perhaps, a development of our ability to understand the nature and character of friendship.

Having argued for taking popular culture seriously, it is of some importance to explore further the matter of why, even among those sympathetic to the foregoing argument, popular culture studies are often relegated to special topics classes taught infrequently and are considered to have a distinctly second-class status within academia. I have argued elsewhere (*Buffy Meets the Academy*) that the primary reason for this is the shape of popular culture studies itself. I will revisit that argument briefly here, and expand some of its implications to address the peculiarities of the universe of Oz. The most singular difference between the two popular culture texts is that the one (*Buffy*) began as a television series that has progressed to written work (e.g., *Season Eight*) while the other (*Oz*) began as a significant literary series before moving to the big screen and stage.

While it is clear that there is not a universally accepted approach to popular culture studies, there is also no universally accepted approach to studies of Socrates, literary criticism, history, psychology, or basket-weaving. When one engages the foregoing (with the possible exception of basket-weaving), however, it is clear that there is a seriousness to the scholarship that is often absent from the treatment of popular culture. Even Faulkner, for example, dabbled in screenplay writing, but it is not his Hollywood career that is fodder for the American Lit course. Scholars engage the text under examination in a deliberative fashion, whatever critical framework is being employed by the scholar. This is often not the case in popular culture studies. Too often, popular culture studies are drowned in fluff.

I tend to divide the field of popular culture studies into five general sorts: Critical Engagement, Theory Exemplar/Corrective, Point of Departure, Cultural Solipsism, and "Isn't that neat?" The "Isn't that neat?" category can, potentially, have a somewhat different character when the discussion is a text that moves from literary to visual instead of one that is almost wholly visual. While a group of friends sitting around watching television might well draw "neat" parallels between the various episodes, the "water cooler" discussion surrounding a text that becomes visual actually harkens back to an ancient phenomenon roundly criticized by Plato — the practice of the "lovers of sights and sounds."

A brief digression into the world of the classical Siskels, Eberts, and Roepers is helpful for our discussion. Imagine ancient theatergoers returning from a stirring performance of *Oedipus, the King*. Gathering in the *agora*, they begin to discuss how well the actors have done in their varying roles, comparing them to previous actors in earlier productions, discussing the sets, the singing of the choruses, and the general tone of the production. With a certain self-satisfaction, they conclude not only that this was a better-than-average performance, but that it lacked some certain panache of the best performances. In other words, what takes place is a conversation that is nearly entirely self-referential with little or no introduction of the apparatus of critical theory. Indeed, these "lovers of sights and sounds" have been fascinated with what Aristotle called "the spectacle," and their reflections are little deeper than superficial.

Such "criticism" is with us still, indeed, will be with us always, however, it sheds little light for all its heat and bother. When discussing a popular culture text as deeply layered and textured as Oz, such a conversation might well be little more than a discussion of how well the movie captures the book, what it leaves out, what it alters, and to what visual affect. Clearly, such criticism is hardly worth the label. All too often, unfortunately, in popular culture studies, it is precisely this sort of work that is offered as popular culture scholarship. Plato's criticism of his ancient adversary is applicable here as well. While the work can seem clever and even quite fun to read, it fails to plumb the depths of a work's meaning precisely because it remains at a superficial level. Before long, this kind of work becomes a self-congratulatory exercise in the self-referential pointing out of neat connections or clever turns of phrase or interesting references. Fortunately, and by design, the essays of this volume explicitly eschew this approach to popular culture studies.

If we have consigned the "lovers of sights and sounds" to the sidelines of scholarship, there is a related form of "examination" of a pop culture text that is more substantial than "Isn't that neat?"— but only slightly. At those times, when it does seem a little more, it can appear as little more than Cultural Solipsism. One of the easiest essays to construct is the one that traces elements of some show or other to other shows that it references. Then, one takes those references and traces them to still others. In some rare cases, the trace comes full circle to the original program under consideration. With Oz, this is even more seductive. *Wicked: A New Musical* almost calls out for the scholar to fall victim. Having left Maguire's *Wicked* at the concept stage, the musical provides a backdrop for a very quick essay that can be constructed tracing origin stories of Dorothy's companions from the later work to the same companions in the former. Such a paper would likely be an interesting read, but would introduce nothing in particular to the scholarly evaluation of either work. Indeed, it would likely present the scholar with obstacles to the study of both texts. While a good bit of fun, perhaps, such work would hardly be considered either original or particularly worthwhile. It is this sort of Cultural Solipsism that often makes popular culture studies seem less than serious and somewhat less than scholarly.

The third popular sort of pop culture criticism is considerably more beneficial than the first two. I call it the Point of Departure approach. With this model, the "water cooler" conversation of the former sort takes on a greater level of sophistication. Here, the popular culture text becomes an artifact, an example that is helpful in advancing one's own views. Thus, watching *The Wizard of Oz*, one devises an example from the journey along the Yellow Brick Road that illustrates, for example, Aristotle's notion of friendship as developed in Book X of the *Nicomachean Ethics*. The popular culture text is reduced to an instrumental role in which whatever meaning it may have within it is lost in the service of explicating a view independent of it.

This Point of Departure approach is helpful, as far as it goes. It is particularly useful as a pedagogical tool. Aristotelian notions of *courage* can be compared and contrasted with the actions of the Cowardly Lion, the notion of *reason* can be compared and contrasted to the Scarecrow's dilemma, and so on. Unfortunately, it is not a way of shedding light on the popular culture text *itself*. The highly popular Philosophy and Popular Culture series generally follows this model, using the popular culture moment as an illumination of the work of some great philosopher. So, Dorothy's plight becomes an illustration of Freud's notions about the nature of dreams and the unconscious. However, the issue for the popular culture critic is this. In this model, the critical attention is not given to *The Wizard of Oz* or *Wicked*. Instead, the attention is Freud and *Oz* is a convenient, but wholly interchangeable instrument. As I have argued elsewhere, this approach to popular culture criticism has the often unintentional consequence of self-negation. If the subject under study is merely an interchangeable and, thus, essentially unimportant feature of a broader conversation, then it is much easier to conclude that *Oz* is essentially unimportant. The troublesome result seems to indict much of the field of popular culture studies by critiquing the way in which much of it proceeds. Such an approach is more substantive than the others, but it still fails to take the text itself seriously enough to justify a separate scholarly investigation of it.

The fourth approach is the Theory Exemplar model. While it has much in common with the Point of Departure model, it has one characteristic that elevates it beyond its cousin. In the Point of Departure approach, *Oz* is an instrument for discussing some theoretical point or other raised by some great thinker within the canon. It is a starting point that is soon abandoned for the more serious conversation that it has spawned of the more important text or concept. On the other hand, the Theory Exemplar recognizes the popular culture text has something of its own to contribute to the conversation. To use *Oz* as an example of a theory, one must first actively engage the text itself. A Cartesian scholar, for example, might quickly note the distinctions between the world as it is perceived and the world as it is; it would, at the same time, be quickly recognized by that same scholar if the text did not actually adequately explicate the view.

The difficulty with this view is similar to the Point of Departure view in that one still uses *Oz* or any other popular culture artifact as a vehicle for illustrating a text other than itself. However, in the serious work that must be done to provide a clear comparison, some measure of critical worth is imputed to the popular culture illumination. At the same time, the text is still largely instrumental and its value is largely that of a tool. It is still unclear whether or not the text *itself* contains anything of value.

It has been my experience in a survey of the literature, both published and presented at various conferences, national and international, that the majority of popular culture studies fall into one of these four models. I take it to be that for these reasons, popular culture studies is often relegated to secondary status within the academy and seen as merely an interesting adjunct or sidebar to other disciplines. This volume, like its *Buffy* predecessor, is itself a critique of that approach to popular culture studies. Further, and more importantly, it is a bit of advocacy for another approach to popular culture texts. I call this approach the Critical Engagement approach.

Some of the essays in this volume fit nicely into the Theory Exemplar approach to popular culture studies. The majority of them, however, stand as independent examinations of *Oz* and the universe it has inspired as texts in themselves and thus employ a Critical Engagement approach. A scholar critically engages a text when she brings her considerable training to the text and asks of the text what it is arguing. The approach is not a matter of discerning ways in which the text may be of instrumental use in some other venue, but rather of asking what intrinsic value may be found. In approaching *Oz* this way, one is not asking, "How can *Oz* be used to discuss good and evil or canon or epistemology?" Instead, one is asking, "What is it that *Oz*, as a text, is arguing about good and evil? What arguments are to be found within it?" One might conclude that the arguments are flawed, that the theories are specious, or that the text is unworthy of serious scholarly engagement. However, such conclusions would be based on the engagement with the text itself, and thus would represent the same sort of scholarship one expects of the philosopher who analyzes Aristotle's *Nicomachean Ethics* or the literary critic who explores Joyce's *Ulysses*.

The Critical Engagement approach is the one most rarely seen in contemporary popular culture scholarship. Why this is is something of a mystery to me. That it is mysterious, however, is in no way a detraction from the view that one should expect the same level of scholarly rigor from critics of popular culture that one expects from historians of Tudor/Stuart England or from archaeologists of ancient Troy. Popular culture studies will continue to suffer from second-class citizen status within contemporary academic scholarship until the majority of the scholarly work is done in this latter way. Failure to engage the text itself reduces the text and its importance to mere instrument. Such self-negating approaches have the deleterious effect of implying the negation of the entire field. The vast wealth of material to be gleaned from the study of popular culture is reason enough to commend its study and to indicate its own intrinsic value. This was the view of Plato and of Aristotle, the founders of perceptive critical and analytical theory. The choice for the modern critic is the same as the choice for our ancient ancestors — a serious engagement with the text or a capitulation to the view that popular culture studies are, at best, an adjunct to true scholarship, or, at worst, a trifling diversion unworthy of scholarly time and attention. It is the hope of the contributors to this volume that the choice to engage the universe of *Oz* as a text is in keeping with the former choice.

Kevin K. Durand

PART ONE

Oz and Literary Criticism

CHAPTER 1

The Emerald Canon

Where the Yellow Brick Road Forks

KEVIN K. DURAND

The canon of the universe of *The Wizard of Oz*, if we can speak of such a thing, can be divided roughly into two epochs — pre–1939 and post–1939. Before the movie roared into theatres, the Oz-verse was a purely literary one. L. Frank Baum's books formed not only its core, but its entirety. Perhaps some scholarly debate might have bubbled up around the question of whether the first book, *The Wonderful Wizard of Oz*, was the core of the canon and the other, following texts were its periphery or if the entirety of Baum's vision was uniformly canonical. Such a conversation might have made a welcome little paper in some fairly obscure academic journal, but it would have been unlikely to raise any fuss beyond those committed to deep literary scholarship applied to the Baum *Oz*-verse.

When the movie exploded on the scene in Technicolor, though, the discussion, had there been one, would have changed somewhat. Questions that always attend the motion picture adaptation of literary texts would perhaps have been the center there, too. How faithfully does the movie render the text? What gets left out? Did you really think that the Wicked Witch of the West would look like Margaret Hamilton? These questions are similar to those raised by fans of the *Harry Potter* series, the *Twilight* series, and any text that gets the movie treatment. While these are interesting questions, to be sure, the *Oz*-verse is really quite different from Potter's England or Bella's great Northwest. The reason for this is quite simple. Since 1939, the movie has set the stage for reading the book, not vice versa. While there is some small subsection of the population that has encountered *Harry Potter* first on the big screen and has only then been enraptured by the texts, the vast majority of those who come to Oz come to it through Judy Garland's "Somewhere Over the Rainbow," long before they encounter the book, and even longer before they realize that there is not just the one, but, indeed, a vast library of books of Oz, also known as The Fabulous Forty.

However, it is even possible to divide the chronology of Oz further. The 1970s saw a revitalization of Oz in the public eye. Not only did the widespread penetration of the television into private homes make the yearly showing of the movie more accessible to more people, but spin-offs and parodies became more commonplace. *The Wiz*, in both its 1975 Broadway production and its 1978 movie incarnation, captured public attention and met some critical success (and ridicule). Whatever the case, the Michael Jackson and Diana Ross duet "Ease on Down the Road" became nearly as widely recognized as its "Rainbow" antecedent. Slightly earlier in the decade, in 1973, Elton John's "Goodbye Yellow Brick Road" became one of his best-selling albums and is often regarded as his greatest work, having been named both to the top 100 British albums (by *Q Magazine*) and top 100 albums of all time (*Rolling Stone*). Musically, Oz has been rarely paralleled in its influence on later popular culture. I daresay, even now, as one reads the Baum books, it is difficult not to hear Garland's vocals or to anticipate the Munchkins' singing welcome to Dorothy. Beyond the soundtrack to Oz that plays in so many minds, I suspect that it is nearly impossible to read *The Wonderful Wizard of Oz* and not see the faces of Judy Garland, Bert Lahr, and Margaret Hamilton, even if the movie characters also seem oddly out of place in the literary work.

Therein lies part of the difficulty in establishing, with any rigor, what amounts to a canon for *Oz*. However, there is yet another difficulty. Much as the 1970s faded as bellbottoms became bootcuts and mirror balls were mothballed, so, too, *The Wiz* has faded into vague memories (if it resides even there) and Elton's music evokes nostalgia as much as any other emotion. As the millennium turned, though, a new addition to the *Oz*-verse shook it up. Gregory Maguire's reimagining the first of Baum's books and the movie from the perspective of the Wicked Witch of the West radically altered some of the time-honored assumptions about both. One of those radical alterations of perception is in the simple fact of naming. The Witch has no name in Baum's books, nor does she have any name apart from her title in the movie. Maguire dubs her Elphaba, a name derived from the initials of the *Oz*-verse's creator — L. Frank Baum become L.F.B., or Elphaba. With a name, she becomes a character with whom the audience is encouraged to identify and with whom even some sense of empathy might be felt. Further, through Maguire's lens, the character of the Wizard, for example, comes into sharper relief, even as it is portrayed in Baum's own work. Maguire's work, then, comes to have some claim on canonical status given that it can radically reshape even the perceptions of the originals.

Oddly enough, were it not for a musical version of *Wicked*, Maguire's books might have been seen as nothing more than interesting adjuncts to the *Oz*-verse, a sort of 21st century *The Wiz*. But, the Tony Award–winning musical took Broadway, and then off-Broadway, by storm, and made stratospheric best-sellers out of Maguire's *Wicked* and the sequel, *Son of a Witch*. Here, too, the original difficulty is encountered. The musical version differs rather markedly from the book, so much so, in fact, that it is almost impossible to see the Elphaba of the musical maneuvering through the book. Thus, what I shall argue in the face of this phenomenological shift in the *Oz* universe is that the movie is canonical within the province of The Wizard of Oz, supplanting the Baum books. It might seem reasonable to argue that the analogous situation would hold within the Wicked universe. However, I argue that, in fact, *Wicked: A New Musical* is actually an adjunct to the musical movie, and while it owes its creative germ to Maguire's *Wicked*, that it owes its storyline to the movie. The odd work out in this view, actually, is *Wicked*. It stands as such a dramatic reimagining that, at this juncture within Oz scholarship, it can be argued to be a canonical branch, separate in important ways from the movie. A consequent of this view is that *The Wiz*, in either of its forms (musical/musical movie), is adjunct to the canonical core, superseded by both the Baum-inspired and the Maguire-inspired texts. However, the 1939 movie continues to stride like a colossus through the *Oz*-verse. In interesting ways, the *Oz* canon is in flux.

Given this widely varied terrain, the scholar of Oz is likely faced with the question of making some decisions about how the terrain can be traversed. In other words, how do we solve the dilemma of incompatibility? Before addressing that question, it is perhaps important to answer a prior one — why is the establishment of a sense of canonical primacy even necessary? Let's address that question since if it turns out that it is unnecessary, then much of the dilemma suggested above dissolves.

To establish a canon is to make a decision about the primacy of one set of texts over another for the purpose of interpreting not only the texts within the canon but all of those connected to it, yet outside of it, as well. An example from classical antiquity can perhaps illustrate what is at stake. During the first three centuries of the Common Era, there was considerable disagreement about what texts should be considered sacred and, thus, authoritative within the burgeoning Christian movement. How, for example, should the infancy gospels be treated? Which gospels should be included and which not? How should letters of Paul be treated, even in those cases where authenticity was in doubt? As an historical matter, it wasn't until St. Athanasius's 39th Festal Letter that the canon of the Christian Bible was listed together in a single place. Up until then, even in the recently popularized Council of Nicaea in 325 C.E., the Christian canon was up for debate.

The difficulties of a canon in flux creates are obvious. Which texts are selected to be the core of the tradition goes a great way toward determining not only how other texts are read but even whether or not they are read. A more particular example will perhaps be helpful. In 144 C.E., a theologian named Marcion cobbled together a set of texts that he argued should be the sacred core of the fledgling Christian movement. The Marcionic canon consisted of the Gospel of Luke, the Acts of the Apostles, and the letters of Paul. Each of these was redacted to remove any positive references made to Jews or the Hebrew tradition. On Marcion's view, Christianity was a radical break from its Jewish roots, so much so that the Christian God and the Hebrew God were not even to be thought the same. It seems clear that if Marcion's view had won the day, all of Christendom, from that day until this, would have been profoundly different because the Marcionic canon was a lens through which the other texts about Jesus was to be interpreted. However, perhaps fortuitously, his view did not win the day. Instead, it was rejected as heresy, and the steps toward the canonization of the set of texts that currently resides in the Christian Bible was well on its way.

This example is not to suggest that the canonization of a text or set of texts in the *Oz*-verse is nearly so important or far-reaching a task. However, the relationship is similar. Perhaps another example, closer to our own century and less portentous in its impact would be helpful. Every department of English in every university has the unenviable task of deciding which books, stories, novels, poems, essays, and the like should be read by a student in order for that student to be considered literate and educated. Some decisions are fairly easy (or, at least tend to be accepted without much debate). For example, Shakespeare gets in. Of course, that then raises the question concerning *which* of Shakespeare's plays makes the cut, but whether or not Shakespeare is included is rarely questioned. A more difficult question might be whether or not George Orwell's *1984* should be included. Or, whether or not Kate Chopin's *The Awakening* has reached the status that it merits inclusion. But the very fact of selecting a set of texts gives them a certain authority and, beyond that, sets them in place as the lens through which even the question "What makes great literature?" is answered by the students for years to come.

Let's take the Shakespeare case. Suppose we choose for inclusion in the literary canon perhaps the most famous of Shakespeare's plays, *Romeo and Juliet*. While it may be true that a rose by any other name would smell as sweet, it is clearly not the case that having read *Romeo and Juliet* that the student has a grasp of the entirety of Shakespeare. Indeed, if one took only that limited background into a reading of the historical *Henry* plays, one would be quite disappointed to discover the general absence of overwrought professions of undying love made from one love-sick teenager to another. But, the inclusion of the former colors the reading of the latter, at least at the outset. This is clearly not to suggest that one cannot then do excellent Shakespearean scholarship if one first encounters *Romeo and Juliet*; however, it is just as clearly the case that the first reading colors later ones.

So, what of *Oz*? Clearly less momentous than the sacred text of the world's largest religion nor as recognized as great literature by the sage heads of academia, does there still remain the need for the canonical conversation? Can we not simply dismiss *Oz* as an entertaining bit of children's literature and move on to the weightier matters of *Two Gentlemen of Verona*? I would argue that given the near universality of the *Oz* phenomenon in popular literature, film, and culture, it is at least worthy of scholarly consideration. And, if it is worthy of scholarly consideration and engagement, then it is a worthwhile exercise to ask how that engagement should proceed. And that question is a question of canon-making and primacy of texts.

At the outset of the essay, I suggested that as an historical matter, the question of a canon of *Oz* doesn't become an issue until following 1939. Thus, there is the cleavage of the *Oz* canon question into pre– and post–1939. In a similar way, that division marks another sort of division — between *Oz* as a strictly literary phenomenon and *Oz* as a more visual/musical phenomenon. So, let us suppose first that there are two different canonical tracks, at the intersection of which we find a dynamic that may well help us to argue that one or the other has primacy as we turn to examine whatever else we find noteworthy in the *Oz*-verse.

If we approach the *Oz*-verse from this twin-track perspective, we can organize the main texts into two groups. Among the first, literary track we find the L. Frank Baum books and Maguire's books; among the second, we find greater variety — the 1939 movie musical; the stage musical, *The Wiz*; the movie musical, *The Wiz*; and the stage musical, *Wicked: A New Musical*. While it may at first seem odd to separate the musical interpretation of the literary text from its literary parent, a fairly cursory viewing of them suggests that in terms of both stylistic content and consistency within the prescribed universe, the musicals have far more in common with each other than they have with their literary parents. And, in turn, Maguire's literary universe looks far more like Baum's than either look like the musical based on them. This sort of phenomenological reading of the ways in which one experiences the *Oz*-verse actually helps us quite a lot when we also recognize that the rather radical shiftings that have occurred over time have also shifted the ways in which the universe is first encountered and interpreted.

The *Oz* canon has transitioned over time, even if we approach the part of the canon that is fairly strictly literary. The Baumian corpus is extensive. From *The Wonderful Wizard of Oz* that opened the series to *Glinda of Oz* that closed it (unless one counts *The Visitors from Oz* that was published in 1960 and adapted from a comic Baum had produced several years earlier), it has always been the case that some of the texts have been much more popular than the others. One need only look at the fact that the first novel captured the imagination of the public, and, in so doing, gave rise to the sepia-toned Kansas of the silver screen. However, no scholar worth repute in his or her discipline would suggest that canonical primacy attended only to the popularity of the work. Let us suppose, for instance, that the second of the *Godfather* movies was far more critically acclaimed and popularly received than the first. This is not an outrageous or unimaginable situation. Indeed, given that both were Academy Award–worthy, one could imagine the second edging out the first in terms of popularity. Let us then suppose the nearly unimaginable — namely, that the third of the series was wildly more popular than the first two. Clearly this was not the case, but in the unlikely, and unfortunate, circumstance that it was, we would not, on the basis of that disparity of popularity, conclude that it was the superior or that it had canonical primacy. Or, in a similar way, though *Episode V: The Empire Strikes Back* and *Star Trek II: The Wrath of Khan* were both more critically and generally more popular than their forebears, one would hardly conclude that they had primacy over *Episode VI* or *The Motion Picture*, respectively. Indeed, one of the most glaring criticisms of George Lucas and his revisitation of *Episode IV* was that changes made to it radically altered the universe of the film. Many critics have suggested that, for example, the change made to the cantina scene when Greedo confronts Han Solo potentially changed the way Solo's character was seen. In the original film, Han fries Greedo at the threat of Greedo's attempt to take him dead or alive. In the "remastering" of the film, Solo only shoots Greedo *after* Greedo has pulled a weapon first. While it may seem more palatable that our hero should not fire first (or draw first) in a confrontation, it is rather more indicative of the rogue character that was imagined in the first version that he should shoot first and slip through the fingers of a bounty hunter clearly intent on doing him harm. While the former is perhaps more noble, the latter is grittier and far more in keeping with the hive of villainy that Obi-Wan describes to Luke.

Another example of this phenomenon is found in the work of J. R. R. Tolkien. *The Hobbit* is far more easily digested than *The Lord of the Rings* trilogy, but Bilbo clearly inhabits the world of Middle Earth constructed by *The Fellowship of the Ring*. My own experience here may well be instructive. I remember well watching the Rankin/Bass production of *The Hobbit*. The cartoon Bilbo and Smaug and the rest are still, to some degree, the visual companion that I bring to the book and to the trilogy. However, no scholar of Tolkien would argue that *The Hobbit* is somehow more canonically prior to the trilogy. Indeed, the first of the trilogy, *The Fellowship of the Ring*, introduces us to a Bilbo and to a ring that, while we long for the backstory, nevertheless, constructs the parameters within which we can read the prequel. The Gollum of *The Lord of the Rings* must be the Gollum of *The Hobbit*. The latter is not necessarily the case. And yet, a brief survey of my students has suggested something that I take to be rather the case instead of an exception. Far more of them have read *The Hobbit* in its entirety than have read the trilogy. So, I suspect it is rather clearly the case that popularity cannot be the sole marker of the primacy of a text within a group of texts that pertain to the same universe. Rather, the earlier of the group as something like the primacy of canon, even if it is the less or least popular of the group.

With this in mind, we can safely suppose that *The Wonderful Wizard of Oz*, occupying primacy of place in the chronology of publication, also enjoys primacy of place for canonical considerations. The map of Oz, found at the outset of the first Baum *Oz* novel is the map of Oz for all. Greater detail and nuance are supplied as the series progresses, but the fundamental shape of the universe is the same. Nothing can be introduced that violates those initial laws of the universe without running the risk of seeming grossly out of place and, thus, compromising the thread of the tale itself. Thus, as the *Oz* universe takes shape, it does so within the parameters of *The Wonderful Wizard of Oz*.

A further example might be of help here. One of the most widely recognized failures of the series of *Star Trek* novels that took up the story of the original crew — *The Entropy Effect*, for example — is that none of the novels that followed the initial foray into the printed world seemed to be constrained by the *Star Trek* universe envisioned by Gene Roddenberry. Several of the texts — *The Vulcan Academy Murders* and *The IDIC Epidemic*, for instance — intentionally were set within the context of the original television series. Others, *Uhura's Song* or *Dreadnought!*, for example — seemed to have little or no connection to either the original series or to the books in the literary series that went before them. This is a phenomenon that is exceptionally common when visual texts become printed series that extend the visual universe. However, the *Oz* books rather remarkably do not fall victim to this dilemma. Instead, they present a single universe that develops and grows rather organically. In this, the initial text has primacy because it is both the foundation for the entire universe *and* because it is the most popular of the bunch.

A consequent of this view would seem to be that *The Wonderful Wizard of Oz* would have canonical primacy along the literary track, and thus, that when concerning oneself with the authoritative view of *Oz*, one must look first to Baum's book. This clearly is a view counter to the one I advanced in the thesis. Thus, it is completely understandable that one might ask, "How might this be?" The simple answer is, "*The Wizard of Oz* changed every-thing."

There are two points to be made here, though, I suppose. The first is that, unlike literary canons that are somewhat fixed (although much argument attends that claim too, I suppose), the canon of the *Oz*-verse is in flux. The second is that even though Maguire's world seems to inhabit Baum's world, it is rather the case that each world is distinct and that rather than being an extension of Baum's *Oz*, Maguire's Oz is radically different, a competitor view of the ethos of the place. Being able to discern the significance of this distinction is reason enough to worry about the proper canon (or, as I have begun to argue, canons) of *Oz*.

Let's return to the view, expressed throughout this essay, that *The Wizard of Oz* changes everything. This seems rather an obvious claim and one without much in the way of detractor. However, it is important to note that the movie so fundamentally alters the perception of the Oz phenomenon, turning it on its head, that it is perhaps difficult to see what the world was like *prior* to the movie. *The Wizard of Oz* exploded on the scene and ushered in a Copernican Revolution to Oz. Prior to Copernicus and, then, Galileo, it was commonly thought that the world was the center of the cosmos, a fixed point, a *terra firma*. So strongly held was this view that when Copernicus had the audacity to suggest that perhaps the earth rotated around the sun and not *vice versa*, he was hauled before the Inquisition and made to recant. Galileo, too, faced such persecution. And, even though he is famously thought to have said under his breath as he was led to life-long house arrest, "It still moves," the received view held sway for another hundred years. Indeed, Giordano Bruno found his time before the Inquisition even more disastrous than his predecessors as he was burned at the stake for refusing to recant. Yet, despite all perceptions to the contrary — after all, it certainly looks like the sun rises in the east and sets in the west each day, like the earth stands utterly still, and like the moon follows its own track of rotation around the earth — even first graders making their first models of the solar system with construction paper and glue sticks know that the sun is the center of things (at least where our own little corner of the galaxy is concerned).

This is not to suggest that the movie's view of *Oz* is "true," while the Baumian corpus is somehow "false." Rather, the analogy is offered as a way of suggesting that the ways in which Baum's work is read after the advent of the movie is so completely altered *by the viewing* of the movie, that the literary works are never really read the same way again. No matter how often one takes the trip through Munchkinland on the page, the Munchkins of the Lollipop Guild and the Lullaby League sing our way along the Yellow Brick Road. As a functional matter, the visual medium has so captured the imagination of generations of viewers that rather than the movie being a convenient visual companion to the book(s), something like the reverse is true — the book has become a literary adjunct to the motion picture. We can argue, perhaps, which set of texts *should* be the canon, but it seems that it is beyond argument that the movie *is* the first piece of the Baum Oz canon, and is first among equals much like the Bishop of Rome is.

One of the consequents of the ascendency of the movie is that much that is of great value and enjoyment within L. Frank Baum's world goes unvalued. From a survey of the scholarly reflections on *Oz*, whether strictly academic or in the more fan-based popular discussions (in which much of scholarly value is to be found), the literary world of Baum's *Oz* has functionally shrunk from fourteen books to one. Given that the movie, *The Wizard of Oz*, strides like a colossus through the Baum-inspired world, and its shadow obscures from sight the universe beyond *The Wonderful Wizard of Oz*, it seems reasonable to ask to what degree its shadow falls over those successors to *Oz*, those works that are clearly the descendents of both Baum's vision and MGM's. Whatever the case there, it seems quite clear that within the province of Baumian *Oz*, the movie has clear canonical primacy.

Before turning to the modern successors of *Oz*, we ought take a moment to discuss those other *Oz* books and authors that comprise what is commonly called "The Fabulous Forty." Ruth Plumly Thomson took up the *Oz*-verse in 1921, the year after *Glinda of Oz* (the last of Baum's books) was published. Similarly, John Neill (the illustrator for Baum's books) and Jack Snow, a Baum scholar, continued the *Oz*-verse, though they tended to abandon characters exclusive to the Thomson universe. However, while these texts enjoyed some popularity in their day and have a loyal following within the world of *Oz* scholars, none of them can really be called "canonical," regardless of the Wikipedia claim to the contrary. This seems clear from merely a brief examination of them. Neither Snow nor Neill seem to consider Thomson's world the *real* Oz, and the reverse also seems true. The only reason for extending canonical status to any of the three is because of the connections the authors had to Baum, himself. This is a slim defense. It would be somewhat akin to suggesting that some of the letters by important members of the early church that are also excluded from the sacred text of Christianity have some claim to canonicity because of the close connection their authors had to the church leaders that went before them. Rather, the entire point of establishing a canon, it seems, is to establish that authoritative lens by which all other writings are evaluated. Thus, the three immediate successors to Baum are clearly secondary to the Baumian originals, and, ultimately, to *The Wonderful Wizard of Oz*, itself.

In turning to the later successors of *Oz*, I think it best to treat them in reverse order; that is, to first attend to *Wicked* and *Son of a Witch* and the musical, *Wicked*, before a brief discussion of *The Wiz*, in both of its forms. One might well expect a similar argument here to the foregoing one. After all, the Tony Award–winning musical seemed to draw attention to Maguire's work in a way that it hadn't enjoyed prior to its adaptation to the stage. Further, the careful reader of Maguire's *Wicked* will readily note that the complex, layered world found there is much more similar to the wondrously complex and quirky world imagined by Baum. Thus, if the analogy is that Baum's work is to *The Wizard of Oz* (the movie) as Maguire's work is to *Wicked* (the musical), then it would follow that since the movie reigns in the first, the musical must in the second. However, I argue here that the analogy, in fact, fails. Indeed, as anyone who has both read the book, *Wicked*, and seen the musical would necessarily see, the analogy fails egregiously.

Let's first apply the popularity test. While the number of those who have seen *The Wizard of Oz* is several orders of magnitude larger than the number of those who've read *The Wonderful Wizard of Oz*, the analogous statement is not true. It would be rather an impressive feat for the musical *Wicked* to outpace the book, viewers to readers. Further, so many of the former were previously among the ranks of the latter. Thus, many went to the musical with Maguire's universe somewhat firmly in place in their minds. It is this phenomenological feature of the two that puts the lie to the analogy. The book, by nearly any measure employed, outstrips the musical as a matter of popular dissemination. This can be put down to two reasons, both of which are rather obvious. First, unlike the movie, the musical has a very limited audience. The number of those who see a Broadway musical, even an award-winning one, during all of its runs (including the high school musicals that often follow on the heels of a successful Broadway show) is far smaller than just the opening weekend for a blockbuster movie. Thus, while *The Wizard of Oz* has captured an almost universal coverage, either on the big screen or the small one, the musical *Wicked* has played to a far, far smaller crowd, even taking into consideration those who have viewed parts of it on Youtube and other internet media. Thus, the popularity test clearly does not play the overwhelming part that it plays in the Baumian world.

The second reason that the analogy fails is related. The musical *Wicked* is portrayed even by those who are diehard fans of it as a very loose adaptation of Maguire's book that owes more to *The Wizard of Oz* for key story elements (the origins of Dorothy's three *Ozian* companions, for instance) than to *Wicked*. While the musical differs from the book in far many more ways than the movie differs from its literary parent, the additional fact that Maguire's book was so clearly a best-seller prior to the musical production, the musical carries the feel of visual companion to the much more layered and nuanced book. Kristin Chenowith's brilliant performances notwithstanding, it is unlikely, without a reprise of the role on the big screen, that she will ever be the household name that Judy Garland continues to be, nor will she be so singularly connected with a role that her name is synonymous with it (as Garland's is with Dorothy). As a musical, the play simply does not have the heft to reduce its parent text to the status of literary companion that the tour de force *Wizard of Oz* did and continues to do to the world of Baum.

Further, we can use this failed analogy to point out just how paradigm-changing the movie was. So effectively does the movie determine our view of the *Oz*-verse, that the musical is hardly even an adaptation of the book. The musical avoids the clever critiques of organized religion that permeate Maguire's version. The political machinations the drive the plot of the book are largely absent from the musical, with Madame Morrible taking on the role of villain while the Wizard is rather an incompetent and bumbling fool. Indeed, it almost seems as if the authors of the musical uncritically accepted the notion that the Wizard was a wonderful wizard, if ever a Wiz there was. This is clearly not the Wizard of Maguire's vision. Additionally, the musical serves to offer origin stories for Dorothy's three companions along the Yellow Brick Road. Elphaba is the source of the Cowardly Lion's cowardice, the Tin Man's lack of a heart (and body of tin), and the Scarecrow's transfiguration from man to straw. Nothing could be more distinct from the text of Maguire's book. Thus, the viewer of the musical is left wondering how this catchy and intriguing musical shares much with its literary namesake beyond the names of some of the characters. Thus, the analogy that the movie is to the book as the musical is to the book fails on almost as many different levels as it is possible to conceive.

This is not to say that the analogy will always be fixed and unchanging. Indeed, there are many reasons why it could change. One could rather easily imagine the crowd attending the 1939 opening of the movie talking about whether or not it would be a faithful rendering of Baum's vision or wondering how a musical could capture such a complex world. Indeed, even after having seen the movie dozens of times, it is not a completely foreign notion to suppose that our 1939 and 1940 counterparts who, having seen the movie, would return home and pick up their copy of *The Wonderful Wizard of Oz* and disappear back into Baum's world, content in the notion that they now had a visual companion for their Oz library. However, such events have not happened to Maguire's world, nor, honestly, do these events seem terribly likely, especially given the utterly radical departure of the structure of the musical from the structure of the book. Though far more lasting in popularity than, say, *The Wiz, Wicked: The Musical* doesn't carry the power of Maguire's vision. Nor does it recapture the power of the 1939 movie musical. Thus, one is left with the vague disconnect that the Elphaba of the musical doesn't quite capture the angst, heroism, and grim resignation of the Elphaba of the book, for example. The musical form simply doesn't have the strength to carry it to the heights of the movie. As a result, the musical forms an interesting, but limited, visual counterpart to the book.

If the argument to this point seems reasonable, what we are left with is a complicated canonical landscape. There are odd and intriguing intersections between literary text and visual adaptation. And, finally, the canon seems to have two tracks, one of which is smaller, but distinctly separate from the older and larger. These tracks are not the ones we might first have expected — literary text to literary text, visual adaptation to visual adaptation. Instead, the tracks are both literary to visual adaptations, though with seemingly opposite directions. In the former, *The Wizard of Oz* creates the lens through which Baum's texts are approached and, ultimately, for good or ill, interpreted. In the latter, the reverse is true — Maguire's *Wicked* creates the universe which gave the musical its seminal idea, but *Oz* gives it life; but, it is reasonable to suppose that Maguire's text is nevertheless the template that determines the strength or weakness its musical incarnation.

However, what shall we do with *The Wiz*? The argument here is rather straightforward, and is reminiscent of the argument concerning the marginalization of Baum's works apart from *The Wonderful Wizard of Oz*. As the Judy Garland movie has overshadowed much of Baum's initial vision and quite nearly obscured all but the first book, so, too, has it obscured *The Wiz*. *The Wiz*, even at the height of its popularity, was never received as much more than a reimagination of the movie. Popularly speaking, *The Wiz* has faded so much from view that one cannot assume that one's interlocutors have ever heard of it, much less seen it. This is clearly not the case with *The Wizard of Oz*. Indeed, the movie musical form of *The Wiz* never challenged *The Wizard of Oz* for anything resembling supremacy in the popular imagination; the stage musical form, similarly, fails utterly to capture the critical or popular acclaim of *Wicked: The Musical*. Part of this must surely be that *The Wiz* has no literary foundations of its own. It is an adaptation of *The Wizard of Oz*, and, thus, is finally incapable of dislodging *Oz* either as a phenomenon in the minds of viewers or as a retelling of Baum's vision. Indeed, *The Wiz* seems utterly disconnected from Baum's world, and rather like a translation of the movie into another vernacular.

Now, the scholar should not discount the role that race plays in the differential reception of the two musicals. Indeed, it is nearly impossible to have a conversation about *The Wiz* without the question of race that it raises. But, independent, ultimately, of race, we can ask ourselves about what it is that *The Wiz* is *trying* to do. *The Wiz* is straightforwardly a melding of *The Wiz-*

ard of Oz and the blacksploitation films of the 1970s. It, itself, is a derivative. Its own promotion was that of a reimagination of the movie aimed at a niche market and targeted, through casting but not concept, to draw a wider audience. However, it only works in the niche *because* of the movie it seeks to adapt; and it only works as a draw to a wider audience because of the substitution of musical stars of the 1970s for Judy Garland, et al. It is, in conception, execution, and promotion, a derivative work. Thus, while it would be foolish for the scholar of *Oz* to ignore *The Wiz* entirely, it would be just as foolhardy to elevate it to anything resembling the canonical status of even those works overshadowed by *The Wizard of Oz* (the movie) and *Wicked* (the book).

Thus, we are left with the conclusion that the *Oz*-verse has a sort of hybrid canon, comprised of distinct, but interrelated tracks; like two star systems, each with its own sun and satellites that present the viewer intriguing similarities, but ultimately do not admit of merger. With this, the Oz scholar can safely conclude that the movie carries canonical primacy within the *Ozian* universe (up to, and including, *Wicked: A New Musical*), that Maquire's *Wicked* has opened an intriguing parallel dimension, whose musical moon has nevertheless been sucked into the movie's gravitational pull, and that *The Wiz*, in either of its forms (musical/musical movie) is adjunct.

CHAPTER 2

Dorothy and Cinderella

The Case of the Missing Prince and the Despair of the Fairy Tale

AGNES B. CURRY AND JOSEF VELAZQUEZ

Introduction

Off to See the Wizard (The Starting Point)

It has become commonplace to refer to *The Wizard of Oz* as a modern American fairy tale. And so we decided to compare *The Wizard of Oz* to a traditional fairy tale to see what the similarities and the differences might be.

As for *The Wizard of Oz* being a fairy tale, this strikes us as somehow obvious, even though we must admit that we lack a precise set of criteria to distinguish fairy tales from non–fairy tales. Baum, in any case, thought it was a fairy tale, since his stated intention was to provide his readers with a "modernized fairy tale, in which the wonderment and joy are retained and the heartaches and nightmares (and moralizing) are left out."[1] And it has generally been received by readers and viewers as a fairy tale.[2] Its characters, in fact, have become standard fairy tale icons, much like Snow White or Sleeping Beauty. And, of course, *The Wizard of Oz* has the standard fairy tale cast of wizards and witches and talking animals and magic shoes, as well as (Baum's disclaimers notwithstanding) the standard fairy tale concern with deep issues about family, maturity, evil, agency, and so on. We realize, of course, that these features are not decisive. *The Odyssey*, for example, has a lot of witches and wizards, and also deals with some deep themes, and yet *The Odyssey* is a myth and not a fairy tale. This is just one example of how criteria to distinguish fairy tales from non–fairy tales can be hard to come by. And yet the witches and wizards, and the deep themes too, do seem to do something to at least suggest that what we have here is a fairy tale. They may not be hard and fast criteria, but they do seem like softer or partial indications.

The traditional fairy tale we chose for purposes of comparison was *Cinderella*. Now, this choice may be a bit surprising (it was to some of our colleagues) but there are actually major similarities between the two stories. The most basic similarity is that both stories involve a conflict between a good mother figure (the fairy godmother, the good witch) and a bad mother figure (the evil stepmother, the wicked witch). In addition to the similarities, though, there is also one major difference: Cinderella finds a Prince, but Dorothy does not. And so the question then becomes: What does this difference signify?

Before we start talking about all this, though, we want to note that we have decided to focus our comparison on the movie version of *The Wizard of Oz* and not on the novel. There are two reasons for this. The first reason is Dorothy's age. In the novel (and particularly in W. W. Denslow's illustrations), she is very young, and this would seem to make a comparison to Cinderella inappropriate. Whereas in the movie, Judy Garland, despite the strenuous efforts of her costumers, is obviously not a small child,[3] but has reached the same ambiguous age of early adolescence as Cinderella. If it be permissible to apply logic to a fairy tale, Cinderella must have been in very early adolescence because (i) the Prince is represented as being her very first crush (ii) her step sisters, who were both older than she, were still of marriageable age, and this at a time when the marriageable age did not last very long. We are mentioning this because if Cinderella is, in fact, in early adolescence, this will move her very close in age to the Dorothy of the movie.

The second reason is the iconic status of the movie. We think it safe to say that, for the last fifty years, it has been the movie that has sparked interest in the book rather than vice versa. If we are interested in the cultural impact of this story, then, it makes sense to focus on the movie and not the novel. It has, in sum, been the ambiguously adolescent Dorothy of the movie, and not the child Dorothy of the novel, who has been a major cultural player. We think, in fact, that a big part of the movie's appeal has been the ambiguous adolescence of its heroine. And if we imagined the movie being remade with a heroine who was, for example, really just an eight year old girl, well, the movie would not be the same — it would not be nearly so interesting.

Follow the Yellow Brick Road (an outline)

This essay will have two parts. Part I (the more specific part) will explore this comparison between *The Wizard of Oz* and *Cinderella*. Part II (the more general part) will then go on to look at *The Wizard of Oz* in the context of other modern fairy tales.[4]

Part I: A Comparison of *The Wizard of Oz* and *Cinderella*

Cinderella and Sigmund (the Underlying Structure of Cinderella*)*

One of the classic interpretations of fairy tales is the Freudian interpretation Bruno Bettelheim provides in his book *The Uses of Enchantment*. We realize that there are other approaches to fairy tales besides the psychoanalytic one. We realize also that, even within the realm of psychoanalysis itself, there are other approaches besides Bettelheim's. We do not want to downplay the importance and value of these other approaches, nor do we want to come off as if we were in a position to argue for the special validity of Bettelheim's approach. However, we would nonetheless ask the reader to allow us, without further effort at justification, to just start with Bettelheim and see where it leads.

According to Bettelheim, *Cinderella* has a structure based on the Oedipus complex, or, more exactly, on the feminine version of the Oedipus complex. This might seem a little odd since the story looks, at first, to be about sibling rivalry. But Bettelheim tells us that the earlier versions of the story contain some sort of improper love between Cinderella and her father[5] and that Cinderella ends up in the ashes and hated by her stepmother as a consequence of this improper love. The sibling rivalry is still there, of course, but it is not the real core of the story. In fact, the sibling rivalry is, to some extent, just a screen for the Oedipal dimension, the evil stepsisters being a symbol of the stepmother, who is herself a symbol of the mother.[6]

In any case, the point that is important for us here is that *Cinderella* is structured around two mother-images. There is the evil mother-image, which is Cinderella's stepmother, and there is also the good mother image. In the Grimm version, this is Cinderella's deceased natural mother, at whose tomb Cinderella prays. In the Perrault version, the deceased natural mother is replaced by a fairy godmother. According to Bettelheim, each of these mother-images has a psychoanalytic interpretation. The evil stepmother represents the mother as seen through the eyes of a young girl's Oedipus complex. In this complex, a girl will feel a rivalry towards her mother, and she will also imagine that this rivalry is felt by her mother. Thus, the mother gets pictured as a terrible figure who hates the young girl and means her harm. On the other hand, the deceased natural mother (or the fairy godmother) represents the mother as the young girl saw her in the pre–Oedipal phase. At this point, there was no rivalry. Thus, the mother is still pictured as completely kind and nurturing and always willing to assist her daughter.

On this reading, the fairy tale presents an itinerary for growing up and successfully resolving the Oedipus complex. When the story begins, we find

Cinderella firmly in the grip of her evil stepmother, i.e., firmly in the grip of the Oedipus complex. But then, as the story unfolds, we see that Cinderella is able to overcome this evil mother figure. She does so by relying on the good mother figure. For it is by praying at her deceased mother's tomb (or through the aid of her fairy godmother) that Cinderella receives the gown and shoes which allow her to be successful at the ball. And so, for Bettelheim, the moral of the story is clear: it is by relying on the good mother-image, which is still buried somewhere in the psyche, that the young girl can overcome the evil mother-image of the Oedipus complex and, by so doing, achieve maturity.[7]

> If we trust the clues presented by Basile's story [an early version of *Cinderella*], then we may say that inordinate love of a father for his daughter and hers for him came first, and her reduction to the Cinderella role by mother or sisters is the consequence. This situation parallels the oedipal development of a girl. She first loves her mother — the original good mother, who later in the story appears as fairy godmother. Later, she turns from her mother to her father, loving him and wanting to be loved by him; at this point the mother — and all her siblings, real and imagined, most of all the female ones — become her competitors. At the end of the oedipal period the child feels cast out; all alone; then when all goes well in puberty, if not sooner, the girl finds her way back to the mother now as a person not to be loved exclusively, but as one with whom to identify.

Besides maturity, she also, of course, obtains the Prince. For Cinderella not only learns to defy her evil stepmother, but she also goes to the ball and then gets married. In psychoanalytic language, when the young girl resolves her conflicted feelings about her mother, she then becomes able to form a loving connection to an outside person. Bettelheim writes,

> Once Zezolla [the heroine of an early version of *Cinderella*] has outgrown the Oedipal age and is ready to have good relations with her mother once again, the mother returns in the form of the fairy in the date tree and enables her daughter to gain sexual success with the King, a non–Oedipal object.[8]

It is important in this regard that Bettelheim reads the Prince as really being an outside person who is not simply reducible to the family system, i.e., the Prince is not simply a father substitute. Bettelheim points here to the scenes (in Grimm) where Cinderella has run back from the ball, dived into the tree or the dovecote, and, unbeknownst to the Prince, sneaked out the other side. For what happens next in these scenes is that Cinderella's father has his servants cut down the tree and demolish the dovecote, hoping thereby to help the Prince uncover Cinderella. Bettelheim reads this as indicating that Cinderella's father is now helping her to transfer her affections from himself to this other person. He continues,

> The Prince, as if recognizing that he cannot win Cinderella as long as she remains emotionally tied to her father in an oedipal relation, does not pursue her

himself, but asks the father to do it for him. Only if the father first indicates his readiness to release his daughter from her ties to him can she feel good about transferring her heterosexual love from its immature object (the father) to its mature object — her future husband. The father's demolishing Cinderella's hiding places — chopping down the dovecote and the pear tree — shows his readiness to hand her over to the Prince.[9]

At this point Bettelheim adds, "But his efforts do not have the desired result." The reason Bettelheim adds this, though, seems not to be because he thinks the father is unsuccessful in loosening the oedipal attachment, but because there are other factors besides this oedipal one that are still holding Cinderella back.

Dorothy and Sigmund (a Comparison of Cinderella and The Wizard of Oz)

There are obvious similarities here to *The Wizard of Oz*. Just like *Cinderella*, *The Wizard of Oz* is also structured around two mother-images. Glinda the Good Witch functions as the good mother-image, and the Wicked Witch of the West functions as the evil mother-image. Glinda, in fact, might actually be Dorothy's deceased mother. Each of the characters in Oz has a counterpart back in Kansas; the Scarecrow, Tin Man and Lion, for example, are the counterparts of the three farm hands. Or actually, this is true for all the characters in Oz except for Glinda, who is the one character who seems to have no counterpart. But maybe, this is our suggestion anyway, Glinda actually does have a counterpart in Kansas too, except that this counterpart is Dorothy's mother whom we don't actually see because she has already died in the Kansas world and only continues to exist as her Glinda counterpart in the world of Oz. Also, just like in *Cinderella*, Dorothy overcomes the evil mother-image with the help of the good mother-image.[10] At the level of psychological structure, in other words, *Cinderella* and *The Wizard of Oz* are remarkably similar stories of growing up.

This same movement from the evil mother-image to the good mother-image also occurs in how Aunt Em is pictured.[11] Aunt Em is a mother substitute, and at the beginning of the film, before Dorothy goes on her adventure, Aunt Em is pictured toward the evil end of the spectrum. She has neither time nor sympathy for Dorothy. She goes even further, brusquely shooing the farmhands away from attending to Dorothy after she falls into the pig pen and even, one could say, using the power of the food she distributes to displace Dorothy. Further, we do not think she tries very hard to save Toto, her Christian scruples notwithstanding.[12] Still more to the point, Dorothy herself feels unsupported enough to run away. But as the story unfolds, Dorothy renegotiates her feelings about Aunt Em, first when she turns back at Professor Marvel's suggestion of her aunt's distress, and then later when she sees a vision of a frantic Aunt Em in the crystal ball at the Witch's castle. By the end of the story, the picture of Aunt Em has changed considerably, and she is now a warm and loving presence by Dorothy's bedside. In the Kansas parts of the story, then, we see an echo of the Cinderella pattern where the heroine moves from the evil mother-image to the good mother-image.

There is also something Cinderella-like in the "Somewhere over the Rainbow" scene. What has just happened is that Aunt Em has shooed away the farmhands who had been crowding around Dorothy and whose attentions she had obviously been enjoying. What happens next is that Dorothy, alone now except for Toto, leans up against some hay bales (a symbol of her rustic isolation) and unleashes her incongruously worldly voice upon a winsome song about how her life might be better in some other place. To fully appreciate this scene, it is necessary to know that farm pin-ups were a popular item at the time the movie was made. In these pin-ups, the model would be posed in a barn, with a pitch fork, or among the hay bales. Dorothy's pose in this scene seems to us to be reminiscent of this farm pin-up tradition.[13] In terms, then, of both its loneliness and its sexual subtext, this scene is not all that different from a scene in which Cinderella, imagined now as a character in a 1939 musical, sings winsomely amidst the pots and pans after her evil stepmother has forbidden her to go to the ball.[14] But where's the Prince? This is the big difference between *Cinderella* and *The Wizard of Oz*. For while Cinderella, at the end of the process, gets a Prince, Dorothy does not.

This absence of the Prince is all the more glaring since, according to the usual canons of fairy tale logic, the Prince should definitely be forthcoming. If you kiss a frog, then you are supposed to get a Prince. Dorothy befriends, in turn, a whole series of frog substitutes: the Scarecrow, the Tin Man, and the Cowardly Lion. But she gets no Prince. If you complete the quest, then you are supposed to get a Prince. And Dorothy, against all odds, does defeat the Wicked Witch and returns to Oz with her broom. But she gets no Prince.

In fact, Dorothy does not even seem to want a Prince. Cinderella obviously wants the Prince. She wants to go to the Prince's ball so desperately that she is willing to enter conflict with her stepmother in order to do so. And in the Grimm version of the tale, she even keeps going back night after night to dance with the Prince again and again, but we see no trace of this in Dorothy. While in Kansas, she wishes for escape, and then while in Oz, she wishes for return, but in neither case do we hear anything about a wish for Princes.

This absence of the Prince seems to us perplexing. Poor Dorothy goes through all the trouble of overcoming one mother-image with the help of the other, and yet she does not get the Prince who is supposed to be the reward for doing this. We wonder if the "Bettelheim logic" still makes sense with the

Prince removed. It does seem, after all, a little incoherent to keep the process itself, while jettisoning the Prince who is the end or goal of that process. Although Bettelheim himself does not actually go into this, it seems to us that the Prince is not only the prize at the end of the process, but also the motivation at the beginning of it. It is, in other words, the desire for the Prince which starts the whole process of maturation off. In the language of the fairy tale, it is the desire to attend the Prince's ball which first brings Cinderella into conflict with her evil step mother and so sends her to her deceased mother (or her fairy godmother) for help. This, it seems to us, makes the point in the text even stronger. For by jettisoning the Prince, *The Wizard of Oz* will be jettisoning not only the end but also the beginning of the psychological structure it is built upon.

Where's Waldo? (Finding a Version of the Prince in The Wizard of Oz)

Actually, in an odd sort of way, the Prince does appear in *The Wizard of Oz*. To explain how, we will make use of an idea from Vladimir Propp and his book *The Morphology of the Folk Tale*.[15]

According to Propp, the important thing when analyzing a folk tale is the function or role, not what particular object happens to be fulfilling that function or role. For example, a standard function in a folk tale is the function of helping the hero in some sort of magical way. This function can be fulfilled by a whole variety of different characters: a kindly old wizard, a magical animal, a fairy godmother, and so on. But according to Propp, the fact that the characters change like this is not that important. The important thing is that it is same function or role, no matter which character is playing it.

Perhaps, then, we should stop worrying so much about the Prince himself, and look instead at what we could call the Prince function.

In *Cinderella*, the Prince performs four functions. These are:

1. The Prince is the object of Cinderella's affections.

2. The Prince motivates the story in the sense that it is Cinderella's desire for the Prince which brings her into conflict with her stepmother, thereby setting everything else in motion.

3. The Prince rescues Cinderella.

4. The Prince is the prize Cinderella wins.

Now, the character in *The Wizard of Oz* who fulfills these four functions is actually Toto:

1. Toto is the object of Dorothy's affections to the point where she is willing to give up her home and run away in order to protect him.

2. It is Dorothy's affection for Toto that brings her into conflict with Miss Gulch, and this conflict then sets off the story that follows.

3. It is Toto who rescues Dorothy by leading her friends to the castle

to save her. It is also Toto who uncovers the Wizard, thus saving Dorothy from the illusion that the Wizard was perpetrating.[16]

4. Toto is the one person whom Dorothy carries back with her from Oz. In fact, the whole story of *The Wizard of Oz* is actually, in this respect, just one long story of how Dorothy gets to keep Toto.

It seems, in sum, that it is actually Toto who functions as the Prince.

All Grown Up? (Images of Maturity in Cinderella *and* The Wizard of Oz)

But look at what the Prince function has become! In *Cinderella*, the Prince is an outside person to whom Cinderella gives herself. In *The Wizard of Oz*, the Prince function is a pet — a lap dog — which Dorothy possesses.

We are obviously not the only ones to have noticed the odd role that Toto plays in this film. In his essay on *The Wizard of Oz* Salman Rushdie has this to say[17]:

> I couldn't stand Toto. I still can't. ... Toto: that little yapping hairpiece of a creature, that meddlesome rug! ... That Toto should be the film's one true object of love has always rankled.

We agree with Rushdie that it is actually Toto who is the secret love focus of the film, i.e., that it is Toto who is the Prince. And we agree, too, with his judgment that Dorothy's love for Toto is actually a problem in the film.

To take all this a little further, we want to suggest that the different Prince functions in *The Wizard of Oz* and *Cinderella* lead to different images of maturity as well.[18] The key, it seems to us, is in where these Prince functions are located.

In *Cinderella*, the Prince function is located completely outside of Cinderella, in the Prince himself, i.e., in a separate person with his own subjectivity. So, if we define maturity as the attitude needed to make contact with the Prince function, then maturity here is a sort of self-donation as Cinderella gives herself to this outside person. Maturity, to drop for a moment the metaphors of Princes and of self-donations, means recognizing another person as genuinely Other and being able to take the risks necessary to open oneself to knowing and being known by this other person.

In *The Wizard of Oz*, by contrast, the Prince function is located at Dorothy's side, in the person of Toto. In fact, making the Prince function into her pet is almost like saying this Prince function is a part of her.[19] And so maturity, or contacting the Prince function, is in this case pictured as a self-possession that ultimately amounts to a sort of closed-off, atomistic self-containment. We have been using a concept of distance, in the sense of the distance between Dorothy and the Prince function. So far we have been using this concept in a pretty intuitive, a pretty rough and ready way. But we can make it a little more precise. And so *Cinderella* creates a relatively large distance between Cinderella and The Prince in two ways. First, the social statuses of princes and of scullery maids are conventionally far apart. Second, the text puts a series of obstacles between Cinderella and the Prince (the step mother, Cinderella's unknown identity), and these obstacles create a distance between them. In the case of Dorothy and Toto we have the same two types of mechanisms, but now operating to create a minimal or zero distance rather than a large one. First, the distance between a pet and his or her owner is conventionally thought to be a very small distance (a pet will, for example, sit on his or her master's lap at night). Secondly, there are no obstacles between Toto and Dorothy, but they belong together, and he is found, often, in her arms. Of course, when Miss Gulch captures Toto that could be seen as an obstacle, but it is not an obstacle in the same sense as the obstacles in *Cinderella*. For what we have with Toto is the interruption of an established relationship rather than, as with Cinderella, an obstacle to forming the relationship in the first place.

This difference shows itself in the different ways the two heroines exhibit courage. Cinderella exhibits courage by defying authority to go to the Prince's ball. Dorothy exhibits courage by slapping the Lion when the Lion threatens Toto. Courage, in the one case, is going dangerously far out of oneself, while, in the other case, it is protecting what is already one's own. There is an interesting link, here, between a failure to move forward into an adult sexual relationship and a move back to that sort of maternal relationship which young girls learn to practice. It is as if the girl who won't start playing at Princes will go back to playing with dolls. Or, to put it more precisely, it is as if the girl who won't start giving herself to Princes will go back to taking care of her dolls — Toto here being a sort of doll of course. The same thing can, by the way, be seen in *Peter Pan* where Wendy and Peter, since they cannot play at being lovers, decide to play at being mother and father instead. This point comes from an article by Stuart Culver where he says,

> Just as her companions learn that what they already have must and will suffice, Dorothy learns to embrace the comfortable enclosure of the whitewashed picket fence and the domestic role it projects for her. The theme of containment is perversely underlined by the casting of Garland, then sixteen, in the role of a seven year old, infantilized and all too obviously contained by her costume and character. If her dream seems to betray an awakening sexual interest in the men around her, it also allows her to reimagine that adolescent desire nostalgically as the simpler relation a child establishes with her dolls and toys, a relationship presented here as more maternal than passionate.[20]

To put it all another way, there is no need for self-donation in *The Wizard of Oz* as the Prince function has now become, in a sense, a part of

Dorothy's own personality. If Toto is in fact the true object of love, then Dorothy does not need to go very far out of herself to find this love object. We agree that one of the problems with *The Wizard of Oz* is its strange sexlessness. And we agree, too, with McGuire's still more disturbing suggestion that this sexlessness is emanating, somehow, from Dorothy. We don't, however, think that the problem is her innocence, exactly. Cinderella, for example, is innocent, but her innocence does not seem to interfere with her desire for the Prince or the Prince's desire for her. We would, therefore, prefer to say that it is not Dorothy's innocence that is the problem, but her self-containedness.[21] In contrast to Cinderella, then, Dorothy is self-contained, already complete, not fundamentally in need of anyone else.[22]

If we assume that both stories are designed to teach young girls the most important lesson and the key to life,[23] then in *Cinderella* that key would be taking the risks which lead to sexual love, while in *The Wizard of Oz* it would be a self-reliance which learns to handle the world. What all the characters in *The Wizard of Oz* learn is that they already possess in themselves all that they need. The Scarecrow learns that he is already pretty smart, the Tin Man that he knew all along how to care, and the Cowardly Lion that he could make himself face his fears on behalf of those he loved, and Dorothy that she always had the power to go where she most wanted to be. None of them, in order to reach completion, needs to make the radical move towards another person that Cinderella makes.

Of course, the characters in *The Wizard of Oz* do form friendships, and of course, these friendships are important. But these friendships do not seem to us to contradict the points we have been making. For these friendships do not, first of all, complete Dorothy.[24] She already has all the brains and heart and courage inside her from the start. And, more importantly, these friendships, with all their comradeship,[25] are still a far cry from the radical self-donation involved in Cinderella's relation to the Prince.[26]

Those Ruby Red Shoes (a Detail Which Confirms the Analysis)

This analysis is confirmed by the detail of the shoes. Both Cinderella and Dorothy move through their respective stories wearing a pair of magic shoes. Very feminine, very beautiful shoes both times. But how they handle these shoes, these symbols of their femininity, is very different.

Cinderella loses one of her shoes, and the Prince picks it up. If we read between the lines, we could say that what is happening here is that Cinderella is giving one of her shoes — and shoes are a very feminine and maybe even a sexual symbol[27] — to the Prince as a gift. And this is a gift that does then bring the Prince, her future groom, to her.

Dorothy, on the other hand, never loses her shoes. In fact, we learn from the Wicked Witch that her shoes cannot come off for, if they do, then she will die. And the effect of these shoes — these magical, superbly feminine, ruby red shoes — is not to take Dorothy forward into marriage and adult life but only backward to her childhood home.

Gregory Maguire's reading of these shoes is similar. This occurs in his novel *Wicked*,[28] which retells the story of Oz from the point of view of the Wicked Witch of the West. In this novel, the shoes are portrayed as instruments of self reliance or unilateral power, but not of sexuality. The shoes originally belonged to the Wicked Witch of the East, whose name was Nessarose. In McGuire's novel, Nessarose was born crippled, and what the shoes do for her is allow her to stand without assistance.[29] There is no suggestion that she wants the shoes to make herself more attractive. And when the Wicked Witch of the West is desperate to get these shoes back from Dorothy, she does not want them because of their attractiveness either. She wants them because they are a family heirloom made by her father and belonging to her sister, of course. She also wants them because they represent a power she does not want to fall into the hands of the Wizard.

The End of the Road (Another Detail Which Confirms the Analysis)

And then there are the endings. *Cinderella* ends with Cinderella marrying the Prince and going off to live happily ever after. *The Wizard of Oz* ends with Dorothy going back to Kansas, vowing to "never ever leave home again." Cinderella moves forward into maturity, while Dorothy moves backward into childhood.

In fact, a colleague of ours, Nancy Billias of Saint Joseph College, suggested that the ending of *The Wizard of Oz* should be interpreted in terms of the Freudian death drive. On her reading, the stasis to which Dorothy returns is a sort of death. Now, we are not sure that we want to accept Freud's death drive theory, but our colleague certainly has a point. For what is the decision of a young girl to immure herself at home except a sort of death? To this point, our colleague added the still more disturbing suggestion that *The Wizard of Oz* is so appealing because something in us is yearning for this death-like stasis too.

All we want to add to this is the idea that the stasis Dorothy comes to at the end is a direct result of her failure to find a Prince. For if she had found her Prince in the Land of Oz, she would not now be returning to Kansas vowing never to leave it again, but would be returning excitedly to invite Uncle Henry and Aunt Em to come to Oz for her wedding feast.

While we are on the subject of endings, we want to note just how bleak the ending of *The Wizard of Oz* actually is. The problem is not just that Dorothy ends up back in the same bleak Kansas from which she began. It is also that, as Terry Staples points out in an online review,[30] Dorothy's little respite from Kansas in the Land of Oz turns out not even to have been real. Still worse, as Staples also points out, is the fact that Toto has not even been saved but is still scheduled to die at the hands of Miss Gulch.[31] Dorothy has not, in fact, brought anything back with her from Oz that will make her capable of stopping this from happening. Literally nothing has been accomplished.

Of course, the movie covers all this over and makes the ending seem happy and optimistic. This is, we think, another way in which the movie appeals, i.e., by sugar-coating the bleakness. In fact, the movie takes the whole trip to Oz — a trip which leads to no Prince, involves a multitude of potentially fatal threats, and ends with a return to the same grey Kansas from which we began — and makes it seem like a wonderful adventure. So much so that a poster advertising the film was even able to call it "the happiest film ever made."[32]

Just Watch Out, My Pretty (Some Objections and Responses)

Our friends and colleagues were (of course) kind enough to raise various questions and objections about these ideas. Questions and objections arose in our own minds, too. So, what we would like to do next is to answer what seemed to be the two most common objections. Our hope is that, in doing so, we will also manage to add the appropriate qualifications to what might have been a bit overstated before.

The first objection says that it is unfair to treat self-donation as a good thing and self-possession as a bad thing. For certainly it is necessary to be self-possessed, to know how to handle the world, to be able to rely on one's own resources, and so on. Besides that, it is necessary to be self-possessed first in order to be self-donative later. Self-possession, in other words, is a necessary developmental step on the way to self-donation. And so we are, in sum, quite wrong to be looking down at Dorothy for being merely self-possessed.

In response to this, we want to say that our complaint is not really with the idea of self-possession itself. We do agree that self-possession is a good thing, and we are happy to see that Dorothy is self-possessed rather than falling apart. But it is just that she is self-possessed in a way that does not seem to have any room for Princes (i.e., Others) in it. And this seems to us a shame, for the Dorothy of the movie is clearly reaching an age where the thought of Princes would be appropriate. It is here that Judy Garland's age becomes a crucial issue. For if she really was only eight or ten years old, then maybe a focus on self-possession alone would be developmentally appropriate. But Judy Garland is so manifestly not eight or ten years old that to see her in her self-contained state, not yearning for or even thinking about her later life beyond Aunt Em and Uncle Henry, no longer seems like maturity, but rather like a sort of failure to move from the self-possessed stage to the self-donative one. And even the objection, with its talk of developmental steps, does admit that self-donation is a higher stage than the stage of mere self-possession. We want, in this regard, to reject the sort of reading which "corrects" the movie in terms of the book, i.e., the sort of reading which says that, because the Dorothy in Baum's novel was only eight or ten, then we should view Judy Garland's Dorothy as only eight or ten as well. We want to reject this sort of reading not just on general principles, but also because we think the movie functions in our culture as its own text, more or less independently of the book from which it was made. Most people who have seen the movie have not, we suspect, also read the book. Therefore, we think we should look at the movie as its own self contained text, and, if we do this, then the Dorothy of the movie is actually as old as Judy Garland looks on the screen — which means that this movie Dorothy is already in early adolescence though still dressing, for some reason, in somewhat younger clothes.

The movie, moreover, presents the ideal of self-possession in a particularly regressive form, where what it means to be truly self-possessed is to decide to go back home and never ever leave it again.[33] This is not a self-possession that seems eager to turn outward again and to experience, once more, the wonders and terrors of the world, but a sort of defensive self-possession that retreats back into a zone of safety.[34] And our point is simply that this might not be the best vision of maturity to be putting forward.

Whatever else is true, *The Wizard of Oz* is undeniably one of our great myths of growing up. We are all invited to think about our own lives and hopes in terms of Dorothy's. And so it seems to us only natural to be a little worried that such a central myth is also such a Princeless one. It is interesting to note in this regard that our other great myth of growing up, the story of Luke Skywalker, is surprisingly similar. It also involves a lot of Oedipal dynamics, which in this case involve the conflict between good father figures (Obi wan, Yoda) and bad father figures (Darth Vader, the Emperor). And it also leaves Luke without any Princess in the end, Leia turning out to be his sister, and, besides, in love with Hans and not with him. Moreover, if we look back to Episodes I, II, and III,[35] we see that it was gaining the Princess that led to the downfall of Anakin Skywalker. Successful Jedis live monk-like existences, needing no Other once their training is complete as The Force alone seems to be enough to nurture them.

The second objection is a feminist one. It says that there is something reactionary and oppressive in holding Cinderella up as an ideal. The whole Cinderella story makes it clear that she is secondary to the Prince. She, the woman, is lowly, while he, the man, is almost unimaginably high and noble.

And what he does, of course, is to reach down and raise her up. Certainly not an image of gender relations we want to be teaching to our children!

In response to this, we want to say, first of all, that we are not putting *Cinderella* forward as our preferred model of gender relations. We do agree with the self-donative aspect of the Cinderella story, for we do believe that maturity means being able to love another person. But just because we agree with the self-donative aspect does not mean that we also agree with all the other unequal aspects of the story. Our approval, then, is limited to the self-donative core, and not to all the trappings of inequality which surround that core.

Secondly, we do not think that the proper response to the inequalities in the Cinderella story is to accept Dorothy, rather than Cinderella, as our feminist ideal.[36] That would be to throw out the baby with the bathwater. In *Cinderella*, we have sexual love occurring in an unequal way. But surely the solution for this is not to look for a cultural icon (like *The Wizard of Oz*) that dispenses with sexual love entirely. For that is not so much a solution as a regression to a previous stage of development. What we need, it seems to us, is not Dorothy, but a new Cinderella who will figure for us a new sort of romance: a romance where sexual passion is not based (as it has been for so long) on the man being of a higher status than the woman and then reaching down to rescue (oh, how exciting) poor dear her.

Finally, while the Cinderella and Dorothy stories are gendered (and heterosexist), our hope is that a self-donative model of maturity is not.

Part II: *The Wizard of Oz* in the Context of Other Modern Fairy Tales

Widespread Disappearances (a Brief Survey of Other Modern Fairy Tales)

The Wizard of Oz is not an unusual or exceptional case. Many of the fairy tales that our society is producing are, under the surface, very similar. One of the little experiments we tried was setting *The Wizard of Oz* back into the context of what we might call its peer group. We defined this peer group as stories which:

(i) are culturally iconic.

(ii) involve a normal heroine who gets caught in a magical world.

(iii) are not simply a retelling of a fairy tale from a previous era.

We included the second criteria, the one about normal girls in magical worlds, because this seemed like the most straightforward way to define the genre (or sub-genre) to which *The Wizard of Oz* belongs. We included the first and third criteria, the ones about culturally iconic stories which are not simply retellings, because we wanted to get stories which are both important and new enough to reflect our modern culture.

The two obvious movies which fit into this peer group are *Peter Pan* and *Alice in Wonderland*. Another colleague of ours, Erica Tucker of the anthropology department of Stonehill College, suggested two children's books: *A Wrinkle in Time* by Madeleine L'Engle and *The Lion, the Witch and the Wardrobe*, by C.S. Lewis Finally, the recent TV series *Buffy the Vampire Slayer* also seems to fit the criteria for, although Buffy is chosen to receive special powers, the show is also careful to insist that she is really just an ordinary California girl.

We realize that this peer group might be too small to yield definitive results. Unfortunately, we did not know what to add to make it bigger. But we do want to begin by admitting up front that the smallness of this sample size makes any results we reach tentative only. In any case, what we found was that, in all these different movies and books, the Prince figure is either absent or, if present, unavailable to the heroine.

To begin with, there simply is no Prince in either *Alice in Wonderland* or in *The Lion the Witch and the Wardrobe*. Of course, Aslan in *The Lion Witch and the Wardrobe* is a very princely figure, but he is obviously not the kind of prince we are talking about here, as he is a religious figure rather than a potential sexual partner for Lucy.

In *Peter Pan* there is a Prince figure: Peter Pan himself. And yet this Prince figure is unavailable to Wendy as Peter has explicitly decided that he will never grow up. It is true that, when Wendy plays the role of mother to the Lost Boys, Peter agrees to play the role of father, but this is only on the condition that it is very clear that the whole thing is just make believe. And so the contact between the Prince and Princess, which should by traditional fairy tale norms be occurring here, fails to actually come off. All we get is two children playing house.

In *A Wrinkle in Time*, Meg does not meet a Prince on her travels, but brings a boyfriend, Calvin, along with her. And this boyfriend is presented less like a Prince, and more like just one of the family. He does not even seem to be the focus of Meg's attention, for she is actually focused on her mission, while his role is merely to supply occasional support and encouragement from behind the scenes. He is nice rather than ravishing. And he seems, if anything, to represent what a boyfriend becomes once the possibility of real princeliness is lost. In fact, when one of us presented, to an eleven year old girl of her acquaintance, the idea that Calvin was Meg's boyfriend, the eleven year old was a little horrified by the idea and continued to insist that Calvin was merely a neighbor.

Finally, in *Buffy the Vampire Slayer,* the good vampire, Angel, is obviously the Prince figure. But although Buffy and Angel do love each other in a very passionate way, an ancient gypsy curse prevents them from ever being together. And so here, too, the Prince is unavailable to the heroine. And the lesson she must learn is not how to gain the Prince and give herself to him, but, rather, how to live without him. And so it does seem, in sum, that many modern fairy tales are Princeless.

We would also like to continue talking about *Star Wars* in this regard. We realize that it does not actually fit into the peer group since it features a hero and not a heroine. But it is both a recent story and also a culturally iconic one. And it does feature a normal person caught in a magical world. Luke is an ordinary boy growing up in an ordinary world until he is, one day, suddenly thrust into the semi-magical world of the Jedi Knights. Maybe it would be interesting, then, to see if the same sort of patterns will hold for heroes as for heroines.

And *Star Wars* does seem to fit the pattern so far, for, as we said a little while ago, Luke does not find a Princess. There is also an interesting parallel here between the earlier episodes of *Star Wars* and *Buffy the Vampire Slayer.* In Buffy's case, it's not just that she and Angel do not in fact get together, but that there is actually a sort of cosmic ban forbidding them to do so. And the one time they do consummate their relationship, it unleashes a "historical badness" that threatens to destroy the world. What is interesting is that similar vast and destructive effects are also unleashed by Anakin Skywalker's forbidden love for Princess Padme. It is almost as if there is something in the very fabric of these fairy tale worlds that gets torn asunder when the heroine possesses her Prince or the hero his Princess.

Like a Fish Out of Water (the Background Sociology of These Modern Fairy Tales)

We also seem to have stumbled upon an odd correlation here. There seems to be a connection between Princelessness on the one hand, and normal heroines caught in magical worlds on the other. We have already seen this connection working in one direction. The examples we have looked at so far do show us a whole series of normal heroines living in magical worlds, all of whom end up without a Prince (as well as one normal hero in a magical world who ends up without a Princess). But does the connection work in the other direction too? In other words, if it is a normal heroine in a normal world or a magical heroine in a magical world, will she then get a Prince?

The answer seems to be yes. Two examples, both recent Disney movies, would be *Mulan* and *The Little Mermaid.* In *Mulan,* we have a normal heroine in a normal world, for Mulan is living in an ordinary, rather than a magical, China. And Mulan does get the Prince at the end of the story. In *The Little Mermaid*, Ariel begins as a magical heroine (a mermaid) living in a magical (undersea) world. She then switches and becomes a normal heroine (an ordinary girl) living in a normal (dry land) world. The point here is that, despite the switching, she is always properly matched to the world, for when she is magical, her world is magical, and when she is normal, her world is normal. And, in a major revision of Hans Christian Andersen's nineteenth-century version of the tale, the modern Disney Ariel gets to keep her Prince too.

We would like, therefore, to suggest the following two correlations:

• If the fairy tale has a normal heroine caught in a magical world, then the Prince will not be available to her.

• If the fairy tale has a normal heroine in a normal world, or a magical heroine in a magical world, then the Prince will be available to her.

These correlations are tentative, of course. We realize that *Mulan* and *The Little Mermaid*, even more than the peer group, do not constitute a large enough sample to begin drawing definitive results. And so the second correlation especially should, in order to be more accurate, read "may be available" rather than "will be available."

We also do not want to pretend to know the meaning of these correlations. However, a first guess would be that they have something to do with displacement or disjuncture. These normal heroines lost in magical worlds are displaced: they are not reliably or comfortably at home in the strange new environments they now find themselves in. And perhaps the point is that this sort of displacement is inimical to the finding of Princes. For perhaps the project of finding a Prince requires more than just an internal self confidence. Perhaps it requires a confidence in the world too. Cinderella, for example, is confident enough that her world will, in the end, still reward merit, that she moves heaven and earth to get to the ball and to dance with the Prince. And she is so at home in the world that she is able (in Grimm's version) to call upon the birds for help in sorting out the peas. And perhaps what our modern (Wizard-of-Oz-like) fairy tales are telling us is that once this sort of confidence is gone; once the heroine is no longer comfortably matched up with her world but now actually disjoined from it, she will lack the secure foundation she would need in order to begin reaching out to Princes.

The King Function (More about the Background Sociology of These Modern Fairy Tales)

Another little experiment we tried was reading these fairy tales as gestalts. In the foreground, there is the heroine and her relation or non-relation to the Prince. In the background, there is the social world as the fairy tale pictures it. And we are using the word "gestalt" because we think there might be a connection between this foreground (the heroine) and this background (her society).

To begin with, we have said that in *The Wizard of Oz* there is no Prince and that Dorothy does not even seem to be pursuing one. Rather, Dorothy is pictured in terms of self-reliance. What we want to say now is that this all makes sense given what sort of world Oz is. It is ruled, after all, by an incompetent and somewhat fraudulent wizard, not to mention the fact that it is beset by a couple of insane witches. Certainly in such a world it would behoove any young girl to put away her thoughts of storybook romance and learn to take care of herself.

In contrast, the world of *Cinderella*, although it does contain the evil stepmother, is fundamentally more stable. There is not only the Prince but also the Prince's father, the King, who is able to provide the ball and then, later, the wedding feast. There is, in other words, an authority in place, and this authority is providing structures that allow the heroine to pursue and then marry the Prince.[37] What we might call high romance is, after all, not an automatic or natural relation, but a relation that requires certain social prerequisites. We realize that we have only gestured vaguely at what those prerequisites are when we use words like stability and structure and authority. Unfortunately, we lack both the space and the learning to analyze these prerequisites in any sort of precise way. And so let us just say that however they should be more precisely defined, it does seem to us that these prerequisites (and hence the possibility) of high romance are much more likely to be available in the world of Cinderella, than in the world of displaced, frightened, wandering Dorothy.

This contrast appears in the locations of the two stories. In *The Wizard of Oz,* the Wizard sends Dorothy back out of doors into the forest.[38] In *Cinderella*, the King invites Cinderella, and all the other young ladies, indoors, into the ball. One story, in other words, takes place in an environment of risk, while the other takes place in an environment of safety. And the point is that only in the latter environment will a young girl have the luxury of devoting herself to Princes and to romance.

We want to put forward, then, as a tentative hypothesis, the following correlations[39]:

• When the King is present, the Prince is available, and the heroine gives herself to the Prince.

• When the King is absent, the Prince is unavailable, and the heroine substitutes self-reliance for self-donation.

These correlations are confirmed by the other books and movies in the peer group. As we said before, in none of these books or movies is the Prince available to the heroine. And it is also true that, just as our correlations predict, in all of these books and movies the King is absent. Wonderland, the world in which Alice lands, is chaotic rather than structured, and the Queen of Hearts, far from being a stable authority, is a deranged tyrant. Never, Never Land is a world of pirates and Indians with no authority capable of protecting the Lost Boys. *A Wrinkle in Time* takes place largely on a planet ruled not by a true king, but by the totalitarian and evil It. Narnia is ruled by the evil figure of the White Witch, while the true king, Aslan, is in exile.[40] And the Sunnydale of *Buffy the Vampire Slayer* is rife with demons and monsters, but lacks any gods or angels.[41]

The *Star Wars* saga fits this same pattern too. To begin with, the King is absent as the galaxy is controlled by the evil Sith Lord, Senator Palpatine. It might seem problematic, at first, to talk here of an absent King, since the universe in *Star Wars* is governed by the Force. But the Force is not a King, being instead the collective product of all living beings. It is, to put it differently, more of an ontological structure than a social authority. And this Force, moreover, does not seem to necessarily be a good and stabilizing structure, since it seems almost equally available for both good uses and for bad.

In any case, given the fact that the King is absent, the story follows just the pattern that the second correlation predicts. Luke is denied a Princess, and, as a Jedi Knight, required to achieve an almost incredible self-reliance. This same correlation is also demonstrated in a sort of reverse fashion by the story of Anakin Skywalker. For when he tries to break out of this pattern and, instead of remaining self-reliant in the absence of a King, takes up a self-donative relation to Princess Padme, he falls victim to the dark side, loses his status as a hero, and becomes the villain instead.

These correlations are also confirmed in another way by *The Little Mermaid* and *Mulan*. As we said before, in both of these movies the heroine does get a Prince in the end. And what is interesting is that both worlds are ruled by a benevolent monarch: King Triton in the one case and the Emperor in the other. In fact, in both cases the heroine actually gets the Prince with the blessings of the monarch.

Of Fairy Tales and Musk Oxen (Still More about the Background Sociology of These Modern Fairy Tales)

But let us come back to the movies and books which are like *The Wizard of Oz*. What we want to say next is that the primary human grouping in these worlds without Princes, or in most of them anyway, is some sort of family-like structure. *Alice in Wonderland* is the one case in which this is not true, for Alice goes through her adventures alone. But in *Peter Pan*, we have the family-like structure of the Lost Boys. And Wendy is actually invited in order to make this family-like structure still more family-like by playing the role of the mother. In *The Wizard of Oz*, of course, Dorothy and her three companions form a sort of substitute family unit. The primary group in *The Lion the Witch and the Wardrobe* actually is a group of siblings, and their primary helpers are a family of beavers. The primary group in *A Wrinkle in Time* is also a family group, with Meg's boyfriend, Calvin, figured as one of the family. *Buffy the Vampire of Slayer* is centered on the substitute family made up of Buffy, Willow, Xander, and Mr. Giles.[42]

Of course it might seem at first that what we have in *The Wizard of Oz* and in *Buffy the Vampire Slayer* are not substitute families but merely groups of friends. We don't, however, think this is really the case. These groups, to begin with, involve persons of both genders, and this is typical of family groups, while friendship groups tend to be single gender affairs. These groups also tend to be together more or less constantly, which is also more typical of family than of friendship groupings. Finally, in *Buffy the Vampire Slayer*, the group involves Mr. Giles who is older and can really be thought of only as the father of the group and not as just one of the gang.—The point seems important to us because family groups are typically tighter than friendship groups in the sense that the family group is the group of last resort when survival becomes an issue. And so to see family groups rather than friendship groups resurfacing in these modern fairy tales strengthens our point about how we are seeing a return to a basic sort of bonding in a situation of instability and threat.

These family-like structures make sense in terms of the unstable worlds which form the background of these stories. In a world filled with uncertainty and threat—in a world ruled by an incompetent wizard and terrorized by a psychotic witch, for example—it is, of course, essential to pull together into a tightly knit group.

And yet this is also what we might call a retreat to an anthropologically more basic structure. For instead of a world of romantic couples, we now have a world of small groups bonded together for purposes of survival. It is almost as if we have stepped back into a time when things like Princes and balls were unthinkable luxuries and when the basic form of community was produced not by love, but by circling the wagons against the dangers of the outside world.

Of course, there are small group structures in *Mulan* and *The Little Mermaid* too. But there is a qualitative shift in what we might call the stature of these small groups. For in both *Mulan* and *The Little Mermaid*, these small groups are downplayed, or, what amounts to the same thing, played for comic effect. In *Mulan*, the small group consists of a cricket, a horse, and a dragon who, for his past failures, has been miniaturized to the point where the fire he breathes can light a match but not much else. There is also the small group of the other soldiers who are played in *Three Stooges* style. And in *The Little Mermaid*, Ariel's small group consists of a little fish, a still smaller crab who has a comically inflated ego, and a gooney bird. These seem, in fact, to be not real small groups so much as the comic vestiges of small groups.

This is quite different from the movies and books in *The Wizard of Oz* peer group. For here the small groups are not so obviously inferior in stature to the heroine. The other children in *The Lion the Witch and the Wardrobe* have basically the same status as Lucy. And the other family members in *A Wrinkle in Time* have basically the same status as Meg. In *Peter Pan*, Wendy's small group would be Peter Pan, the Lost Boys, and Tinkerbell, and none of these seem to be obviously inferior to her. It is interesting in this regard that Tinkerbell is not turned into some sort of cute comic stereotype, but acts intelligently and even heroically. In *The Wizard of Oz*, the Scarecrow, Tin Man and Cowardly Lion are Dorothy's roughly equal companions. Just looking at this issue in terms of size, they are all the same size as Dorothy or larger, whereas in *Mulan* and *The Little Mermaid* we have small groups consisting of creatures much smaller in size than the heroine.[43] And finally, in *Buffy the Vampire Slayer*, Buffy's high school friends, despite the fact that she is clearly the leader, still have a rough equality with her, and Giles, as her watcher, has a status which is actually higher.

And this difference seems to make sense in terms of the other correlations we talked about before. In *Mulan* and *The Little Mermaid*, we have both Prince and King, which means that the small groups are not so important and can therefore be demoted to comic status. In the movies and books which are like *The Wizard of Oz*, though, there is neither Prince nor King, and so the small groups, as the only real group left, become overwhelmingly important and cannot be demoted. This leads us to our final two correlations:

• If the Prince is available and the King function is in place, the small group structures will be vestigial or comic.

• If the Prince is not available and the King function is not in place, the small group structures will be central rather than vestigial.

Star Wars fits this pattern too. As we said earlier, there is no Princess available for Luke, and he lives at a time when the Empire is ruled by evil men. And, just as the second correlation above predicts, Luke's comrades (his small group) play a role that is central rather than vestigial.

It appears, in sum, that *Star Wars* fits all the same correlations as *The Wizard of Oz* and its peer group. Perhaps, then, these fairy tale patterns are not really as gendered as they might seem, i.e., perhaps they can apply to both heroes and to heroines. Luke, it seems, is Dorothy's late-born twin brother.

*From Cinderella to Dorothy to Spiderman (a Tentative Hypothesis
Concerning the Literary History of the Fairy Tale)*

The overall picture is pretty bleak. We seem to have a whole group of modern fairy tales where the heroine gets no prince and so has no possibility of marriage; where, although an ordinary girl, she gets caught up in a world of magic always a little beyond her grasp; where there is no king function and the world is consequently unstable and dangerous; and where the romantic couple is replaced by a small group clinging desperately together in the face of external threats.

Because of this underlying bleakness, we think that it is probably not quite accurate to think of these modern fairy tales as a continuation of the old fairy tale tradition. It might be more accurate to think of them as the *despair* of the old fairy tale tradition. Sure there was a lot of heartache in a fairy tale like *Cinderella*, but there was also the Prince, the ball, the King, the marriage, and the chance for the happily ever after. In a modern fairy tale like *The Wizard of Oz*, however, there are none of these things. *The Wizard of Oz* is the destitution of all those features that made the Cinderella world, despite its injustice and its pain, a hopeful one.

And this, we want to suggest, explains the next step in the fairy tale tradition: the step to superheroes like Batman, Superman, and Spiderman. Superheroes seem to us to represent a violent reaction to the despairing world of the modern, Wizard-of-Oz style, fairy tale. One of the typical human responses to despairing situations is violence. It is also typical in such situations to dream of violence. And we suspect that it is this dream of a violent solution to despair that we are seeing in the modern superhero stories.

It is interesting, in this regard, to note some similarities between the superhero world and the world of Oz. As our sample of superhero movies, we selected *Superman, Superman Returns, Batman, The Dark Knight, Spiderman, Spiderman 3*, and (in line with our interest in cases where the gender switches) *Catwoman*. We realize that, given the large number of superhero movies, and especially the vast comic book literature, this sample size is still very small, and we hope it does not introduce too many inaccuracies.

In any case, in both Oz and the superhero world, the Prince or Princess is generally unavailable. For Dorothy, there simply seems to be no Prince on the horizon, while for the superheroes, the Princess (or in Catwoman's case, the Prince) seems to be both dazzlingly visible and yet also just a little out of reach. The one clear exception to this is the first Batman movie which ends with Vickie Vail being chauffeured off to meet Batman.[44] But in *The Dark Knight*, Batman does not get to keep Rachel Dawes,[45] the fundamental problem being his dedication to his self-appointed role. Similarly, at the end of

Catwoman, Prudence Phillips walks away from the very handsome Thomas Lone, citing her role as Catwoman as the reason for the breakup. And at the end of the first Spiderman movie, it seems to be his Spiderman role which causes Peter Parker to push Mary Jane Watson away. By the time we reach *Spiderman 3,* though, things have gotten more complex, and when the movie opens Peter and Mary Jane are actually dating. But they soon face unprecedented challenges, and the movie chronicles a botched marriage proposal as well as Spidey's exploring his dark side at Mary Jane's expense. The movie ends ambiguously, with the pair dancing in a jazz club, Mary Jane tearful, after she has just sung about being through with men. Finally, although Superman does not quite manage to get together with Lois in the first *Superman* movie, by the time of *Superman Returns* he has had at least enough of a relationship with her to have produced a son. Unfortunately, he does not know about this son and leaves on a multi-year foray to the ruins of Krypton. By the time he returns, Lois has moved on to a stable domestic relationship with Richard. While she is still in love with Superman and does tell him of their son, the final scenes show Superman imparting to the little boy the same words that sustained him in his own father's absence.

In both Oz and the superhero world, there is a disjuncture between the character and his or her setting. Dorothy is a normal girl caught in a magical world, while the superheroes are magical people caught in a normal world. These are reverse cases, of course, but to our mind the important thing is that in both cases the character and world are failing to match.

Of course, the word "magical" might not be quite right here. What magic amounts to in a modern tale is, in fact, a vexed question.[46] But whether "magical" is the right word or not, we hope it is obvious enough that all the superheroes are "super" because of some fantastical exception about them. Whether this comes from a difference in planetary origin (Superman), a freak accident of technology (Spiderman), astronomical wealth coupled with a pathological need for vengeance (Batman), or possession by an ancient deity (Catwoman), each of these characters is mismatched.[47]

In both Oz and the superhero world, there is the lack of a King function.[48] Oz is ruled by an incompetent wizard and evil witches. Gotham City is ruled, more or less, by criminals. The New York of Spiderman is a pretty criminal place too, albeit on a smaller scale. And it is a place where many of the institutions — the media, the military, the big corporations — are more or less corrupt. There is the goodness of Uncle Ben and Aunt May, of course, but they are not ruling figures, and, far from being able to introduce order into the world, their puissance stops at being able to provide a small island of refuge from it. Catwoman's world is dominated by an evil corporation whose beauty products destroy the health of those who use them. And Metropolis, though its institutions do not seem as corrupted as in some of these other worlds, still has a lot of evil characters: including many small time criminals and a criminal mastermind bent on replacing North America with a continent of his own construction.

There is a difference between Oz and the superhero world when it comes to the issue of small group structure. *The Wizard of Oz* places Dorothy in the small group consisting of The Scarecrow, Tin Man, and Cowardly Lion, but the superheroes tend to be much more alone. Batman, the most human in terms of his powers, has the closest thing to a group structure. There are Alfred, his butler and confidante, Mr. Fox, his business manager and arms supplier, and the future Commissioner Gordon, with whom he shares intelligence. But even Batman, when it comes to actual combat, tends to fight alone. And the small group is still more superfluous for the magical Spiderman, who lacks even Batman's coterie, and has only his slowly developing relationship with Mary Jane to rely on. Catwoman, also magical, is also pretty much alone: neither her best friend Laura nor her potential boyfriend knows who she really is, and all she gets is a bit of general advice from the older woman who owns the magical cats. Finally, Superman, the most alien, is also perhaps the most alone, being accompanied only by the occasional disembodied voice of his father offering him advice.[49] But although this diminished importance of the small group is a difference between the superhero world and the world of Oz, it is a difference that does make sense. For if the superhero story is proposing mythological violence as a solution to despair, then the superhero, the possessor of this overwhelming violence, will no longer need a group of equals as his assistants. The main point is that, except for this one difference, a difference which is moreover an expected one, the world of Oz and the world of the superhero are remarkably similar.

The easiest way to interpret this similarity would be to simply say that both types of stories are responses to a similar bleakness and despair. When we come right down to it, a movie like *The Wizard of Oz* where the bleakness is covered over with a borrowed fairy tale charm, and a movie like *The Dark Knight* where the bleakness is covered over with the dream of violence, are not, perhaps, so very different.

But maybe we can risk a slightly stronger statement than just that these two types of stories are similar responses to similar conditions. For it is also true that there is a time sequence here: superhero stories come after stories like *The Wizard of Oz*. To take just one example, the print version of *The Wizard of Oz* came out in 1900, while *Superman* did not appear in print until 1939. In terms of movies, *The Wizard of Oz* appeared in early versions in 1910, 1914 and 1925, with the iconic version appearing in 1939. *Superman*, in contrast, did not hit the screen until 1951.[50] So, instead of just saying that these two types of stories are connected, maybe we should say that the later type (superhero stories) actually developed out of the former type (modern fairy tales like *The Wizard of Oz*). Perhaps the method of covering over the bleakness with fairy tale charm began to wear thin, so we needed to turn to the still stronger medicine which dreams of violence provide.

Our last conjecture, then, is that what we are seeing is a three-stage history in the evolution of the fairy tale. The first, or Cinderella, stage contains fairy tales where the Prince is available and happiness is at least a possibility. The second, or Oz, stage contains modern fairy tales where there is no Prince and no happiness, but where the characters bond desperately together against a chaotic and dangerous world — the whole being covered, however, in a fairy tale optimism and charm. The third, or Dark Knight, stage contains superhero tales in which overwhelming violence is presented as the only viable solution to this despair.

Notes

1. See L. Frank Baum, *The Wonderful Wizard of Oz*, "Introduction," online at http://www.literature.org/authors/baum-l-frank/the-wonderful-wizard-of-oz/introduction.html.

2. George A. Dunn suggests that Baum's philosophy of fairy tales differs substantially from other modern models, particularly Tolkien's and Chesterton's, but notes that the movie, at least, reverts to more traditional fairy tale assumptions. See "The Wonderful Smallness of Evil in Oz," in *The Wizard of Oz and Philosophy: Wicked Wisdom of the West*, edited by Randall E. Auxier and Philip S. Seng (Chicago, IL: Open Court, 2008), 149–166.

3. It is interesting to note in this regard that, in a previous movie version released in 1925, Dorothy is explicitly said to be 18 on the day the cyclone hits. We are indebted for this fact to Philip S. Seng and his article "A Sort of Homecoming: Growing up with Dorothy" in *The Wizard of Oz and Philosophy: Wicked Wisdom of the West*, edited by Randall E. Auxier and Philip S. Seng (Chicago, IL: Open Court, 2008), 249.

4. We would like to take a moment to thank those colleagues whose conversations have helped us develop our ideas. They are: Nancy Billias, of Saint Joseph College in West Hartford Connecticut, and Scott Cohen and Erica Tucker of Stonehill College in Easton Massachusetts. We would also like to thank Nancy Billias in a special way for her patience in reading through a draft of this paper and for her many helpful suggestions. Agnes's husband brought a true fanboy's eye for detail to the discussions of superheroes and *Star Wars*, enriching them considerably, and we are grateful. We would also like to thank the participants at the conference on "The Yellow Brick Road in the 21st Century" for their many interesting and helpful comments. "The Yellow Brick Road in the 21st Century" conference was held June 26–28, 2009, at Henderson State University in Arkadelphia, Arkansas.

5. Bruno Bettelheim, *The Uses of Enchantment: The Meaning and Importance of Fairy Tales* (New York: Vintage Books, 1977), 245.

6. Bettelheim, 249. The word "symbol" is our term, which we have used in an effort to keep our language simple. Bettelheim actually uses the technical term "displacement."

7. Bettelheim, 248.

8. Bettelheim, 245.

9. Bettelheim, 264.

10. Although he does not make the comparison to *Cinderella*, the structure of good versus bad mother images is also talked about by Jerry Griswold in the second part of his article about Oz. See: Jerry Griswold's "There's No Place but Home: *the Wizard of Oz*," in *The Anti-*

och Review, vol. 45, no. 4, Autumn 1987, 468–473. There are many interesting additional features of Griswold's analysis which we, unfortunately, do not have time to go into here.

11. This is also noted by Jerry Griswold. See: Jerry Griswold, "There's No Place but Home: *the Wizard of Oz*," in *The Antioch Review*, vol. 45, no. 4, Autumn 1987, 468.

12. Aaron Fortune similarly reads both Ant Em and Uncle Henry as only half-hearted in their defense of Dorothy. See "There's No Place Like Home: Dorothy Gale's Relations," in *The Wizard of Oz and Philosophy: Wicked Wisdom of the West*, edited by Randall E. Auxier and Phillip S. Seng (Chicago, IL: Open Court, 2008), 278.

13. Reproductions of some farm pin-ups can be found at: http://hayinart.com/2004_03.html/; for Betty Grable on the farm, see: http://bettygrable.net/betty-grable-photos-color/betty_grable_color_3; for Betty Brosmer, see: http://www.flickr.com/photos/36387135@N00/2494187564/; and: http://www.flickr.com/photos/36387135@N00/2494187600/; for one by Al Buell, see: http://www.thepinupfiles.com/images/f-ab06.jpg.

14. The original Wizard of Oz novel, though not the movie, contains a further surface similarity to *Cinderella*. For in the novel Dorothy is actually imprisoned for a while by the Wicked Witch, who makes her do kitchen work.

15. Translated by Laurence Scott. First and second editions published together by the University of Texas Press.

16. Or perhaps it would be more accurate to say that Dorothy is freed from this illusion *up to a point.* For Stuart Culver points out that the characters continue to embrace the fantasy of the wizard's power even after they know full well that it is merely humbug. Culver then connects this to Adorno and Horkheimer's notion of "enlightened consumerism" where consumers still feel compelled to buy the things they see through. See: Stuart Culver, "What Manikins Want: *The Wizard of Oz* and *The Art of Decorating Dry Goods Windows*," *Representations* 21, Winter 1988, 97.

17. We have removed the italics from the first sentence in the quote. The essay is called "A Short Text About Magic." And it is from the book *The Wizard of Oz* by Salman Rushdie, published by BFI in 1992. The quote is from pages 17–18. The whole passage goes like this: "I thought one other thought, which I had better confess now, as it gave me a sneaking regard for the Wicked Witch, and, some might say a secret sympathy for all persons of her witchy disposition which has remained with me ever since. *I couldn't stand Toto.* I still can't. As Gollum said of the hobbit Bilbo Baggins in another great fantasy: 'Baggins: we hates it to pieces.' Toto: that little yapping hairpiece of a creature, that meddlesome rug! (I should point out that I felt this way about Toto even when I still had hair of my own.) L. Frank Baum, excellent fellow, gave the dog a distinctly minor role: it kept Dorothy happy, and when she was not, it had a tendency to "whine dismally": not an endearing trait. It's only really important contribution to the narrative of Baum's story came when it accidentally knocked over the screen behind which the Wizard stood concealed. The film–Toto rather more deliberately pulls aside a curtain to reveal the great Humbug, and in spite of everything I found this an irritating piece of mischief making. I was not surprised to learn that the canine actor playing Toto was possessed of a star's temperament, and even, at one point in the shooting, brought things to a standstill by staging a nervous breakdown. That Toto should be the film's one true object of love has always rankled. Useless (though satisfying) to protest: nobody, now, can rid me of this turbulent toupee."

18. We are, of course, not pretending to talk about maturity in its entirety. We recognize that what we are talking about here is one aspect of maturity only.

19. Toto can be read as being a part of Dorothy in another way too, i.e., he can be read as representing her feistiness and spunk. And this interpretation leads to the same result as the one in the text. For on this interpretation, too, Dorothy's love for Toto would have something a little self-contained — something, in fact, a little narcissistic — about it. The idea that Toto can be read as a symbol of Dorothy's own feistiness can also be found in Jerry Griswold's article. See: Jerry Griswold, "There's No Place but Home: *the Wizard of Oz*," in *The Antioch Review*, vol. 45, no. 4, Autumn 1987, 469.

20. See Stuart Culver, "What Manikins Want: *The Wizard of Oz* and *The Art of Decorating Dry Goods Windows*," *Representations* 21, Winter 1988, 99.

21. See Gregory Maguire, *Wicked: The Life and Times of the Wicked Witch of the West*, (New York: Harper, 2007), 497.

22. Aaron Fortune talks about something similar. He contrasts the atomistic characters in Oz with the more relational characters in Kansas. This allows him to read the ending of *The Wizard of Oz* in a positive way: Dorothy moves from atomism to relatedness. And all we want to say about this is that Fortune is not talking about relatedness in the same sense we are. For he is talking about relatedness in a general or communitarian sense, while we are talking about relatedness in the sense of sexual pair bonding. And although Dorothy may be learning something about the virtues of relatedness in a general sense, she is not (and this is our point) doing, or even getting close to, any pair bonding. See Aaron Fortune, "There's No Place Like Home: Dorothy Gale's Relations" in *The Wizard of Oz and Philosophy: Wicked Wisdom of the West*, edited by Randall E. Auxier and Phillip S. Seng (Chicago, IL: Open Court, 2008), 279–283.

23. And, as one of the participants at the conference on "The Yellow Brick Road in the 21st Century" reminded us, it is not just young girls, but young boys too who watch *The Wizard of Oz* to learn about self-reliance. ("The Yellow Brick Road in the 21st Century" conference was held June 26–28, 2009, at Henderson State University in Arkadelphia, Arkansas).

24. They don't seem to complete the other characters either. For these friendships seem to be friendships between already complete people. What The Scarecrow learns, for instance, is not that, even though he himself has no brains, he can nonetheless rely on the brains of his friends. If this were actually the case, then The Scarecrow really would be incomplete and his friendships really would serve to complete him. But it doesn't work like this. For what the Scarecrow actually learns is that he has brains already. And so he is already complete and all that happens is that The Wizard helps him to realize this.

25. For an argument that the friendships in Oz are not even really as wonderful as they look see Aaron Fortune, "There's No Place Like Home: Dorothy Gale's Relations" in *The Wizard of Oz and Philosophy: Wicked Wisdom of the West*, edited by Randall E. Auxier and Phillip S. Seng (Chicago, IL: Open Court, 2008).

26. An index of this is the relatively painless breakup of the friendship between Dorothy and her companions at the end of the movie. There is a little sadness to be sure, but no trauma. This is a sign that all we really had here were four already complete persons in a temporary and affectionate alliance. Cinderella could certainly not have been separated from her Prince with so little psychic damage.

27. Bettelheim in fact says that the shoes represent the vagina. See Bettelheim, 265, 268–271. Here is a passage from page 265: "A tiny receptacle into which some part of the body can slip and fit tightly can be seen as a symbol of the vagina. Something that is brittle and must not be stretched because it would break reminds us of the hymen [Bettelheim is here referring to the glass shoes of the Perrault version]; and something that is easily lost at the end of a ball when one's lover tries to keep a hold on his beloved seems an appropriate image for virginity, particularly when the male sets a trap — the pitch on the stairs — to catch her."

28. Gregory Maguire, *Wicked: The Life and Times of the Wicked Witch of the West* (New York: Harper, 2007).

29. To be more precise, the shoes don't exactly do this by themselves, but do it as a result of a spell cast on them by Glinda, the Good Witch.

30. Here is the whole of the relevant passage from Staples' review: "This idea of validating a dream or fantasy by having some of the actors play two characters, one in each world, is common to a range of films (e.g. *The Five Thousand Fingers of Doctor T*), the convention being that, when the child wakes up, he or she is holding something tangible from the dream world which proves that it is as real as home. In addition, a film-child returning from another world usually has some newly acquired self-confidence or skill which makes it possible to solve the problem which first created the need for escape. In *The Wizard of Oz* neither of these things happens. Dorothy does not produce the ruby slippers to prove — even to herself — that Oz really is 'a place, not a dream'; and, more disturbingly for a perceptive child in the audience, she does not bring with her from Oz anything that will help her solve the problem of Miss Gulch. Whether or not this was the makers' intention, part of the film's 'heartache' comes from the

fact that, though the Wicked Witch has been disposed of, Miss Gulch is still alive; and the legal warrant condemning Toto to death, which was what caused Dorothy to wish to fly away over the rainbow, is still in force when she comes back." See: www.answers.com/topic/the-wizard-of-oz-1939-film.

31. This point about how Toto is still slated to die is also made by Aaron Fortune in his article "There's No Place Like Home: Dorothy Gale's Relations" in *The Wizard of Oz and Philosophy: Wicked Wisdom of the West*, edited by Randall E. Auxier and Phillip S. Seng (Chicago, IL: Open Court, 2008), 278–279.

32. See www.movieposter.com/poster/MPW-29628/Wizard_of_Oz.html.

33. This turning inward can also be looked at from the political context of an isolationist ideal in response to the advent of World War II: everything needed was at home and the greater world is best left alone. For a related discussion see Jerry Griswold, "There's No Place but Home: *the Wizard of Oz*," in *The Antioch Review*, vol. 45, no. 4, Autumn 1987, 473–475. A summary of what he says on these points can also be found at "Penn Tags: Tags: Isolationism," University of Pennsylvania Library, http://tags.library.upenn.edu/tag/isolationism.

34. Salman Rushdie also complains about how the great outward adventure towards Oz is cancelled by the movie's ending. See Salman Rushdie, "A Short Text About Magic" in *The Wizard of Oz* by Salman Rushdie, published by BFI in 1992, 55–57. Our only caveat vis a vis Rushdie is that even the trip to Oz is not quite as outward moving as it appears since it does not involve Dorothy making the really outward movement that establishing a relationship with a Prince would involve.

35. We are assuming here that we can treat these earlier episodes as part of the *Star Wars* canon.

36. For a feminist's account of why Dorothy does not really qualify as a feminist ideal, see "Wicked Feminism" by Pam R. Sailors, in *The Wizard of Oz and Philosophy: Wicked Wisdom of the West*, edited by Randall E. Auxier and Phillip S. Seng (Chicago, IL: Open Court, 2008), 289–291.

37. Cinderella's father also plays a sort of stabilizing role in the story. He does at the beginning bring Cinderella a gift along with the gifts he brings to her stepsisters (this is from the Grimm version). And as Bettelheim points out and as we discussed above, he does try to help the Prince find Cinderella and so helps her transfer her affections from himself to the Prince.

38. We are indebted to Salman Rushdie for pointing out how almost all of the action in *The Wizard of Oz* occurs out of doors. See, "A Short Text About Magic" in Salman Rushdie, *The Wizard of Oz* (London: BFI, 1992), 33.

39. We wish to reiterate what we said in the section of objections and replies, i.e., that although we are reporting these correlations as being what we found in the material before us, this does not mean that we ourselves are necessarily endorsing the patriarchal and heterosexualist tone of what we found.

40. Of course, in the brief epilogue at the end of the novel, Narnia is ruled, if not by Aslan himself, then at least in the spirit of Aslan. What is interesting, though, is that once an Aslan-inspired regime has been established, the ordinary children with whom we began become princes and princesses.

41. Of course there is the famous scene where a miraculous snowfall arrives just in time to save Angel's life. This sort of divine intervention, though, seems to be pretty much a one time thing. Perhaps there is also a reference to the possibility of a deity in the scene where Riley arrives at the church as vampires are overrunning it, for when Buffy questions him later about what he was doing there, he replies simply that he was "going to church." If this is a reference to a deity, though, it is pretty oblique, since it is not like the deity actually stepped in to stop the vampires in His or Her own person. Finally, it is also of course true that Glory is a goddess. But, characteristically for this show, she is an evil goddess with limited powers, and no good goddesses seem ever to appear.

42. For a laudatory treatment of the groups in *Buffy* and *Angel* as substitute families, see Jes Battis, "Buffy the Vampire Slayer and Angel," in *Blood Relations: Chosen Families* (Jefferson, NC: McFarland and Co., Inc., 2005). For our more suspicious analysis, see Curry and

Velazquez, "'Just a Family Legend': The Hidden Logic of *Buffy's* 'Chosen Family'" in *Buffy Goes Dark: Essays on the Final Two Seasons of* Buffy the Vampire Slayer, edited by Lynne Y. Edwards, Elizabeth L. Rambo, and James B. South (Jefferson, NC: McFarland and Co., Inc., 2008), 143–166.

43. It has been pointed out to us that this point is not absolutely true 100 percent of the time. For example, Tinker Bell, who is in the non-vestigial group surrounding Wendy, is actually smaller than Wendy. In the reverse direction, the horse who is in the vestigial group surrounding Mulan, is larger than she is. But even though this rule about sizes is not 100 percent true, it does seem to be generally or for the most part true.

44. It is interesting to note, though, that even here their moment of finally coming together is not shown. And Alfred in fact informs Miss Vail that Batman is liable to be somewhat delayed.

45. This change from Vickie Vail to Rachel Dawes points up a feature that makes it difficult to establish any firm conjectures concerning superheroes: many of the storylines are set in alternate universes where events that are different from or even contradictory to a major storyline are nonetheless explored. *The Dark Knight* represents such an alternate storyline. We are indebted to Agnes's husband for stressing to us the importance of this fact.

46. For a reading of much of Baum's magic as sorts of technology, see George Dunn, "The Wonderful Smallness of Evil in Oz," in *The Wizard of Oz and Philosophy: Wicked Wisdom of the West*, edited by Randall E. Auxier and Phillip S. Seng (Chicago, IL: Open Court, 2008), 149–166.

47. Of all these characters, the least magical seems to be Batman, since his special powers are derived from technology and wealth, and not from the fact that he himself is somehow different than an ordinary human. And yet, at the same time as we want to admit that Batman might not fit the magical pattern, we would also like to point out that he has used his wealth and technology to transform himself, at least in appearance, into a human-animal hybrid — which is a pretty magical sort of creature to be.

48. An interesting fact in this regard is the number of orphans involved in these stories. Dorothy, of course, is an orphan. And, at least as far as he knows until he's already well into his adventures, so is Luke Skywalker. Superman, Batman and Spiderman are all orphans too. The only case that might be different is Catwoman, for the movie does not tell us whether her parents were still alive when she was growing up.

49. While *Superman Returns* depicts Lois and Richard saving Superman's life after Lex Luther stabs him with a shard of kryptonite, Superman's work remains essentially a solo affair.

50. To take another example, Peter Pan first appeared in print in 1902 (in the novel *The Little White Bird*) and on the screen in the iconic Mary Martin version in 1953. Batman, in contrast, appeared in print in 1939, and on the screen (television) in the late 1960's. (Information from Internet Movie Database and Jamie Colville, "The History of Superhero Comicbooks," http://www.geocities.com/Athens/8580/Hist1.html).

Works Cited

Auxier, Randall E., and Philip S. Seng. *The Wizard of Oz and Philosophy: Wicked Wisdom of the West*. Chicago, IL: Open Court, 2008.

Battis, Jes. *Blood Relations: Chosen Families in Buffy the Vampire Slayer and Angel*. Jefferson, NC: McFarland and Co., Inc., 2005.

Bettleheim, Bruno Bettelheim. *The Uses of Enchantment: The Meaning and Importance of Fairy Tales*. New York: Vintage Books, 1977.

Culver, Stuart. "What Manikins Want: *The Wizard of Oz* and *The Art of Decorating Dry Goods Windows*." *Representations* 21, Winter 1988.

Curry, Agnes, and Josef Velazquez. "'Just a Family Legend': The Hidden Logic of *Buffy's* 'Chosen Family.'" In *Buffy Goes Dark: Essays on the Final Two Seasons of Buffy the Vampire Slayer*. Ed. Lynne Y. Edwards, Elizabeth L. Rambo, and James B. South, Jefferson, NC: McFarland and Co., Inc., 2008.

Fortune, Aaron. "There's No Place Like Home: Dorothy Gale's Relations." *The Wizard of Oz and Philosophy: Wicked Wisdom of the West.* Chicago, IL: Open Court, 2008.

Griswold, Jerry. "There's No Place but Home: *the Wizard of Oz.*" In *The Antioch Review,* vol. 45, no. 4, Autumn 1987.

Maguire, Gregory. *Wicked: The Life and Times of the Wicked Witch of the West.* New York: Harper, 2007.

Rushdie, Salman. "A Short Text About Magic." In *The Wizard of Oz: An Appreciation.* London: British Film Institute, 1992.

Seng, Philip, "A Sort of Homecoming: Growing up with Dorothy." In *The Wizard of Oz and Philosophy: Wicked Wisdom of the West.* Chicago, IL: Open Court, 2008.

CHAPTER 3

Psychospiritual Wizdom

Dorothy's Monomyth in The Wizard of Oz

JENÉ GUTIERREZ

Since the film premiered in 1939, *The Wizard of Oz* has been the subject of numerous interpretations. In 1964, Henry Littlefield's *American
Quaterly* essay entitled "The Wizard of Oz: Parable on Populism" espoused a
political connection, illustrating the story's alignment with Populism. Gregory Renault offers a Marxist interpretation in "Over the Rainbow: Dialectic
and Ideology in *The Wizard of Oz*," arguing that the story is a response to
advanced capitalism. In "Waiting for Godoz: A Post-Nasal Deconstruction
of *The Wizard of Oz*," David Downing argues theologically that the film is
"one of the most devastating exposés of institutional religion ever to reach the
screen" (qtd. in Nathanson 11). Notable as the quintessential coming-of-age
story, *The Wizard*'s most common analytical approach seems to be psycho-
analytical. David Magder considers *The Wizard* a "parable of psychotherapy,"
while critics Daniel Dervin and Harvey Greenberg probe *The Wizard's*
Freudian subconscious levels of meaning (Nathanson 8–11). Paul Nathanson
and Gita Dorothy Morena analyze the film through the lens of Carl Jung's
collective unconscious and archetypes in *Over the Rainbow: The Wizard of
Oz as a Secular Myth of America* and *The Wisdom of Oz: Reflections of a Jun-
gian Sandplay Therapist*, respectively.

Based on L. Frank Baum's children's tale *The Wonderful Wizard of Oz*
(1900), the movie maintains its appeal even more than fifty years after its
release. The American Film Institute recognizes *The Wizard of Oz* in many
of its lists: it ranks #1 in the 2008 Top Ten Fantasy Movies, #3 in the 2006
Greatest Movie Musicals and #6 in the 1998 list of 100 Years, 100 Movies ("AFI
Ten Top Ten"). What is the timeless, universal appeal of this movie? The
answer could lie in the film's blending of one of the oldest and most preva-

lent patterns of storytelling — that of the monomyth, or hero's journey — with the ageless aspects of the human psyche. Utilizing this approach, *The Wizard of Oz* demonstrates the psycho-spiritual journey of its heroine, Dorothy.

Mythology and psychology/psychoanalysis have an intimate connection. Sigmund Freud elucidates this link in *The Interpretation of Dreams*, writing, "[...]symbolism is not peculiar to dreams, but is characteristic of unconscious ideation, in particular among the people, and it is to be found in folklore, and in popular myths, legends, linguistic idioms, proverbial wisdom and current jokes, to a more complex extent than in dreams" (qtd in Campbell 19). Furthermore, in Jung's *The Structure and Dynamics of the Psyche*, he writes,

> Just as some kind of analytical technique is needed to understand a dream, so a knowledge of mythology is needed in order to grasp the meaning of a content deriving from the deeper levels of the psyche[....] The collective unconscious — so far as we can say anything about it at all — appears to consist of mythological motifs or primordial images, for which reason the myths of all nations are its real exponents. In fact, the whole of mythology could be taken as a sort of projection of the collective unconscious [qtd in Jung 39].

In the preface to *The Hero with a Thousand Faces*, where he first describes the monomyth, Joseph Campbell writes,

> It is the purpose of the present book to uncover some of the truths disguised under the figures of religion and mythology by bringing together a multitude of not-too-difficult examples and letting the ancient meaning become apparent of itself[....] But first we must learn the grammar of the symbols, and as a key to this mystery I know of no better modern tool than psychoanalysis. Without regarding this as the last word on the subject, one can nevertheless permit it as an approach [vii].

In other words, the primordial symbols and stories of mythology reflect the primordial symbols associated with the unconscious. One such story frequently found across cultures is the hero's journey, or monomyth.

Joseph Campbell derived the term "monomyth" from James Joyce's *Finnegans Wake*, the first work for which he offered a mythical reading (Underwood 16). Campbell defines his term: "A hero ventures forth from the world of common day into a region of supernatural wonder: fabulous forces are there encountered and a decisive victory is won: the hero comes back from this mysterious adventure with the power to bestow boons on his fellow man" (30). Campbell's structure is formulated in the broadest terms, meant as a framework of the typical hero's journey, with departure, initiation, and return as the essential elements of this journey (121). Well-known examples of this myth can be found in religious mythology, such as the stories of the Buddha and Jesus Christ, in the stories of Greco-Roman mythological figures such as

Odysseus and Prometheus, and in many films, including *Star Wars, E.T.*, and *The Lion King*.

The Wizard of Oz follows the course of the hero's journey in the structure of "Departure," "Initiation," and "Return" which Campbell describes in *The Hero with a Thousand Faces*. This structure also mirrors the three-act structure of the film. In Act One, during the "Departure" stage, Dorothy demonstrates three definitive steps of the hero's journey: the Call to Adventure, the Refusal of the Call, and the Belly of the Whale. Shortly into the movie, Dorothy becomes aware of her "Call to Adventure" in the form of a song. Campbell writes, "But whether small or great, and no matter what the stage or grade of life, the call rings up the curtain, always, on a mystery of transfiguration — a rite, or moment, of spiritual passage, which, when complete, amounts to a dying and birth" (51). For Dorothy, she strongly feels the urge to escape her bleak, sepia-toned Kansas farm after her family dismisses her and tells her to "find [her]self a place where [she] won't get into any trouble." When Dorothy sings "Over the Rainbow," she explicitly entertains this call to adventure. She longs for a place of perfection, harmony, and peace — a place for herself. When Dorothy runs away and meets Professor Marvel, she engages the "Refusal of the Call" phase of her adventure.

In the "Refusal of the Call," the hero experiences second thoughts and personal doubts about the challenge ahead, converting the adventure into its negative. Dorothy's escape evokes a sense of readiness to begin the adventure ahead, but she refuses this call when she meets Marvel. He advises her to go back home, and Dorothy heeds this advice. Upon returning home, however, Dorothy encounters the tornado which ultimately pushes her into the adventure. Campbell says that sometimes in the monomyth, the heroine's inner turmoil and character conflicts manifest in the landscape around her (*Joseph Campbell and the Power of Myth*). The tornado in *The Wizard of Oz* performs this function adequately. Dorothy wants to leave; then, she wants to stay. Her sense of peace, or home, is unbalanced, and this inner turmoil manifests as outer turmoil. Eventually, a window frame in her house knocks Dorothy unconscious, and she is sent into "The Belly of the Whale."

During this stage, the sphere of rebirth is symbolized in the worldwide womb image of the belly of the whale: "The hero [...] is swallowed into the unknown, and would appear to have died[....] Instead of passing outward, beyond the confines of the visible world, the hero goes inward, to be born again" (Campbell 90–91). In *The Wizard of Oz*, Dorothy's unconscious dream images manifest after the window frame knocks her out. Until the end of the movie, the audience does not know that Oz is Dorothy's dream, and for all intents and purposes, could believe that she has died. Dorothy clearly embarks on an inward journey, as her entire adventure occurs within her unconscious.

In Act Two, or the "Initiation" stage of this monomyth, Dorothy encounters "The Road of Trials," "Apotheosis," and "Atonement with the Father" phases outlined by Campbell. As soon as Dorothy arrives in Oz, she begins her succession of trials. In this stage, Dorothy must decide who she can and cannot trust, and her skills and powers are tested to prepare for conflict ahead. In Munchkin City, Dorothy meets an influential ally in Glinda the Good Witch of the North and her most influential enemy, the Wicked Witch of the West. She also faces her first test of the adventure — embarking on her journey alone down the Yellow Brick Road to meet the Wizard of Oz who knows how to get her home. Down this road, she meets her three key allies: the Scarecrow (brainless), Tin Man (heartless) and Cowardly Lion (gutless) who are equally interested in meeting the Wizard to provide them with the attributes they believe they lack. Because Dorothy is dreaming, all of the characters that Dorothy encounters are archetypes of her unconscious which she must discover and assimilate; she must reconcile the good witch, bad witch, brainless, heartless, and gutless aspects of her unconscious with her consciousness in order to complete her journey.

Dorothy encounters the "Apotheosis" phase of her journey when she commits the selfless act of throwing a bucket of water onto the Scarecrow, only to melt the Wicked Witch of the West. During this phase, the hero transcends dualities and becomes free from all fear (Campbell 151). Because of her selfless act, she transcends the duality of good and evil by unintentionally eliminating the Wicked Witch from Oz and her unconscious. This frees Dorothy of all fear, and she ventures back to the Wizard with the Witch's broomstick, able to make her "Atonement with the Father" and transcend dualities of tyranny/mercy and authority/subservience. This atonement consists of the reconciling of these dualities of the father-like authority figure. When Dorothy and her friends meet the Wizard of Oz for the second time, they all demonstrate the fearlessness gained during the Wicked Witch's elimination and stand up to him when he refuses to help them. Dorothy says, "If you were really great and powerful, you'd keep your promises!" During this confrontation, another aspect of Dorothy, Toto, reveals "the man behind the curtain." Toto, Latin for in totality, reminds Dorothy that she always has everything she needs within her, consciously or unconsciously, and he serves to transcend the duality of separate/wholeness which Dorothy perceives at the beginning of the film. Toto, as an extension of Dorothy, also transcends the tyranny/mercy and authority/subservience dualities by revealing the truth of the identity of the Wizard, who is "a very good man ... just a very bad wizard."

Act Three of the movie represents the "Return" stage of the hero's journey. Dorothy experiences Campbell's "Freedom to Live," "The Magic Flight," and "Master of the Two Worlds" during the end of the movie. In the "Freedom to Live" stage, the hero reconciles the individual consciousness with the universal will through the "realization of the true relationship of the passing phenomena of time to the imperishable life that lives and dies in all" (238). For Dorothy, this occurs when she relates what she has learned: "I think that it, that it wasn't enough just to want to see Uncle Henry and Auntie Em. And it's that, if I ever go looking for my heart's desire again, I won't look any further than my own backyard. Because if it isn't there, I never really lost it to begin with." Here Dorothy realizes that she contains the totality of her heart's desires and, with the knowledge of her self-journey, is prepared to return "home" with the assistance of her magic slippers. Her "Magic Flight" is precipitated by Glinda's blessing and she returns "home," awakening with her renewed sense of self. When she awakens and insists that her experience was not a dream, but a real place, she demonstrates her "Mastery of the Two Worlds." During this phase, the hero must not contaminate the principles of the one world with those of other, while permitting the mind to know the one by virtue of the other (Campbell 229). While her family tells her she only experienced a dream, Dorothy persists and says, "Doesn't anybody believe me?" Just as her family concedes, "Of course, we believe you," Toto jumps onto the bed. This action reminds Dorothy of her mastery of the two worlds, and she says, "But anyway Toto, we're home!" The end of her journey culminates with her acceptance of the two worlds and her realization that no matter where she is, she is always "home."

The spirituality of Dorothy's journey is mostly reflected in her goal throughout the movie, which is to return "home." For Susan Mackey-Ellis,

> Home is often the literal home from which the hero sets out, but more significantly, it is a state of mind or a way of seeing not possible before the hero departs. The hero's quest not only often requires a journey home to the place from whence the hero departed, it also necessitates a journey home to a state of being or consciousness that was within the hero's heart all along [135].

The Wizard of Oz clearly illustrates both this literal return home, but also the state of mind which Dorothy learns was with her all along. Mackey-Ellis continues,

> The transconsciousness, or the state of unity with the Spirit sought by the heroes of all ages, is an evolution, paradoxically to a place that has always existed (soul-knowledge) but which could never be fully realized without questing in the realm of consciousness (ego), unconsciousness (pre-ego), and imperfect human activity (shadow/sin, death, and separation) [24].

This also corresponds to Jung's idea of individuation. For Jung, individuation is the journey toward wholeness and completion (Underwood 21). Mackey-Ellis's transconsciousness mirrors Jung's individuation as they both seek to unify aspects of the unconscious. Although not overtly religious, both Campbell and Jung's work "engage in what could be called a 'natural history' of religious myth, symbol, and sentiment, a *natural* history that seeks to honor the function of the religious imagination without granting it a *super-natural* authority" (14).

The spirituality of *The Wizard of Oz* is further reflected by the use of the mantra-like phrase, "There's no place like home." In Eastern religions, the mantra is a "syllable, word, or verse considered to possess mystical or spiritual efficacy, and repetition of or meditation on a particular mantra can induce a trance-like state in the participant and can lead the individual to a higher level of spiritual awareness" ("Mantra"). Clearly, Dorothy's mantra induces a transformation which demonstrates her greater sense of awareness; she cannot return home without the aid of this "sacred utterance." Also, with regard to Eastern-influenced spirituality, Joey Green claims, "Ultimately, Dorothy attains satori, the Zen experience of 'awakening.' She finds her true Self, her higher consciousness, her ultimate Oneness with the cosmos, her home" (18). Regarding Western-influenced spirituality, Christian author William Bausch argues that Dorothy's search for home is a metaphor for the search for "God," writing, "Like all myths, the hero-adventurer myth encapsulates the traditional signposts of the human spiritual journey. The three phases of the journey — departure, struggle, return — describes what happens to us as well when we evolve from self-centeredness to an awareness of the spiritual self" (8). These authors advocate differing spiritual discourses of Dorothy's journey, but the similarities with each other, Campbell, and Jung cannot be ignored. The search for Self, individuation, transconsciousness, satori, and "God" are reflections of each other manifesting in different levels of discourse.

Campbell and his colleagues best fit under the classification of universalists, while his critics are considered particularists. Universalists emphasize the similarities among phenomena, while particularists emphasize the differences (Segal 81). According to Robert Segal, neither side necessarily denies the findings of the other; the ultimate difference is temperamental. While one group asserts the importance of similarities, the other argues for the importance of differences:

> But to argue for either particularism or universalism, both sides would have to agree on the starting point: on what constituted the *surface* similarities and differences. In all likelihood, universalists would deem the differences superficial and the similarities deeper; particularists, the reverse. Each side would likely dismiss the other's *conclusions* at the mere *starting point*" [84].

Therefore, the arguments between the two groups prove ultimately futile.

While differences between mythologies, psychoanalyses, and spiritualities abound, there can be no denying the alignment of these elements in *The*

Wizard of Oz. To account for the film's far-reaching success across cultures, age, gender, and religions, a framework of universalism is most applicable. The film follows, almost exactly, the structure of the monomyth which Campbell identifies; this myth not only reflects images of the unconscious and Jung's process of individuation, but also mirrors the spiritual quest which heroes throughout time have undergone.

Works Cited

"AFI: 10 Top 10: The Wizard of Oz." *American Film Institute*. 2008. 12 May 2009 http://www.afi.com/10top10/moviedetail.aspx?id=7892&thumb=1.

Bausch, William J. *The Yellow Brick Road: A Storyteller's Approach to the Spiritual Journey*. Mystic, CT: Twenty-Third Publications, 1999.

Campbell, Joseph. *The Hero with a Thousand Faces*. Princeton: Princeton UP, 1973.

Green, Joey. *The Zen of Oz*. Los Angeles: Renaissance, 1999.

Joseph Campbell and the Power of Myth. Joseph Campbell, Bill D. Moyers, George Lucas, and Catherine Tatge. New York: Mystic Fire Video, 2001.

Jung, C. G., Joseph Campbell, and R. F. C. Hull. *The Portable Jung*. Viking portable library. Harmondsworth: Penguin, 1976.

Mackey-Ellis, Susan. *The Hero and the Perennial Journey Home in American Film*. Philadelphia: UP Press, 2001.

"Mantra." *Encyclopædia Britannica*. 2009. Encyclopædia Britannica Online. 12 May 2009, http://www.britannica.com/EBchecked/topic/363001/mantra.

Nathanson, Paul. *Over the rainbow: the Wizard of Oz as a Secular Myth of America*. McGill Studies in the History of Religions. Albany: State Univ. of New York Press, 1991.

Segal, Robert A. "Joseph Campbell the Perennial Philosopher: An Analysis of his Universalism." *Paths to the Power of Myth: Joseph Campbell and the Study of Religion*. Daniel C. Noel. New York: Crossroad, 1990.

Underwood, Richard A. "Living by Myth: Joseph Campbell, C.G. Jung, and the Religious Life-Journey." *Paths to the Power of Myth: Joseph Campbell and the Study of Religion*. Daniel C. Noel. New York: Cossroad, 1990.

The Wizard of Oz. Dir. Victor Fleming. Based on book by Lyman Frank Baum. Perf. Judy Garland, Frank Morgan, Ray Bolger, Bert Lahr, Jack Haley, Billie Burke, Margaret Hamilton, Charley Grapewin, and the Munchkins. MGM, 1939. VHS, Warner, 1999.

CHAPTER 4

"Come out, come out, wherever you are"

How Tina Landau's 1969 Stages a Queer Reading of The Wizard of Oz

RONALD ZANK

Since its publication in 1900, L. Frank Baum's *The Wonderful Wizard of Oz* has been a favorite for adaptation, both to the stage and film, with the first theatrical version debuting in 1902 and the famous MGM film version in 1939. There have been revisionist iterations, such as the Black musical *The Wiz* in 1975, which utilized soul, rhythm and blues and funk music to tell the story, or the musical prequel, *Wicked*, based on Gregory Maguire's novel of the same name, which some have viewed as a more feminist view of *Oz*. In *Something for the Boys: Musical Theater and Gay Culture*, critic John M. Clum noted: "*The Wizard of Oz* has been discussed many times as an allegory of gay experience,"[1] and perhaps this is why it is quoted in other gay-themed theatrical works like Tony Kushner's *Angels in America*. Perhaps it is because, as writer John Carlyle suggests, "Dorothy's desire to fly over the rainbow to a place of perfection and to escape from troubles struck an instant chord."[2] And while *The Wizard of Oz* has been read as gay allegory, it has seldom (if ever) been adapted or staged literally as such. Tina Landau's play *1969, or Howie Takes A Trip* is one of the few plays to make this depiction overt, for, as Scott T. Cummings described it, "[t]he play combines Dick Cavett's interview with Janis Joplin, touchstone tunes of the day [...], cross-dressing characters from *The Wizard of Oz*, classroom and locker room vignettes, psychedelic lighting, and a parody of high-school choreography to generate a genuine nostalgia 'trip.'"[3] The male characters of the play take on the lines, personae, and actions of Dorothy, the Scarecrow, the Tin Man, the

Cowardly Lion and the Wizard from the film. I would argue that Landau's play, unlike others that directly adapt or quote *The Wizard of Oz*, stages a queer reading of the film, rendering what was camp or covert to the gay and lesbian community overt or queer to a more general audience.

The play *1969* was first performed at the 18th Annual Humana Festival of New American Plays in 1994. In her introduction to it, playwright and director Tina Landau explained that Jon Jory, Producing Director of the Actors Theatre of Louisville (home to the Humana Festival), "had heard about several projects I had done by inviting a group of actors to come into a rehearsal room with me and create a piece from scratch. With this alternative way of 'writing' in mind, he took the brave step of asking me to come to Louisville with nothing but a group of people and an idea."[4] The resulting play is an examination of the year 1969 (the year of Judy Garland's death) through the experiences of a group of high school seniors, including music, television, the Vietnam War, the Black Power movement, women's liberation, and drug use. One student in particular, Howie, comes to recognize himself as gay through the events of the play, dodges his military induction, and flees to New York just in time for the Stonewall rebellion, which is usually identified as the triggering event in the modern Gay Rights movement.

It is not merely the exploration of a cultural moment that makes *1969* worthy of examination. The play itself has seldom been produced and has received almost no critical attention since its initial performances at the Humana Festival, nor is it mentioned in Jeffrey Ullom's history of the Festival's new plays. Fraser Sherman's detailed study, *The Wizard of Oz Catalog*, which documents *Oz* adaptations on stage, film and television, both domestic and international, has no entry for *1969*.[5] This may be due to few productions or little critical attention to the *Oz* aspects of the script, resulting in less general knowledge of the script's existence. As director/playwright Landau notes, "[t]he written text of *1969* represents just one layer of several that actually make up the piece."[6] She describes the importance of other "tracks" to be read, specifically the staging and the sound score (music and effects). As she cautions, "the aural world was continual and seamless and the physical choreography was complex. It's hard to imagine this piece merely by reading it."[7] Perhaps this challenge has resulted in fewer productions after the initial Louisville run, and thus limited scholarship. Furthermore, given its seemingly singular status by embodying a queer reading, additional study seems warranted. Initially, I will look at the importance of *The Wizard of Oz* and Judy Garland to gay men and what it means to "queer" a text like the film. More importantly for the purposes of this study, I will utilize a close reading of the text analyzing how Howie reflects Dorothy/Judy Garland and fellow tragic diva, Janis Joplin. In addition, I will examine the "queer" relationships between

Howie and his classmates, as compared to Dorothy's *Oz* companions: Logo/the Scarecrow; Robbie/the Tin Man; Curt/the Cowardly Lion; and his teacher, Royce, with the Wizard; finally ending with Howie's escape to the "Village of Odds," Greenwich Village. This will demonstrate how they take images and lines from the film of *The Wizard of Oz* and reframe them, transforming them from something read as "camp" in the film to being staged as overtly "queer" in Landau's play.

Before examining how *1969* stages a queer reading of *The Wizard of Oz*, it is necessary to define what a queer reading is and how notions of queer and camp relate to the film. Alexander Doty, in his essay, "There's Something Queer Here," "propose[s] *queerness* as a mass culture reception practice that is shared by all sorts of people in varying degrees of consistency and intensity," and goes on to posit, "basically heterocentrist texts can contain queer elements, and basically heterosexual, straight-identifying people can experience queer moments."[8] Susanne Luhmann states that, "Queer ... transgresses the boundaries between queer and straight, partly by deciphering queer content and subtexts in ostensibly straight narratives, partly by pointing to the overlap between heterosexual and homosexual practices."[9] Thus, if all audiences can experience queer moments, and take note of queer content, to do so is to provide a queer reading. It is important to distinguish how this differs from (or is similar to) the notion of camp. Henry M. Benshoff and Sean Griffin suggest the two ideas are similar, asserting, "[l]ike queer reading practices in general, camp created a subject position from which urban gay men could revise a text's original meanings, and thus it strongly figured in the creation of a sense of shared community."[10] Yet Corey K. Creekmur and Alexander Doty make an important distinction, pointing out that: "[c]amp was also, for some time, an 'insider's' attitude and knowledge, a means not ... of disseminating information about who (or what) was in — that is, in the life (homosexual), in the know, au courant, avant-garde, or, to use a later term, hip."[11] This definition of early versions of camp locate it as knowledge hidden from the presumed mainstream, privileging the homosexual point of view, while in contrast, the more contemporary definition of queer allows this awareness to anyone who chooses to be aware of it. Critic Nikki Sullivan also emphasizes the excesses of camp, stating that it "is most often associated with parody, exaggeration, theatricality, humour, and insofar as it foregrounds the performative character of gender, sexuality, race, class, and so on."[12] This contrasts with a more multi-faceted definition of queer, which destabilizes and subverts assumed binaries of gender and sexuality by suggesting there are other, "in-between" options regarding culture and identity. Thus, camp puts greater emphasis on humor and extreme, or as Eve Sedgwick (quoting Robert Dowidoff) queries: "What if whoever made this was gay too?"[13] and privileging an "insider" knowledge. In contrast, queer can signify anyone or any-thing outside the perceived mainstream or status quo, including (as David Savran suggests) the "renovation of camp,"[14] or the aware (presumed) hetero-sexual observer.

Operating from these definitions then, what would qualify as a queer or camp reading of *Oz*? Film critics Benshoff and Griffin suggest the queer view-ers respond to films about "social outsiders. Perhaps the best example of this type is *The Wizard of Oz* (1939), a fantasy about a young girl who escapes a drab rural existence only to find a fascinating urban world in which anything is possible."[15] To cite a more elaborate example that references camp but could also be read as queer, Creekmur and Doty offer:

> To take a privileged example from camp's (counter) canon, MGM's wholesome children's fantasy *The Wizard of Oz* is a story in which everyone lives in two very different worlds, and in which most of its characters live two very different lives, while its emotionally confused and oppressed teenage heroine longs for a world in which her inner desires can expressed freely and fully. Dorothy finds this world in a Technicolor land "over the rainbow" inhabited by a sissy lion, an artificial man who cannot stop crying, and a butch-femme couple of witches. This is a reading of the film that sees that film's fantastic excesses (color, cos-tume, song, performance, etc.) as expressing the hidden lives of many of its most devoted viewers, who identified themselves "as friends of Dorothy."[16]

Yet, while the fantasy element in the film is important, Raymond Knapp sug-gests that it is the use of real actors rather than animation that makes them more empathetic, "because we invest in them as performers, especially those we recognize from other films. Thus, for example, we connect with Dorothy *and* Judy Garland, who is both making the transition into stardom and delay-ing the transition into adulthood."[17] For many in the gay community, Gar-land and her character became emblematic of the film.

This connection with Dorothy and Garland is important, for as Ben-shoff explains it, "her *Wizard of Oz* character even became a code word within the era's queer subcultures: one could ascertain whether another man was homosexual by euphemistically asking 'Are you a friend of Dorothy's?'"[18] Fol-lowing her firing by MGM in 1950 and a suicide attempt not long after, Gar-land became synonymous with "survivor," especially when she sang and particularly for gay men. As Michael Bronski describes it, "[w]hen she sang she was vulnerable. There was a hurt in her voice that most other singers don't have—[Janis] Joplin did, Nina Simone does—and an immediacy that gave the impression that it was *her* hurt, not merely the hurt in the song or in the persona of the singer."[19] Garland's pain was reinforced by the annual televi-sion broadcast of *The Wizard of Oz* that began in 1959, forcing the Garland of the 1950s and 60s, struggling with addictions, weight gains and failed marriages, to always be compared with the young Garland of the past. These broadcasts encouraged young "friends of Dorothy" to watch her television specials and crowd her concerts until, as critic Caryl Flinn explains it, "[t]he ostensible birth of gay activism at Stonewall ... [was] precipitated by the death of camp icon Judy Garland."[20] The evening of Garland's funeral, "members of the New York City Vice Squad [came] under fire, from beer cans, bottles, coins, and cobblestones, as they [tried] to arrest some of the regulars at the Stonewall Inn in Christopher Street."[21] While this revolt by drag queens and other patrons was not a direct effect of Garland's death, the death of Judy Garland, favorite of the gay community and quintessential survivor, added to atmosphere of the politically charged year the Gay Rights movement began — 1969.

The experiences of Howie, the lead character in *1969*, typify it as a work of "coming out" literature, identified as such since "one of the plot lines will be the growth of awareness in the narrator of attraction to his or her own gender."[22] In the third scene of the play, Howie describes being called "faggot," and confesses:

> So that was the first time I heard the word "faggot" but I had to wait until I got to the safety spot of my own house before I could look it up, there's no place like home you know, and there it was, the truth, right there in the dictionary: a bundle of twigs.[23]

At this point, Howie's awareness is so minimal that he does not understand the difference between this archaic definition and the more contemporary slang for homosexual. Over the course of the play, the audience witnesses his physical attraction to a male classmate (Curt, the one who called him "faggot") and Howie's struggles with his with strong, romantic feelings towards his outspoken male teacher. In one of the final scenes, he refers to himself as a "faggot"[24] and even describes growing up wanting to be Dorothy. One scene is Howie's dream of the prom, at which he dresses as Dorothy. Even in that first monologue he quotes perhaps Dorothy's most famous line from *The Wizard of Oz*, "there's no place like home," yet his naiveté about the slang word "faggot" marks him as innocent regarding the world, much like Dorothy.

Expanding Howie's identification as "queer," he is paralleled not only with Dorothy, but also with Janis Joplin. Like Garland, Joplin is another alleged bisexual singer with chemical dependency issues, and much as Garland died of an overdose in 1969, Joplin suffered a similar fate in 1970. The play *1969* begins with a recording of Joplin's famous interview with Dick Cavett, in which he asked her what high school was like:

> Voiceover Janis: They laughed me out of class, out of town, and out of the state. So I'm goin' home.[25]

Using the word "home," Landau connects Joplin with Dorothy's famous utterance, "there's no place like home,"[26] a line also repeated by Howie in his first monologue. Howie, like Joplin, is laughed at by classmates. There is an additional connection between Dorothy, Janis, and Howie, since Howie's school activities include being in choral music classes,[27] identifying him as a singer like them. When interviewed about his future goals for the yearbook, Howie's first response is "To become Janis."[28] This reminds us of Michael Bronski's assessment of Garland: "There was a hurt in her voice that most other singers don't have — [Janis] Joplin did."[29] Howie does not sing in the course of the play, yet he is mentioned as a singer, as Garland and Joplin were. Moreover, both singers have been rumored to be bisexual, marking them as "queer" and thus doing the same for Howie by association.

This Dorothy/Janis/Howie conflation is reinforced when Howie dreams of his prom. The stage directions tell us the music is "Janis' 'Maybe' " while the prom theme is announced as "Somewhere There's a Place for Us Over the Rainbow,"[30] combining the most famous song from *The Wizard of Oz* with a lyric from *West Side Story*, both of which describe an imaginary better world where everyone gets along and there is not trouble. His male classmates appear in the dream as the Scarecrow, Tin Man, Cowardly Lion trio and ask Howie, "Dorothy — are you coming with us?"[31] before putting him in a dress like Dorothy's. Thus, in his dream, Howie transforms his friends into their *Oz* personae, references Garland's most famous song, "Over the Rainbow," and even garbs himself as Dorothy. This transformation is crucial, for in the film, the farmhands are transformed by Dorothy's subconscious into her colorful companions, while Dorothy herself remains unchanged. Howie apparently feels differently, needing to don a dress to belong or fulfill an imagined heterosexual paradigm with Royce. Moreover, there is only mention of the dress, no wig or makeup, so the image is not Howie in drag or Howie trying to *become* Dorothy, but merely the boy Howie in a dress, again marking Howie not simply as gay, but queer. Each of the other characters, according to the stage directions, "turns into"[32] their *Oz* counterpart while Howie is in between his own persona and that of Dorothy. All of this occurs to a Janis Joplin recording, again conflating Joplin with Judy (as Dorothy) with Howie.

There are some striking similarities and inversions between the Scarecrow of the film and Howie's classmate, Logo, in Landau's play. In the film, the Scarecrow is the one Dorothy meets first in Oz and will miss "most of all"[33] when she leaves. By contrast, Howie and Logo do not seem especially close, with Howie often using Logo's given name, Lester, rather than his nickname, Logo. Even the nickname "Logo" comes from the Greek "Logos," meaning word or speech, and is associated with reason or divine wisdom,[34] suggesting both the Scarecrow's search for a brain, but also perhaps implying that Logo already has "brains." Indeed, in classroom scenes Logo and Howie are presented as the most intelligent males in their class, while Curt and Robbie seem less likely to offer opinions or participate in discussions. "Logo" even echoes "Scarecrow," with both names ending with a long "o" sound. Logo remarks to Howie, "Shit, it's tedious being stuck up here all day long,"[35] paraphrasing Scarecrow's first conversation with Dorothy, when he is hanging from the pole. In the film, Dorothy takes the Scarecrow on her trip to the Emerald City because he requests it, while in *1969* it is Logo who inverts this pattern and takes Howie on several drug "trips," at his request. In addition, while the Scarecrow goes to the Emerald City seeking brains, Logo feels he has already been enlightened by his drug use, explaining to Howie that it will "[b]low your mind — you'll you'll you'll open up to so much shit, and beauty, man."[36] The Scarecrow helps rescue Dorothy from the narcotic effects of the poppy field, while in *1969*, Logo supplies the LSD for Howie's various "trips," including his first one, where he "looks up into a cascade of red poppies which fall on him,"[37] with Logo reassuring Howie afterward of their friendship. That said, when Howie is fearful of his medical exam for the draft and seeks out Logo for more LSD, he does warn Howie, "man, you shouldn't take this shit in the state you're in"[38] but hands over the LSD anyway. The Scarecrow reveals the only thing that scares him is a lighted match, though he tells Dorothy he would "face a whole box full of them for the chance of getting some brains."[39] Logo, in contrast, does not fear matches, for a matchbox is, in fact, where he stores his LSD tabs and he even asks Howie, "hey, you got a match?,"[40] perhaps suggesting he fears nothing.

Film critic Alexander Doty recounts how some have suggested the Scarecrow represents bisexuality[41] with his directional advice to Dorothy, "[o]f course, people do go both ways,"[42] and Logo, while evidencing no bisexual tendencies, does tell a story of being mistaken for a little girl due to his long hair as a child.[43] Moreover, rather than a label like "bisexual," Logo proposes a strong binary for humanity as he and Howie take LSD: "[t]he world is divided into two types of people, man — straight and hip."[44] In the slang of 1969, his meaning is not our contemporary notion of straight and gay (with "straight" meaning heterosexual), but the ones who are willing (i.e., are "hip") or unwilling to do drugs (i.e., are "straight"). Yet, this also echoes Creekmur and Doty's definition of camp as insider knowledge, privileging those, "in the life (homosexual), in the know, au courant, avant-garde, or, to use a later term, hip"[45]; thus, while not marked as gay or bisexual, Logo is still queer. Yet, while the Scarecrow is informed by the Wizard that he already has brains, the same could be said for Logo were it not for his extensive drug use. He explains how "[s]ome of us acid-crawlbacks want to stand and be counted, too. Now if only I could find my feet."[46] This notion of finding one's feet echoes the scene in the film where the Scarecrow is helpless, having been attacked by the Wicked Witch's Flying Monkeys: "[t]hey tore my legs off and they threw them over there. Then they took my chest out and then they threw it over there"[47] While both Logo and Scarecrow are intelligent, it takes little to physically incapacitate either character, though Logo does so by choice, and losing his feet is a metaphorical state. He recommends that Howie learn, "the hippie smile — wide-eyed, big grin, chock full of wonder — and just a hint of brain damage,"[48] as a strategy for coping with the police but also connecting with other "hip" (i.e. queer) people. While the Wizard told the Scarecrow what he lacked was not brains, but a diploma, the audience is left to wonder if Logo will, in fact, receive his.

Any hint of romance in the film of *The Wizard of Oz* might be found between Dorothy and the Scarecrow, for when departing Oz, she tells him, "I think I'll miss you most of all,"[49] perhaps due to her knowing him the longest, having met him first. This connection does not seem to carry over for Logo and Howie in *1969*. Instead, the play depicts a strong emotional bond between Howie and his former best friend, Robbie, who is associated with the Tin Man. One scene includes the recitation of a poem Howie has written, accompanied by the stage directions: "During the following, we see a series of 'snapshots' of Howie and Robbie as they grow from inseparable childhood friends into estranged young adults."[50] These "snapshots" include Robbie and classmate Curt ignoring Howie at school and Robbie taking a group picture which excludes Howie, suggesting that Robbie is indeed "heartless." Even Landau's choice of the name "Robbie" for the character brings to mind another iconic, non-human metal man of late 1950s and early 1960s popular culture, Robby the Robot, who first appeared in the film *Forbidden Planet* in 1956 and was featured in numerous films and television shows in the years following.[51] In their final scene together, Robbie reminisces with Howie about how when they were children they watched *The Wizard of Oz* on television together, remembering, "how I always wanted to be the Tinman"[52] and describing how "I spent all this time alone, banging on my chest ... trying to see if it [his heart] was there or not," realizing, "I guess I kind of, you know ... related to him or something freaky like that,"[53] suggesting that even as a child he wondered if he, like the Tin Man, lacked a heart and the associated emotions. Since the broadcasts began in the late 1950s, Robbie and Howie could have seen them annually since childhood. However, while Logo seems intelligent but addled due to drug use and Curt seems initially to have no fear, Robbie does appear somewhat insensitive or "heartless." Yet, examined more closely, in their first scene together, Robbie warns against drug use, "Howie, ya don't want that shit, do you?"[54] He also apologizes for the dissolution of their friendship, acknowledging, "Look, Howie, I know I haven't been around a lot recently —... I'm sorry, Howie.'"[55] Despite their estrangement, it is to Robbie that Howie reveals his military induction, and, when he decides to run away, Robbie is the only friend to whom Howie bids farewell. When Howie admits he will be dodging the draft and refers to himself as a "faggot," Robbie does not even react. Instead, he changes the subject and reminds Howie of their annual viewing of *The Wizard of Oz* as children and his own desire to be the Tin Man while both speak of Howie's urge to be Dorothy. They recreate the Oz characters' dialogue of departure, ending with the Tin Man's line, "Now I know I've got a heart ... 'Cause it's breaking."[56] While not necessarily romantic, though critics like Benshoff refer to "the rather effeminate Tin Man from *The Wizard of Oz*,"[57] there is certainly a strong emotional attachment between Howie and Robbie, indicating that Robbie/Tin Man (rather than Logo as Scarecrow) is the one Howie will miss "most of all" because of having known him the longest (like Dorothy and the Scarecrow) and because, even with his concern for being heartless, he expressed pain at his friend's imminent departure and an acknowledgement of their childhood fascination with their respective *Oz* characters. For these reasons, Robbie can also be viewed as queer.

Perhaps the greatest reconfiguring of Dorothy's companions is Curt, an African-American classmate that Howie imagines as the Cowardly Lion. Regarding the film, some gay audience members identified with the Lion's lines, such as "born to be a sissy."[58] Others shared the difficulties film critic Alexander Doty's described from watching the Cowardly Lion in his late teens, "I hadn't come out to anyone, and he seemed to be too out: flamboyant, effeminate, and self-oppressive."[59] This interpretation stands in sharp contrast to Landau's character, Curt. The most athletic of the students, star of the track and football teams, he is also physically attractive and African-American. In an extended scene in the locker room, he play-fights with his classmates, snapping a towel and paraphrasing the Coward Lion's first appearance in the film, offering to fight the Scarecrow and Tin Man, or rather, Logo and Robbie: "'Shit, man, put 'em up. Put 'em up. Which one of you is first? Ahhh — pulling a towel on me, eh? Oh, scared, eh? Come on, get up and fight ya' shivering junkyard. Come on you lopsided bag of hay."[60] In the film, of course, this bravado is short-lived, and the Lion's cowardly nature is immediately revealed when Dorothy strikes him. In Landau's play, Curt appears to be as fearless as he seems, though when questioned for the yearbook about his greatest fear, he confesses, "[b]lowing my chance for a football scholarship."[61] Logo questions why he is not fighting and protesting with others in the Black Students Alliance, even imagining how he himself would act and be involved if he were Black (in a speech somewhat reminiscent of the Cowardly Lion's song, "If I Were the King of the Forest"), finally asking, "What's your hangup, man, what're you so afraid of!"[62] Curt responds by threatening Logo and slamming him into Howie's locker, proclaiming: "You look like the little scairty cat 'round here, bro—"[63] So, even though Curt has offered a playful performance of the Cowardly Lion's lines, he distinguishes between himself and Logo, labeling the latter scared and cat—a much more diminutive version of a lion—and threatening physical harm. Robbie explains to Logo that the Black Students Alliance is pressuring Curt to join, "but he's, I don't know, he's playing it safe."[64] This discussion of Curt's actions seem to hint at a vulnerability, and indeed, Landau gives him dimension through a monologue describing his secret desire to join his fellow students, but also his related fear, or even cowardice, about the rejection that might accompany such a move: "I am part of the American experience and hey, I don't know, maybe there's no way I can bridge the gap. What if I'm not ... accepted.... What if I'm like ... a whole different species?[65] For the most popular student, "playing it safe" is close to admitting fear, though Curt only admits his fear of not being accepted to himself and the audience.

Regarding Curt's more direct relationship to Howie, he explains how Curt called him "faggot" on the first day of high school, elaborating that they did not know each other, but Curt was the most popular student, "so you see he popularized this activity, I mean that of hating me, so everyone wanted to get into the act."[66] Nevertheless, Howie cannot help but watch Curt, transfixed in his physical attraction, as he dresses in the locker room. Curt does seem relatively fearless to Howie and others, and by making the Lion of her piece an African-American student, Landau almost seems to be suggesting some primitivist vision, associating him with an African "animal," the lion, making him the object of Howie's sexual desire rather than the emotional involvement Howie feels towards Robbie or Royce. Perhaps this portrayal even projects into *The Wizard of Oz*'s history in 1974 with the all–Black adaptation, *The Wiz*. Indeed, in Howie's dream vision of the prom, the stage directions describe Logo and Robbie in tuxedos, dancing with the only females in the cast, Roz and Stefanie, when "Curtis arrives as the Cowardly Lion and sings 'If I Were King of the Forest.'"[67] If the whole number is indeed performed, it ends with the Lion asking, "What have they got that I ain't got?" to which his companions respond, "Courage!"[68] Such an admission by Curt and accusation by his peers would fulfill a fantasy for Howie, by making Curt vulnerable and subject to ridicule. What is more, since Curt "arrives as the Cowardly Lion" and begins singing, he and Howie are the only male students not seen dancing with women (both of whom are assumed to be Caucasian), and Curt is dressed as an animal rather than in more "civilized" formal wear, performing a comic, self-deprecating number—almost a minstrel performance for the other students. This is clearly Howie's dream of the prom, since it makes Curt a ridiculous, animalistic figure admitting his own fear. Yet, outside of Howie's dream, while not a "friend of Dorothy's"/Howie's, Curt does serve his purpose, by functioning as an object of Howie's sexual desire and supplying him the vocabulary "faggot," which he uses to identify himself both alone and with Robbie. What is more, though it is 1969 (just a few years after integration of the schools) and Curt is African-American, he is identified as "the most popular guy in school"[69]; yet, his monologue voices his concern that he might be "a whole different species,"[70] and he admits when dealing with school authorities, "I'm confused man ... alright?,"[71] all of which marks him as queer as well.

In the *Oz* scenario, one of the more troubling figures is the Wizard himself, for he is, for most intents and purposes, a con artist. Yet, he also has the most in common with Dorothy, for both are outsiders, brought to Oz by chance. His counterpart in *1969*, Royce Martinson, is quite the opposite. He is a graduate of the same high school eight years earlier, thus close to the students in age. He is known by a series of nicknames, including Royce the Voice (for imitations of radio disc jockeys), Mr. Wizard (after the television science show host), and as he tells the audience, "Clark Kent, because [my students] say when I get excited and take off my tie, I turn into Super-Teacher."[72] Each of these characters can be compared to the Wizard of the film. By associating Royce with a disc jockey, it imagines him as a disembodied voice emerging from the radio, face unseen, somewhat like the Wizard when he is merely a disembodied head and amplified voice in the throne room. The association with Clark Kent emphasizes duality, suggesting a "mild-mannered" persona with an additional secret identity that is more colorful, powerful and theatrical. In actuality, Clark Kent is the opposite of the Wizard, for while Superman possesses amazing powers and merely pretends to be the weak, mortal Kent, the Wizard is not "Oz, the great and powerful," but merely a human from the Midwest, like Dorothy, who *pretends* to be a powerful being, prompting the question of whether Royce has power he is hiding or if he is pretending to be powerful. Certainly, the duality suggests secrets and a hidden nature. Obviously, the Wizard of Oz in the film is invoked by the students calling Royce, Mr. Wizard. At the same time, it is also the name of a children's television host who came to prominence in the late 1950/early 1960s and was noted for his amazing and seemingly miraculous science experiments performed on television, like the theatrical techniques utilized by the Wizard in the film to impress those in his throne room. However, while the Wizard of Oz is revealed to be a humbug, Mr. Wizard would actually show children the science behind the amazing feats he accomplished. The television tricks were often very simple and involved household items.[73] By the same token, Royce encourages his students to "expand your minds," in some ways revealing the construction of his power, but also hiding some of his frustration and disappointment with the school administration. He tries to be his students' friend, encourages them to apply for college and announces that there will be a pop quiz the next day. He invites them to attend foreign films at the local art cinema and call him by his first name. He also reveals that he plans "to go to finish grad school and ... of course ... my novel."[74] Rather than "the man behind the curtain," this "Mr. Wizard" is seemingly one of the most open characters in the play. Yet, his insistence that his students use his first name or a nickname, his closeness in age to them, his revelation of plans like pop quizzes and socializing with students outside of school, his creative activity like playing guitar and novel-writing, his intent to finish graduate school, all place him in an in-between, queer state — not quite teacher, not quite student. Indeed, he reveals to the audience that he wants "to get the in-betweeners to consider college"[75] to protect them from the military draft. The "in-betweeners" are not the top of the class, which will certainly go to college, or the bottom of the class, who will not go to college and will be drafted, but the ones in between, i.e. the queer ones.

In relation to Howie, one of his goals is "to have Royce notice me,"[76] and when Howie envisions his dream prom, he imagines dancing with his intellectual and romantic fantasy, Royce, rather than Curt, the object of his sexual desire. Royce is described as wearing a mask; perhaps the mask suggests that Royce is, in fact, gay himself, or has other secrets "behind the curtain." He is the only one of the male characters who is never described as dressing as his film counterpart, the Wizard, for the prom. When Royce cares for Howie during a bad LSD trip, Howie sends him a thank you letter afterward:

> Still Royce, the sound of your voice stays in my mind
> that night appears in my dreams—
> gives shape and color to these words, these sentences,
> whatever theme I write, whatever thought flies by,
> With all love and respect ... Howie.[77]

This letter is intercepted by Curt and handed over to school authorities. Given its "queer" content — it is written in verse, it references color and a shared night, and is signed "love" — it is misinterpreted as a love letter between them. Royce is fired and moves to New York City. Like the Wizard in the film, Royce departs because he has little choice.

Thus Howie, labeled as gay by the rumors, nearing graduation but facing the draft, runs away to New York as well. Like Dorothy, he must travel under his own power, without the Wizard's help. Throughout *1969*, Howie conflates New York with Oz, specifically Greenwich Village, declaring it "the polar opposite of this place," and exclaiming "I just want to get out of there

... this unreal suburban landscape,"[78] even urging "[w]e have to get to Emerald City!"[79] when pursued by police. Few remember that in the film, *The Wizard of Oz*, Dorothy runs away, and it is only at the urging of Professor Marvel/ The Wizard that she returns home, although she is still transported by the tornado. Theatre critic Ben Brantley, following a similar summary, explains:

> The kid has many exciting adventures but continues to yearn with a bottomless pang for the idea of something called home. Yes, that is the plot of "The Wizard of Oz." It is also the life story of countless numbers of gay men and lesbians who fled what Tina Landau, the writer and director, describes in the play "1969" as the "vast map of normalcy" that is much of America. Many of them found their own Oz on a northeastern island called Manhattan.[80]

Certainly, the film is famous for Dorothy's return home, but as writer John Carlyle expresses: "I did not want Dorothy to go home to Kansas! When she had to say goodbye to her Land of Oz companions, I felt that I would explode with sorrow."[81] Many gays and lesbians felt as Carlyle did and did not return home, but made New York their home.

The final scene, labeled "Coda/Transition to Stonewall," somewhat mirrors the first Oz scene of the film. Howie asks where he is, and a Puerto Rican drag queen who identifies herself as Glinda the Good Witch tells him, "The Village of Odds."[82] When she asks his name, unlike his film counterpart, Howie makes one up, calling himself "Timothy," echoing both the name Dorothy as well as suggesting 1960s counterculture figure Timothy Leary. While Dorothy had no reason to reinvent herself, Howie does, to avoid the military, his parents, and his past. He is shocked to learn that, unlike the ending of *Oz*, this scenario is not a dream. Despite the prominence of the good and wicked witches in the film, this is the only appearance of one in *1969*, and in the original production Glinda was likely played by the same actor who played Howie's teacher, Royce. Glinda offers "Timothy" a place to sleep, explaining, "everyone is welcome here, you know."[83]

In his queer reading of *The Wizard of Oz*, John M. Clum admits, "Oz has dangers, as does living in the urban gay ghetto, but they're mitigated by the fabulousness of the place. There Dorothy and her queer friends build their own family."[84] However, *1969* differs from the famous film, for while Dorothy does not recognize the farmhands as her colorful friends until returning home/awaking, Howie is well aware of both the male companions of his high school life and their *Oz* counterparts. Rather than reinvent them to help him in New York, he has left both behind, and perhaps Glinda is the first of his truly queer friends with which he will build a family. Thus, the *Oz* scenario is reinvented specifically for a performance of queer identity, with shifts to Dorothy/Howie's relationship to the Tin Man, Scarecrow and Cowardly Lion characters. In addition, the Wizard figure is made one of the most honest on stage; Glinda is reconfigured as a Puerto Rican drag queen, and the Oz Howie sought is real — as long as he reinvents himself. Dorothy's adventures in Oz are precipitated by her unwilling transport in the tornado and the subsequent accidental murder of the Witch of the East. Tina Landau's *1969* stages a queer reading of *The Wizard of Oz* for audiences by depicting Howie "taking a trip" which brings him away from his past and former companions to find the very specific place he heard and dreamt about. At the end of Landau's play, the "tornado" of the Stonewall riots and the gay rights movement are just about to begin. Fortunately for Howie, "it wasn't a dream,"[85] and "Timothy" is home.

Notes

1. Clum, *Something for the Boys*, 153.
2. Carlyle, *Under the Rainbow*, 24.
3. Cummings, "Review," 1994.
4. Landau, *1969*, 180.
5. Sherman, *The Wizard of Oz Catalog*.
6. Landau, *1969*, 180–181.
7. Ibid., 181.
8. Doty, "There's Something Queer Here," 72 .
9. Luhmann, Susanne. "Queering/Querying Pedagogy?,"146.
10. Benshoff and Griffin, *Queer Images*, 69.
11. Creekmur and Doty, *Out in Culture*, 2.
12. Sullivan, *A Critical Introduction to Queer Theory*, 193.
13. Sedgwick, *Epistemology of the Closet*, 156.
14. Savran, *A Queer Sort of Materialism*, 57.
15. Benshoff and Griffin, *Queer Images*, 101.
16. Creekmur and Doty, *Out in Culture*, 3.
17. Knapp, *The American Musical*, 68.
18. Benshoff & Doty, *Queer Images*, 101.
19. Bronski, "Judy Garland and Others," 202–203.
20. Flinn, "The Death of Camp," 433.
21. Ross, "Uses of Camp," 309.
22. Bosman and Bradford, *Gay, Lesbian, Bisexual, and Transgendered Literature*, 109.
23. Landau, *1969*, 185.
24. Ibid., 214.
25. Ibid., 182.
26. Langley, *The Wizard of Oz*, 107.
27. Landau, *1969*, 183.
28. Landau, *1969*, 195.
29. Bronski, "Judy Garland and Others," 202–203.
30. Landau, *1969*, 200.
31. Ibid.
32. Ibid.
33. Langley, *The Wizard of Oz*, 106.
34. Woolf, *Webster's New Collegiate Dictionary*, 677.
35. Langley, *The Wizard of Oz*, 195.
36. Landau, *1969*, 195.
37. Ibid., 196.

38. Ibid., 208.
39. Langley, *The Wizard of Oz*, 42.
40. Landau, *1969*, 195.
41. Doty, *Flaming Classics*, 52.
42. Langley, *The Wizard of Oz*, 38.
43. Landau, *1969*, 190.
44. Ibid., 203.
45. Creekmur and Doty, *Out in Culture*, 2.
46. Landau, *1969*, 203.
47. Langley, *The Wizard of Oz*, 80.
48. Landau, *1969*, 203.
49. Langley, *The Wizard of Oz*, 106.
50. Landau, *1969*, 188.
51. Imdb.com.
52. Landau, *1969*, 214.
53. Ibid.
54. Ibid., 184.
55. Ibid., 185
56. Langley, *The Wizard of Oz*, 105.
57. Benshoff & Griffin, *Queer Images*, 149.
58. Langley, *The Wizard of Oz*, 54.
59. Doty, *Flaming Classics*, 50.
60. Landau, *1969*, 193.
61. Ibid., 195.
62. Ibid., 193.
63. Ibid., 193.
64. Ibid., 193.
65. Ibid., 199.
66. Ibid., 185.
67. Ibid., 200.
68. Langley, *The Wizard of Oz*, 71.
69. Landau, *1969*, 185.
70. Ibid., 199.
71. Ibid., 211.
72. Ibid., 187.
73. Woolery, *Children's Television*, 241.
74. Ibid.
75. Ibid.
76. Ibid., 195.
77. Ibid., 207.
78. Ibid., 213.
79. Ibid., 215.
80. Brantley, *The New York Times*.
81. Carlyle, *Under the Rainbow*, 24.
82. Landau, *1969*, 218.
83. Ibid.
84. Clum, *Something for the Boys*, 10.
85. Langley, *The Wizard of Oz*, 106.

Works Cited

Benshoff, Harry M., & Sean Griffin, eds. *Queer Images: A History of Gay and Lesbian Film in America.* New York: Rowman & Littlefield Publishers, Inc., 2006.

Bosman, Ellen, and John P. Bradford. *Gay, Lesbian, Bisexual and Transgendered Literature: A Genre Guide.* Edited by Robert B. Ridinger. Westport, CT: Libraries Unlimited, 2008.

Brantley, Ben. "CRITIC'S NOTEBOOK: Why Oz Is a State of Mind in Gay Life and Drag Shows." *The New York Times,* June 28, 1994, Section C, page 15.

Bronski, Michael. "Judy Garland and Others: Notes on Idolization and Derision." In *Lavender Culture.* Ed. by Karla Jay and Allen Young. New York: New York University Press, 1994.

Carlyle, John. *Under the Rainbow: An Intimate Memoir of Judy Garland, Rock Hudson and My Life in Old Hollywood.* New York: Carroll & Graf, 2006.

Clum, John M. *Something for the Boys; Musical Theater and Gay Culture.* New York: Palgrave, 1999.

Creekmur, Corey K., and Alexander Doty, eds. "Introduction." *Out in Culture: Gay, Lesbian, and Queer Essays on Popular Culture.* Durham: Duke University Press, 1995.

Cummings, Scott T. "Review." *Theatre Journal,* Vol. 46, No. 4 (Dec 1994), pp. 545–548.

Doty, Alexander. *Flaming Classics: Queering the Film Canon.* New York: Routledge, 2000.

_____. "There's Something Queer Here." *Out in Culture: Gay, Lesbian, and Queer Essays on Popular Culture.* Durham: Duke University Press, 1995.

Flinn, Caryl. "The Deaths of Camp." In *Camp: Queer Aesthetics and The Performing Subject.* Ed. by Fabio Cleto. Ann Arbor: University of Michigan Press, 1999.

Knapp, Raymond. *The American Musical and the Performance of Personal Identity.* Princeton: Princeton University Press, 2006.

Landau, Tina. *1969 or Howie Takes a Trip.* In *Humana Festival '94 The Complete Plays,* edited by Marisa Smith, 179–219. Louisville, KY: Smith and Kraus, 1994.

Langley, Noel, L. Frank Baum. *The Wizard of Oz: Screenplay.* New York: Faber Children's Books, 2001.

Luhmann, Susanne. "Queering/Querying Pedagogy? Or, Pedagogy Is a Pretty Queer Thing." *Queer Theory in Education.* William F. Pinar, ed. Mahwah, NJ: Lawrence Erlbaum Associates, Publishers.

"Robby the Robot." The Internet Movie Database. 19 August 2009. http://www.imdb.com/character/ch0013436/

Ross, Andrew. "Uses of Camp." In *Camp: Queer Aesthetics and The Performing Subject.* Ed. by Fabio Cleto. Ann Arbor: University of Michigan Press, 1999.

Savran, David. *A Queer Sort of Materialism: Recontextualizing American Theater.* Ann Arbor: University of Michigan Press, 2003.

Sedgwick, Eve Kosofsky. *Epistemology of the Closet.* Berkeley: University of California Press, 1990.

Sherman, Fraser A. *The Wizard of Oz Catalog: L. Frank Baum's Novel, Its Sequels and Their Adaptation for Stage, Television, Movies, Radio, Music Videos, Comic Books, Commercials and More.* Jefferson, NC: McFarland & Company, 2005.

Sullivan, Nikki. *A Critical Introduction to Queer Theory.* New York: New York University Press, 2003.

Ullom, Jeffrey. *The Humana Festival: The History of New Plays at Actors Theatre of Louisville.* Carbondale: Southern Illinois University Press, 2008.

Woolery, George W. *Children's Television, The First Thirty-Five Years, 1946–1981.* Metuchen, NJ: Scarecrow Press, 1983–1985.

Woolf, Henry Bosley, ed. *Webster's New Collegiate Dictionary.* Springfield, MA: G. & C. Merriam Company, 1977.

CHAPTER 5

"Something between higgledy-piggledy and the eternal sphere"

Queering Age/Sex in Shelley Jackson's Patchwork Girl

EMILY A. MATTINGLY

American writer and artist Shelley Jackson's now-classic electronic hypertext *Patchwork Girl* (1995) is multiple, slippery. A hypertext with neither an unambiguous narrative trajectory nor a clear-cut conclusion, *Patchwork Girl* presents a web of intertextual allusions to various theoretical, historical, and fictional works, including Mary Shelley's gothic novel *Frankenstein* (1818) and L. Frank Baum's illustrated children's book *The Patchwork Girl of Oz* (1913). We, as readers, navigate *Patchwork Girl*'s complex network of allusions without knowing what we will read next. As we navigate *Patchwork Girl*, we become hyperaware of— and, perhaps, frustrated by — this hypertext's lack of a clear beginning, middle, and end. In her influential study "Flickering Connectivities in Shelley Jackson's *Patchwork Girl*" (2005), feminist literary critic N. Katherine Hayles describes how we read *Patchwork Girl* in just these terms, and she interprets very literally the work's rhetorical comparison between "hyperlink" and corporeal, memorial inscription, or "scar":

> The user inscribes her subjectivity into the text by choosing which links to activate, which scars to trace. Contrary to the dictates of good taste and good writing, the scars/links thus function to join the text with the corporeal body of the user who perform the enacted motion that bring the text into being as a sequential narrative [159].

How readers engage *Patchwork Girl* is, in many ways, driven by their respective interests and curiosities about which links to click next.[1] Depending on which paths of links readers choose to follow, the lexias' meanings change. Though we navigate *Patchwork Girl* in circles and often repeat which links we follow and which lexias we read, we, as Hayles suggests, eventually organize the hypertext into some kind of sequential narrative so that it makes sense to us. We may organize *Patchwork Girl* into a linear narrative in our minds, but, as we read this hypertext, we realize the following: Jackson's work invites us to think about linear narrative structures as a narrative option, not a narrative rule. This circular reading and repetition, then, draws readers' attentions to *Patchwork Girl's* performative nature.

In her often-cited 1997 talk at MIT, "Stitch Bitch: The Patchwork Girl," Jackson shared with her audience that *Patchwork Girl* reflects her following preference: "My favorite texts loiter, dawdle, tease, pass notes, they resist the linear, they pervert it" (251). For Jackson, such texts — or, examples of "bad writing," as she calls them — exemplify "everything that for centuries has been damned by its association with the feminine" (248). Electronic hypertexts are particularly damned. Because they often have numerous reading paths and multiple narrative entry points, Jackson notes, electronic hypertexts are "amphibious vehicle[s], good for negotiating unsteady ground, poised on [their] multiple limbs where the book clogs up and stops, [they] keep in motion" (246).[2] Such hypertexts are "what literature has edited out: the feminine" (248).

Perhaps not surprisingly, Jackson believes that hypertexts allow her to forge new possibilities for reconfiguring femininities. Specifically, she suggests that *Patchwork Girl*, as a hypertext, opens a performative and metacritical space where she can critique traditional masculinist print narratives. Such masculinist narratives subordinate various feminine bodies and subjectivities, Jackson argues, because the patriarchal realm of language reinforces them. For Jackson, both *Patchwork Girl's* non-linear structure and intertextual makeup subvert this language. In her essay "What if Frankenstein('s Monster) Was a Girl?: Reproduction and Subjectivity in the Digital Age" (2008), feminist scholar Jenny Sundén suggests that readers eventually learn "to give up the search for the True Story — which never existed anyway" (160). In other words, when we begin to read *Patchwork Girl*, we look for linear narrative lines. Because we are conditioned to want masculine narratives, we look for a transparent narrative progression that fulfills our expectations for what "good writing" looks like. We want clearly-marked chapters and numbered pages. We want a story that we can follow from beginning to end, a story that is "stable." The more links we follow and the more lexias we read, however, the more we are confronted by the feminine.

Patchwork Girl's intricate web of lexias and links, however, is not particularly groundbreaking. Indeed, in "What if Frankenstein('s Monster) Was a Girl?," Sundén observes that "*Patchwork Girl* was born when hypertext theory had reached its peak" (155). Jackson's hypertext, Sundén notes, is "a progeny of this moment in the history of hyperfiction" (155). Like many other hypertexts during the mid–1990s, *Patchwork Girl*, Sundén suggests, "takes great pleasure in the process of letting the narrative capacities of the medium merge with the narratives being told through writing spaces, the most obvious example being the mirroring of scars and links" (155). Moreover, *Patchwork Girl's* feminine performance, in many ways, reflects early and mid–1990s feminist hypertext artists' and writers' interests in complicating feminine subjectivities and bodies.[3] Many 1990s feminist hypertexts artists and writers, like Jackson, were deeply invested in both challenging masculinist print narratives and performing various femininities in hypertext. Specifically, in her study "Feminist Digital Aesthetics: The Everyday and Yesterday" (2007), media scholar Caitlin Fisher notes that many of these feminist hypertext artists and writers revisited 1970s feminists' interests in creating feminist revisions of various classic print texts, exploring domestic spaces, and consciousness-raising (154). Moreover, Fisher notes that several of Jackson's female contemporaries were interested in using their work to "disrupt understandings of the boundaries of feminist theory" (155). "[T]hrough their performance of feminist theories," Fisher suggests, Jackson's contemporaries used their hypertexts to create spaces that were both "as much about feminism's past as about its present" and "disrupt[ed] the easy linear developmental tale of the feminist then to the feminist now" (157). These women were interested in exploring the potentially productive relationships between feminist content and electronic hypertext form.

Queer/Feminine/Hypertext

Jackson's work is notable precisely because of how we engage her depictions of various feminine subjectivities and bodies through Storyspace — the software used to create *Patchwork Girl*— and the computer screen. Moreover, considering *Patchwork Girl's* perceived place within the larger history — both feminist and otherwise — of hypertext, I suggest that Jackson's work is notable because it exploits the content/form relationship between the illegible feminine subjectivities and bodies Jackson depicts. In her essay "Subject to Change: The Monstrosity of Media in Shelley Jackson's *Patchwork Girl; or, A Modern Monster* and Other Posthumanist Critiques of the Instrumental" (2006), feminist scholar Laura Shackelford suggests the following about Jackson's complex depictions of femininity:

> [*Patchwork Girl* acknowledges] the multiplicity within the category of the feminine that compromises social systems' and subjectivities' attempts to stabilize a single gendered identity, as well as the material complexity of physical bodies — their lack of identity, sameness, or stability — marks the limits to a masculinist

illusion of instrumental mastery. Foregrounding these limits, *Patchwork Girl* opens up the possibility of a different grammar, one that would enable nonoppositional, nonbinary differences rather than require the subjugation of difference and of a logic of [masculine] possession that attempts, but inevitably fails, to secure the reproduction of the same [89].

As this quote from Shackelford suggests, Jackson's hypertext is deeply invested in creating a narrative space that upsets various restrictive sexed and gendered identity constructs. According to Shackelford, Jackson's depictions of the patchwork girl — *Patchwork Girl's* feminine protagonist who is made of various sewn-together human and animal parts collected from various gravesites — denaturalizes such constructs. Jackson's depictions of the patchwork girl's volatile corporeality and history bring into question how bodies are materialized. Such depictions of the patchwork girl, in other words, reveal how seemingly stable sex and gender categories are naturalized through discursive repetition by introducing sex/gender alternatives and disrupting such repetition.[4] Much of this disruption, Hayles suggests in "Flickering Connectivities," stems from the patchwork girl "having been assembled and not born, with no chance to grow into the adult she now is" (165). Specifically, the patchwork is made of body parts from several women, men, and a cow: her liver comes from Roderick, a gay fabrics importer who lived with his partner in the English countryside; her left breast comes from Charlotte, a woman who "squirted" her "extra milk on her dying babies" ("left breast"); her vagina comes from Eleanor, "a lady very dextrous with the accoutrements of femininity" ("right arm"); her veins come from Helen, a "quiet and malleable young woman" ("veins"); and her lower intestine comes from an unnamed cow. The patchwork girl's piecemeal body underscores her illegible femininity.

Indeed, the patchwork girl's illegible femininity destabilizes binary gender logics, but is she, as Hayles assumes, an adult? Put differently, is her illegible femininity always already adult because she was, as Hayles suggests, "assembled and not born"? More specifically, does the patchwork girl's assembled body and history only question how adult bodies and adult femininities are materialized? Even the patchwork girl asks herself the following: "What is the age of the resurrected body?" ("resurrection"). In posing these questions, I draw attention to how feminist scholars often investigate how the patchwork girl's illegible femininity complicates sex and gender categories, but overlook how age operates — or, does not operate — in Jackson's work. Indeed, scholars have yet to explore how *Patchwork Girl* intervenes in contemporary knowledge production that both creates and upholds a strict child/adult binary — a binary that, in many ways, relies on a strict, sequential model of age and normative developmental stages.

Feminist scholars' oversight of how age operates in Jackson's hypertext,

I argue, is symptomatic of contemporary feminist scholarship's tendency to imagine children as both asexual and innocent. Specifically, in his influential essay "Feminism, Child Sexual Abuse, and the Erasure of Child Sexuality" (2004), Steven Angelides suggests that, since the 1980s, "childhood sexuality" often "figure[s] only as an oxymoron" (142). Angelides suggests that this oxymoron stems from post–1980s feminist interests in child sexual abuse and child pornography. Feminist discourses of child sexual abuse, Angelides argues, compromise childhood sexuality because it either "ceases to be sexuality, or else the use of terms such as *sex play* and *sexual experimentation* works to disqualify it" (154; author's emphasis). Indeed, in feminist scholarship, tropes of sexual innocence haunt children. And, if feminist scholars do discuss children's sexualities, they typically imagine children as asexual and oversimplify, trivialize, or downplay their sexual expressions as innocent games.[5]

Such feminist discourses, then, often reinforce a strict age/sex divide between children and adults. By reinforcing this binary, adults are figured as sexual and children as asexual. In other words, many contemporary feminist discourses of sexuality "collapse the axis of sexuality into that of age" (163). Such a collapse, Angelides argues, upholds a "linear and sequential model of age stratification premised on distinct chronological, spatial, and temporal stages of biological and psychological development" (163). This collapsing of age/sex, I believe, is exactly what happens in feminist scholars' criticism of *Patchwork Girl.* By assuming that the patchwork girl is an adult, scholars both deny that *Patchwork Girl*'s depictions of sex between the patchwork girl and various other characters are anything other than depictions of "adult sex." Such assumptions ignore Jackson's hypertext's complex illustrations of intergenerational sex and multi-generational bodies. Moreover, such assumptions ignore age constructs' relationships to power.

"In its poststructuralist and deconstructive variations, queer theory," Angelides maintains, "offers an important corrective" to the linear model of age, binary constructions of age/sex, and, in particular, the oversimplification of childhood (164). Specifically, according to Angelides, such "queer critical interventions highlight the importance of examining the *signifiers* of 'childhood,' 'adolescence,' and 'adulthood,' and thus the analytic *axes* of age and sexuality, in the same frame of analysis" (164; author's emphasis). Through such a queer lens, we begin to see that even how we engage *Patchwork Girl* is inextricably linked to how we engage the patchwork girl's illegible femininity and her non-sequential age, and vice versa. Indeed, when we navigate Jackson's hypertext, we do not engage the patchwork girl as a subject who relies upon linear narrative lines that determine her subjectivity. Rather, we engage her as an unstable subject who exists only through and during her hypertextual narrative construction.

Such construction, I suggest, underscores how *Patchwork Girl* is a thoroughly queer text that revels in its own queer, feminine performance. Specifically, I suggest that Jackson's hypertext reflects gender scholar Lynne Huffer's discussion about "queer performativity." In her essay "'There is no Gomorrah': Narrative Ethics in Feminist and Queer Theory" (2001), Huffer suggests the following:

> Queer performativity ... openly acknowledges its own linguistically constructed status, where the emergence of the speaking subject coincides with the moment of utterance of the speech act itself. Thus, while both narratives and performatives produce subjects, narrative depends on a retroactive legitimation of the subject position through the temporality of narrative grammar, while performativity admits that the subject it speaks in the present moment of the utterance is the only subject there is [9].

Considering Huffer's discussion about queer performativity, I suggest that *Patchwork Girl* is a queer text because it simultaneously foregrounds its own constructedness and "openly" constructs the patchwork girl's volatile identity categories. As a queer text, *Patchwork Girl*, as I will later explore, is both self-conscious of its "amphibious," queer, feminine natures and how this amphibiousness is necessarily linked to the patchwork girl's multiplicities.

Curiously, however, scholars have yet to explicitly explore *Patchwork Girl*'s queerness. More pointedly, although feminist scholars often explore how Jackson's work complicates gender binaries, these scholars are reluctant to acknowledge how *Patchwork Girl* operates as a queer text. As my earlier discussion about how feminist scholars situate *Patchwork Girl* within a larger history of feminist hypertexts created during the 1990s suggests, Jackson's exploration of feminine subjectivity is often read only as a feminist exploration. For these scholars, then, Jackson's depictions of complex feminine subjectivities and bodies are simply feminist concerns that preclude queerness. And, while several scholars who investigate Jackson's hypertext mention the various "lesbian" relationships that the patchwork girl has with different women, their discussions, quite ironically, overlook how queer theory may be a fruitful lens through which to examine *Patchwork Girl*.[6] Here, I do not wish to suggest that feminist scholars' deep engagements with *Patchwork Girl* are neither useful nor productive. However, I do suggest that, by overlooking how *Patchwork Girl* may be read as a queer text, these scholars ignore much of the transformative possibilities imbedded within Jackson's work. Indeed, using a queer lens to investigate *Patchwork Girl* allows us to move beyond feminist scholars' sometimes flat discussions about normative and non-normative femininity in Jackson's hypertext. Exploring *Patchwork Girl* through a queer lens is especially productive because it invites us to both interrogate how Jackson's work complicates the normative age/sex binary and better explore this text's complex depictions age. Moreover, a queer lens allows us to examine how queer discourses of age inform Jackson's depictions of various queer feminine sexualities. Ultimately, such a lens encourages us to complicate the age/sex binary that feminist scholars often implicitly uphold in their respective critical discussions about *Patchwork Girl* and rethink Jackson's hypertext's place within feminist literary and media scholarship.

Queer Couplings, Queer Stanzas

I suggest that *Patchwork Girl's* depictions of queer couplings offer particularly fruitful insights into how Jackson's work complicates the age/sex binary. In particular, *Patchwork Girl's* portrayal of the queer relationships between the patchwork girl and Mary and Elsie, respectively, foreground this hypertext's deep interest in exploding this binary and challenging normative feminine constructs.

To begin my exploration of *Patchwork Girl's* queer couplings, I first turn to Jackson's depictions of the patchwork girl and Mary. Mary—a fictional version of Mary Shelley—writes/sews the patchwork girl. Keeping her creation a secret from her husband, Percy, Mary pieces the patchwork girl together late at night by candlelight. While assembling the patchwork girl, Mary feels like she is "sewing a great quilt, as the old women in town do night after night, looking dolefully out their windows ... and imagining [Mary's] sins while their thighs tremble" ("written"). These older, sexually frustrated women fantasize about Mary having sex with Percy—or, perhaps, even masturbating—as they sew. Indifferent to these women's sexual curiosities, however, Mary keeps on with her work. "[T]his creature," Mary thinks to herself as she diligently continues creating the patchwork girl, is "a brash attempt to achieve by artificial means the unity of a life-form—a unity perhaps more rightfully given, not made..." ("sewn"). Mary feels "interrupted" ("sewn"). She feels much like how the patchwork girl's body looks: patched together. In many ways, then, her "brash" effort to make the patchwork girl whole and unified is an attempt for her, too, to feel whole and unified.

Mary imagines that the patchwork girl will be a version of the ideal Romantic child: innocent, close to nature, uninhibited, simple, carefree, and virtuous.[7] Specifically, Mary wants the patchwork girl to be the Romantic child that she feels she never was—or, could be—as a girl. She wants the patchwork girl to "grow up" into a coherent, proper woman who she feels she is not. "[W]hen I was a child I laid a piece of paper over a tombstone," Mary notes, "and rubbed a bit of charcoal back and forth [...] until the winged skulls and disconsolate maidens emerged ... as if summoned up from my own bewildered and superstitious soul" ("learn"). Even as a child, Mary knows that she is expected to grow into proper (heterosexual) feminine womanhood from a proper (asexual, though, at the same time, heterosexual) feminine girlhood. Mary identifies with the "disconsolate maidens" and felt like she "summoned" them. As a girl, Mary is haunted by the image of the Romantic child, and feels that her own girlhood fell short of the Romantic ideal because she remembers her "bewildered" sexual feelings toward the women on the tombstone. Deep down, Mary knows that the Romantic child is an ideal child that never truly existed in the first place, a child that is always already a construction, a figment of the Romantic imagination. Nevertheless, as she constructs the patchwork girl, she hopes to bring to life a Romantic child and make material the ideal she always wanted to experience herself.

Sexual desire, however, also drives her fantasy to create the patchwork girl. Just like the older women who longingly look at her window at night as she sews/writes, Mary stays up late into the night, driven by her own sexual frustration. Mary "craves" the patchwork girl's company and her creation is motivated by "the fierce mad engine that is throbbing inside [her] serene life, staining [her] underclothes..." ("crave"). She is turned on by the idea that the patchwork girl—as a supposedly Romantic child—is sexually "innocent." Her sexual interest in the patchwork girl, I suggest, reflects James Kincaid's following observation in his highly controversial study *Erotic Innocence: The Culture of Child Molesting* (2000):

> As for innocence: at one point a theological trope, in the nineteenth century it became more and more firmly attached to this world and to this world's sexuality. It was, further, a characteristic that outran any simple physical manifestation: innocence became a fulcrum for the post–Romantic ambiguous construction of sexuality and sexual behavior. On the one hand, innocence was valued deeply and guarded by criminal statutes (albeit often bendable ones); on the one hand, innocence was a consumer product, an article to possess, as a promise to the righteous and the reward to the dutiful. It came to you in heaven or in marriage, a prize. We were trained to adore and covet it, to preserve and despoil it, to speak of it in hushed tones and in bawdy songs [15].

As Kincaid suggests, discourses that construct Romantic childhood innocence are always imbued with sexual fantasies. Such discourses that construct childhood innocence, as mentioned in my earlier discuss about contemporary feminist discourses, haunt us today. Indeed, we construct discourses of innocence that, quite ironically, fetishize innocence. We covet innocence, we fantasize about it. We eroticize children—especially girls—in the same moment we imagine that they are asexual. We imagine children's sexual otherness and lack—an otherness and lack that keeps them "safely" separate from "fully" sexual adults. Mary's desire to create a Romantic child, then, is also a queer desire to materialize her innocence fetish and appease the "fierce hunger under her stays" ("she").

On the surface, we may read Mary's relationship with the patchwork girl as mother and daughter coupling. After all, Mary calls the patchwork girl her "child" ("appetite"). However, Mary does not see herself as a mother. She, instead, sees herself outside of the heterosexual reproductive framework that constructs the child. Indeed, when the patchwork girl comes to life, she calls herself a "would-be parent" ("appetite"). This "would-be parent" role exists completely outside of the heteronormative parental and, more specifically, maternal role. This role resists parenthood, and, at the same time, creates a queer time/space in which Mary can both have a "child" and not be tied to heterosexual reproduction or motherhood. When Mary calls herself a "would-be parent," she resists normative constructs of time and space based on heterosexual reproduction. As queer theory scholar Judith Halberstam argues in her *In a Queer Time and Place: Transgender Bodies, Subcultural Lives* (2005), "[r]eproductive time and family time are, above all, heteronormative time/space constructs" (10). Mary resists both reproductive and family time. Rather, Mary constructs a queer time/space for herself in which, as Halberstam notes, "the separation between youth and adulthood quite simply does not hold" (174). Mary, then, is not ageless, per se. However, Mary's age does not fit into the normative child/adult binary.

Even though Mary herself complicates heteronormative time/space constructs, she still sees the patchwork girl strictly as a Romantic child. Mary loves when the patchwork girl runs through the hills near her home, "stamping," "hallooing," "jumping," and "laughing" like she is a Romantic child who is connected to nature ("appetite"). Turned on by the patchwork girl's carefree nudity as they roam the forest together, Mary thinks the patchwork girl looks like a "hoyendish child of overgrown proportions [when] she tears the confining garments from her form" ("appetite"). Despite the passing years, for Mary, the patchwork girl remains much like a Romantic child: "exuberant, ferocious, loving, and unhinged" ("infant").

Curiously, even at the same time Mary thinks of the patchwork girl as a Romantic child, she recognizes that the patchwork girl's body is made of body parts that belonged to people and an animal who were very different ages upon their respective deaths and who died at different times. Mary also realizes that "[s]craps of memories" that are attached to the patchwork girl's various body parts "blow through her mind like bits of patterned cloth" ("infant"). Initially, for Mary, such memories and body parts do not sway her attraction to the patchwork girl. Indeed, at first, Mary views the patchwork girl as "infant"-like because her normative linear age suggests that she is only a few years old ("infant"). When Mary and her creation have sex, however,

Mary soon realizes that the patchwork girl is not the mythical Romantic child she first envisioned. After they have sex, Mary believes that the patchwork girl is neither sexually "innocent" nor a child. Much like Mary, the patchwork girl does not fit into the child/adult binary. The patchwork girl undermines Mary's erotic fantasy that she is completely a child and, therefore, asexual. Soon after Mary's fantasy comes to an abrupt end, Mary shows no interest in the patchwork girl and the patchwork girl leaves her home. Upon leaving, the patchwork girl sinks into a deep depression. She describes her depression as such: "After Mary and I parted, I became depressed, suffering a kind of post-partum blues in reverse" ("Aftermath"). Disillusioned by Mary's long-time insistence that her creation is a Romantic child, the patchwork girl feels that she not only loses Mary, but that she loses herself. She is no longer defined by Mary's ideal Romantic child, and is suddenly overwhelmed by her fragmented body and history — a body and history that has no "script," no norm, no ideal.

Eventually, after parting with Mary, the patchwork girl moves from England to New York City. While in New York, the patchwork girl lives with Madam Q, an elderly, straight-talking spiritualist who makes her earn her keep by participating in séances. After several years of living with Madam Q, the patchwork girl grows restless and "hopscotches" to Los Angeles ("interim"). Frustrated by her "chequered nature" ("passing"), she hopes that her journey west will both help her shed her pieced together body and history and allow her to "grow into [her much-desired] oneness" ("cut and paste").

Once in Los Angeles, the patchwork girl works as a plumber and lives alone in a cramped apartment, which she fills with tacked-up photos of beautiful celebrities and her extensive collection of stuffed giraffe toys and figurines. When not at work, the patchwork girl spends hours by herself in her bathroom. Desperate for smooth, uniformly colored, scar-free skin, she often sits in her bathtub and stares at the photos of the celebrities on her bathroom walls as she douses her scars with acid, snips away at scar tissue with scissors, and scours her body with pumice stones and facial scrubs. The patchwork girl, however, does not simply want to erase the networks of scars that fuse together her various body parts to make herself feel physically whole. Rather, she wants to create a corporeal tabula rasa, a clean slate on which she can write — or, rewrite — a new past.

Uncomfortable with her complicated, patched history, then, the patchwork girl wants to buy someone else's past. She believes that another's past will satisfy her need for a history that is both coherent and "unified under the aegis of I" ("I"). In search of such a past, she follows a young woman, Elsie Hull, down a busy Los Angeles street and offers to buy her history. Elsie agrees to the patchwork girl's sales pitch and gives the patchwork girl a photo album.

Believing that the past is "just a nasty habit of thought," she closely reads the album and memorizes various details from Elsie's life ("cut and paste"). Particularly interesting to the patchwork girl are details from Elsie's childhood:

> Her past was perfect for me.... I acquired the house I was born in and the blurred corner of my bedroom window. I acquired the red light of a flashbulb in my wide five-year-old eye, a blink at ten, a scowl at twelve. I acquired half a street sign:— ST ST. I acquired a B&W curtsey in a new grey dress held out at knee-length, and the same dress in a sandbox, revealed to be green, and flirting about the top of scrawny thighs ["photo album"].

The patchwork girl's interest in Elsie's childhood reflects her desire to become "historical" ("photo album"). Upon noting that "[l]ife once did flow toward death, parents engendered offspring, time moved from the beginning to the end," the patchwork girl feels that she is like "a disturbance in the flow" ("born"). The patchwork girl, in other words, feels that her body — and the piecemeal history attached to her body — disrupts the normative, linear, sequential model of age stratification. She believes, then, that buying Elsie's history — and, in particular, Elsie's girlhood — will allow her to transpose a linear model of age onto her own body/history.

Indeed, the patchwork girl does not fit into a linear model of age. When we look closely at Jackson's depictions of the patchwork girl in Los Angeles, we see that her complex illustrations of her assembled protagonist are often rife with imagery associated with childhood and, in particular, girlhood. The patchwork girl "hopscotches" across the country from New York to Los Angeles and many of the stuffed giraffes in her apartment are "fuzzy baby toys" ("passing"). Just as many young girls post their favorite television, music, sports, and movie stars on their school locker doors and bedroom or bathroom walls, we see the patchwork girl tack photos of celebrities on her apartment's walls. We frequently see the patchwork girl in her bathroom, an often rigidly gendered space that many late twentieth-century and contemporary feminist scholars discuss in relation to girlhood and femininity.[8] Images of the patchwork girl as a child or doing child-like things, however, are always paired with discussions about her "adult" age. For example, after she meets Elsie, the patchwork girl notes to herself that the "motley effect of [her] patched skin has lessened with age and uniform light conditions, though [she is] still subtly pied" ("I am"). She also states that she has "lived in [her] frame for 175 years" and that, "[b]y another reckoning, [she has] lived many lives (Tituba's, Jane's, and others') and [is] much older" ("I am"). Although she may be 175-years-old when she meets Elsie, the patchwork girl's body does not age, wrinkle, or look older, per se. Rather, her body looks much like it does when she is first assembled. The patchwork girl's body is multi-generational, a generational spectrum that queers normative, age-specific signifiers.

The patchwork girl desperately wants to become "a real woman," and, for her, part of becoming "real" is passing through a linear, coherent girlhood into adult womanhood ("craft"). However, as suggested by the fragmented nature of the aforementioned excerpt from *Patchwork Girl* detailing Elsie's girlhood memories, she does not buy a girlhood that she can ever fully know or fully incorporate into the new, smooth body that she tries to create in the privacy of her bathroom. Specifically, this excerpt reveals that the patchwork girl only really purchases visual snippets of Elsie's childhood: Elsie's girlhood bedroom, half of the street sign that marks where Elsie lived as a girl, images of Elsie's eyes that are obscured by a camera's flash. She buys images of one of Elsie's girlhood dresses that, in one black and white photo, seems grey and modest, then, in a color photo, seems green and revealing. In both of these photos, Elsie's own girlhood sexuality seems like a specter, an apparition. The patchwork girl, much to her eventual disappointment, has in her possession only partial images of a coherent girlhood that never existed, a girlhood that does not even fully belong to Elsie.

Much like the patchwork girl's body, this photo album is an elaborate collage. Nevertheless, Elsie's photo album serves as material evidence of a past and makes the patchwork girl feel like she now has a linear history that physically exists independently of her crazy quilt-like body. This evidence, she briefly believes, provides her with the visual memories that make her feel real, complete, and undivided. Through the combination of her own manipulations on her body and Elsie's photo album, the patchwork girl feels "that [she] put [her new body and history] together so neatly" ("tic"). However, her body slowly begins to fall apart. One morning, after suffering through an evening of nightmarish, prophetic dreams about her organs disbanding from her body, she wakes up and runs outside. As she stands in her backyard, her body explodes, erupting into a bloody mess. After gathering her body parts, she makes her way to her bathroom and calls Elsie to come help her. After Elsie's initial shock of seeing the patchwork girl sitting in a bathtub brimming with "a warm reddish slurry of bathwater and blood" wears off, she, too, gets into the tub:

> Elsie [is] immersed in me, surrounded by fragments, but somehow she held them. I [am] gathered together loosely in her attention in a way that [is] interesting to me, for I was all in pieces, yet not apart. I felt permitted. I began to invent something new: a way to hang together without pretending that I was whole. Something between higgledy-piggledy and the eternal sphere ["I made myself over"].

In "Flickering Connectivities," Hayles suggests that the above excerpt reveals the moment in which the patchwork girl "realizes that if she is to cohere at all it cannot be through unified subjectivity or a single narrative line" (166).

Exploring her own body in the tub, the patchwork girl both acknowledges and accepts that "she is always already fragmented, ruptured, discontinuous" (165). Drawing from Hayles's study, in her essay "Subject to Change," Shackelford makes similar observations. Indeed, much like Hayles, Shackelford argues that this bathroom is the first moment in Jackson's hypertext in which the patchwork girl "finds a way to make [her] parts meaningful that does not aspire toward a union, conjoinder, or wholeness" (91).[9] Specifically, the above excerpt, Shackelford notes, shows the patchwork girl slowly recognizing that her body, history, and memory are neither whole nor will they ever be whole.

When the patchwork girl accepts that she exists "between higgledy-piggledy and the eternal sphere," she begins to celebrate her multiple subjectivities and fragmented body. Unlike the patchwork girl's earlier experiences in her bathroom in which she violently tries to erase her scars, the bathtub experience with Elsie reveals to her that the way she feels about her body and past does not have to be haunted by "wholeness." As the patchwork girl sits with Elsie in the blood-filled bathtub, then, the bathroom shifts from a space in which to self-inflict violence and feel shame into a space in which to celebrate her fragmented body. Sitting together in the tub with Elsie, the patchwork girl's body becomes "supple," her "furniture parts [become] mellow as wax and [her] joints and junctures, long turned to proper purposes, [bend] past their right angles into impossible obliquities, or [find] curves not known to their before-uses" ("I made myself over").[10] For the first time since she was animated, the patchwork girl feels comfortable with her fractured memories. This sense of comfort she now feels allows her to explore her body's range of movement in ways that she always resisted because such movement reminded her that she is chimerical.

When read together, both Hayles's and Shackelford's critical discussions about the patchwork girl's new-found acceptance of her multiplicity emphasize how Jackson's hypertext complicates, amongst other things, corporeal boundaries and feminine subjectivities. We see in this bathtub scene that Jackson's hypertext disrupts seemingly stable sex, gender, and age constructs by queering the normative discourses that construct the illusion of such stability. The patchwork girl's and Elsie's relationship is a primary example of how Jackson's hypertext calls attention to such disruption. Indeed, the patchwork girl desires wholeness, but the harder she tries to force herself to become whole by erasing her scars and substituting Elsie's supposedly coherent childhood memories for her own, the more she, according to Hayles, "erupts into crisis" (165). The patchwork girl's crisis, put differently, stems from her refusal to accept herself as an assemblage. The more she tries to transpose Elsie's supposedly coherent childhood onto her own history, the more she — quite literally — falls apart.

Exploring her body in the tub, the patchwork girl notes that she is "many things before [she becomes] something like human again, and all the while Elsie [is] magnificent, like a woman in a fairy tale, holding her true love tight, though she turn badger or wildcat or asp" ("I made myself over"). Though self-acceptance does not come easy for the patchwork girl, and she, according to herself, is like a dangerous animal who does not want to be touched, Elsie stays with her. Sitting together and embracing each other in the bloody water amongst floating body parts, the patchwork girl and Elsie become lovers. Indeed, according to Shackelford, these characters' "mutual immersion" in the tub water is a "metaphor for their sexual exchange" (91).

As such an exchange, then, this bathtub scene revises the Western fairy tale narrative tradition that typically ends in a happily-ever-after, heterosexual coupling. Although she does not specifically discuss *Patchwork Girl*, feminist fairy tale scholar Cristina Bacchilega notes in her groundbreaking study *Postmodern Fairy Tales: Gender and Narrative Strategies* (1999), such revisions often work on the following two levels:

> Postmodern revision is often two-fold, seeking to expose, make visible, the fairy tale's complicity with "exhausted" narrative and gender ideologies, and by working from the fairy tales' multiple versions, seeking to expose, bring out, what the institutionalization of such tales for children has forgotten or left unexploited. This kind of rereading does more than interpret anew or shake the genre's ground rules. It listens for the many "voices" of fairy tales as well, as part of a historicizing and performance-oriented project [50].

In its entirety, *Patchwork Girl* is not simply a revisionary fairy tale, per se. I quote Bacchilega at length here, however, because she helps us, as readers, better understand how this bathtub scene re-envisions, queers the normative fairy tale narrative. Elsie is "like a woman in a fairy tale" because she holds onto the patchwork girl and overlooks her supposed abject grotesqueness. However, she is neither a stereotypical, self-sacrificing, virginal martyr who forfeits her sexual agency for a heroic, prince-like figure, nor is she a prince-like figure who rescues the patchwork girl from (self-)destruction. Rather, Elsie helps the patchwork girl understand that normative femininity is a myth, a construction. This bathtub scene is not constructing a tidy ending and upholding sexed/gendered/aged myths. This bathtub scene exposes what is left from such narratives: multi-generational, intergenerational queer sex. Not only does this scene rewrite a fairy tale-like narrative that includes such queer sex, but this scene suggests that, by having sex with Elsie, the patchwork girl begins to accept her feminine multiplicities. Moreover, this sex scene completely explodes the age/sex binary that, in many ways, haunts the patchwork girl throughout Jackson's hypertext.

When the patchwork girl sits in the tub with Elsie, then, her resolution to create a "way to hang together without pretending that [she is] whole" disrupts how femininity has been written on her body. She no longer tries to cohere to normative sex, gender, and age categories. She no longer feels that she needs to "grow" into feminine womanhood from an idealized feminine girlhood. The patchwork girl describes what she discovers about herself after her bathtub experience with Elsie as such:

> I had lived longer than anyone I knew of, without palpitations or forgetfulness. I would live even longer, no doubt. I thought, if my life has no foreseeable end, if the shape and reach of it is unknown to anyone, then what I know of lives from books and conversation has no bearing on my case. If I clung to traditional form with its ordered — to youth, adolescence, middle age and senility — I belonged in the grave. I'd be like black holes and other zombies that live on their own extinguished matter, turn all light back into themselves, live a non-life without time in the aftermath of time, chewing on themselves. I could be a kind of extinguished wish for a human life, or I could be something entirely different: instead of fulfilling a determined structure, I could merely extend, inventing a form as I went along ["what shape"].

I quote *Patchwork Girl* at length here because this passage, I would argue, underscores how this hypertext destabilizes normative linear age constructs. Indeed, when we pair the above excerpt with my earlier discussion about both the patchwork girl's move from New York to Los Angeles and her subsequent relationship with Elsie, we begin to realize that the patchwork girl's body and illegible feminine subjectivity complicate the supposedly strict child/adult binary. As her above description of what she discovers about herself suggests, she accepts that she has neither a clear beginning — or, birth — nor a clear, foreseeable ending — or, death. She realizes that she does not "[cling] to traditional form with its ordered stanzas" and finds such stanzas restrictive, even boring.

By embracing her fragmentation, the patchwork girl disidentifies with normative femininity. Through such disidentification, she creates an alternative, subversive way to express her femininity — a way that embraces her multigenerational body. The patchwork girl, in other words, accepts that she is an assemblage and begins to forge a flexible, constantly-changing, multiplicitous femininity for herself that compliments her sewn-together body and complicated history. When the patchwork girl recognizes that her corporeal assembly — and the respective histories and memories of the women, men, and even cow that are imbedded in her assembly — allows for her contradictions, then, she celebrates how her contradictions and illegible femininity destabilize binary gender logics and these restrictive logics' attachments to bodies. She realizes that normative femininity is a myth, a construction that she does not fit into.

Notes

1. As Hayles notes in her book *Electronic Literature: New Horizons for the Literary* (2008), "agency is distributed between conditions established by the media and embodied responses of humans who interact with the media" (129). However, Hayles makes clear, distributed agency "does not mean agential power is absent" (129). More pointedly, Hayles states the following about distributed agency:

> Indeed, in this framework, the points of intervention expand to include those who fashion the hardware and build the software, those who use the software to create works of electronic literature, and those who interact with electronic literature as users/players. Media technologies do not come into existence by themselves any more than bodies do [129].

In other words, we navigate *Patchwork Girl* by clicking on links and reading lexias that interest us. However, reading *Patchwork Girl* is not a "free-for-all" in which there are no organizing principles that govern how we read this hypertext. Indeed, the hypertext often guides us — in ways that we can neither see nor predict — to particular links.

2. For further information about both the differences and relationships between print texts and electronic hypertexts, see N. Katherine Hayles's insightful essay "Print is Flat, Code is Deep: The Important of Media-Specific Analysis" (2004).

3. Most notably, Australian artist and writer Linda Dement published her popular hypertext *cyberflesh girlmonsters* in 1996. Dement's hypertext, much like Jackson's *Patchwork Girl*, explores monstrous, multiple feminine embodiments and subjectivities.

4. For further information about discursive repetition and disruption, see Judith Butler's influential philosophical treatise *Gender Trouble: Feminism and the Subversion of Identity* (1990).

5. Importantly, in her essay "Growing Sideways, or Versions of the Queer Child: The Ghost, the Homosexual, the Freudian, the Innocent, and the Interval of Animal" (2004), Kathryn Bond Stockton notes that, at the same time we think of children as asexual, hegemonic discourse also conveniently imagines them as heterosexual (283).

6. For a discussion about lesbian politics in *Patchwork Girl*, see Shackelford's "Subject to Change."

7. For further information about "the" Romantic child, see James Kincaid's later-mentioned *Erotic Innocence*. Also, see children's literature scholar Anne Higonnet's influential study *Pictures of Innocence: The History and Crisis of the Ideal Childhood* (1998).

8. For more information about girlhood and bathrooms, see Celia Cowie's and Sue Lees's article "Slags or Drags" (1981). Also, for an extensive discussion about femininity, girlhood, bathrooms, and the abject, see feminist children's literature scholar June Cummins's study "Hermione in the Bathroom: The Gothic, Menarche, and Female Development in the Harry Potter Series" (2008).

9. Here, Shackelford's analysis of the patchwork girl's and Elsie's bathtub experience echoes feminist literary critic N. Katherine Hayles's influential essay "Flickering Connectivities in Shelley Jackson's *Patchwork Girl*" (2005). Specifically, in this essay, Hayles suggests the following:

> This resolution, in which the monster realizes that if she is to cohere as all it cannot be through unified subjectivity or a single narrative line, leads to [the lexia] "afterwards," in which the monster decides that the only life she can lead is nomadic[...]. Thus the narrative pattern of her life finally becomes indistinguishable from the fragmentation and recombination of the digital technology that produces it [166].

10. In her description of the patchwork girl's bathtub experience with Elsie, Shackelford suggests that following: "Comparing her morphology ... to the 'joints and junctures' in furniture, the patchwork girl marks this 'remaking' as an intervention in the rules of differentiation that ... organize and materialize her understanding of her body..." (91). Here, however, Shackelford misreads Jackson's depiction of "furniture parts" ("I made myself over"). Indeed, "furniture parts" is a direct reference to L. Frank Baum's *The Patchwork Girl of Oz*. "Furniture parts" is actually a reference to Baum's Scrap's brain.

Works Cited

Angelides, Steven. "Feminism, Child Sexual Abuse, and the Erasure of Child Sexuality." *GLQ: A Journal of Lesbian and Gay Studies* 10.2 (2004): 141–77.

Bacchilega, Cristina. *Postmodern Fairy Tales: Gender and Narrative Strategies.* Philadelphia: University of Pennsylvania Press, 1999.

Baum, L. Frank. *The Patchwork Girl of Oz.* 1913. New York: Dover, 1990.

Butler, Judith. *Gender Trouble: Feminism and the Subversion of Identity.* New York: Routledge, 1990.

Cowie, Celia, and Sue Lees. "Slags or Drags." *Feminist Review* 9 (1981): 17–31.

Cummins, June. "Hermione in the Bathroom: The Gothic, Menarche, and Female Development in the Harry Potter Series." *The Gothic in Children's Literature: Haunting the Borders.* Eds. Anna Jackson, Karen Coats, and Roderick McGillis. New York: Routledge, 2008.

Fisher, Caitlin. "Feminist Digital Aesthetics: The Everyday and Yesterday." *Fluid Screens, Expanded Cinema.* Eds. Janine Marchessault and Susan Lord. Toronto: University of Toronto Press, 2007.

Halberstam, Judith. *In a Queer Time and Place: Transgender Bodies, Subcultural Lives.* New York and London: New York University Press, 2005.

Hayles, N. Katherine. *Electronic Literature: New Horizons for the Literary.* Notre Dame, IN: University of Notre Dame Press, 2008.

_____. "Flickering Connectivities in Shelley Jackson's *Patchwork Girl.*" *My Mother was a Computer: Digital Subjects and Literary Texts.* N. Katherine Hayles. Chicago and London: University of Chicago Press, 2005.

_____. "Print Is Flat, Code Is Deep: The Importance of Media-Specific Analysis." *Poetics Today* 25.1 (2004): 67–90.

Higonnet, Anne. *Pictures of Innocence: The History and Crisis of the Ideal Childhood.* New York: Thames and Hudson, 1998.

Huffer, Lynne. "'There is no Gomorrah': Narrative Ethics in Feminist and Queer Theory." *differences: A Journal of Feminist Cultural Studies* 12.3 (2001): 1–32.

Jackson, Shelley. *Patchwork Girl.* Watertown, MA: Eastgate, 1995.

_____. "Stitch Bitch: The Patchwork Girl." *Rethinking Media Change: The Aesthetics of Transition.* Eds. David Thornburn and Henry Jenkins. Cambridge, MA: MIT Press, 2003.

Kincaid, James R. *Erotic Innocence: The Culture of Child Molesting.* Durham, NC: Duke University Press, 2000.

Shackelford, Laura. "Subject to Change: The Monstrosity of Media in Shelley Jackson's *Patchwork Girl; or, A Modern Monster* and Other Posthumanist Critiques of the Instrumental." *Camera Obscura* 21.3 (2006): 62–101.

Shelley, Mary. *Frankenstein.* 1818. New York: Bantam, 1991.

Stockton, Kathryn Bond. "Growing Sideways, or Versions of the Queer Child: The Ghost, the Homosexual, the Freudian, the Innocent, and the Interval of Animal." *Curiouser: On the Queerness of Children.* Eds. Steven Bruhm and Natasha Hurley. Minneapolis: University of Minnesota Press, 2004.

Sundén, Jenny. "What if Frankenstein('s Monster) Was a Girl?: Reproduction and Subjectivity in the Digital Age." *Bits of Life: Feminism at the Intersections of Media, Bioscience, and Technology.* Eds. Anneke Smelik and Nina Lykke. Seattle and London: University of Washington Press, 2008.

CHAPTER 6

No Place Like the O.Z.

Heroes and Hybridity in Sci-Fi's Tin Man

KRISTIN NOONE

In 2007, the Sci-Fi channel reimagined *The Wizard of Oz*, creating the grim fantasy wasteland of the O.Z. ("Outer Zone"), where the Wicked Witch commands a reign of terror, prostitutes inhabit the Emerald City, and the figure of Dorothy herself, unknowingly, once helped cause the ruin of the land. In this new incarnation of L. Frank Baum's tale, each of the four classic protagonists — Dorothy, the Scarecrow, the Tin Man, and the Cowardly Lion — is recreated as a newly hybrid figure, both human and monstrous at once, in the shapes of the otherworldly DG, the half-brained Glitch, the iron-suited Wyatt Cain, and the empathic Raw. In this new Oz, their otherness becomes, paradoxically, the means of preservation of the world, as only these dislocated characters are capable of foiling the Witch's plot. In this way, along with the unresolved tensions at the ending of the mini-series, *Tin Man* seems to suggest an uneasiness about these quintessentially American mythic heroes at the beginning of the twenty-first century. Dorothy and her friends may save the world, but may not ever truly find home in it again.

In the Introduction to the *Annotated Wizard of Oz*, Michael Patrick Hearn observes that "the deceptively simple story of Dorothy's adventures in the marvelous land of Oz has resonated for young and old since it was first published in 1900. *The Wizard of Oz* has entered American folklore; it reflected and has altered the American character."[1] L. Frank Baum's original text has, in the century following its publication, been translated not only into various languages worldwide, but into new media, from the 1939 musical film with Judy Garland to *Wicked: A New Musical*, based on Gregory Maguire's novel *Wicked*, itself an adaptation of Baum's tale. The Sci-Fi channel mini-series thus enters into a long tradition of Wizardly re-envisionings in popu-

lar culture. To rewrite *The Wizard of Oz* as science fiction, however, is an⌉
unusual move. Certainly Baum's original work, and its previous adaptations,
are often more readily classified as fantasy; a discussion of Oz, for example,
appears in Leslie Stratyner and James R. Keller's essay collection *Fantasy Fiction Into Film*. It is worth noting, however, Stratyner's and Keller's comments
on the nature of fantasy film: "There has always been and will always be a
considerable imaginative distance between the page and the screen. As fantasy concerns itself with the fantastic (that is, elements of plot and character
that are outside the realm of possibility), the imaginative distance between
those symbols ... is potentially far greater."[2] Istvan Csicsery-Ronay, Jr., has
offered a strikingly similar definition of science fiction in *The Seven Beauties
of Science Fiction*: science-fictional thinking, he claims, is always characterized by gaps and hesitations "between conceiving of the plausibility of historically unforeseen innovations in human experience and their broader ethical
and social-cultural implications and resonances."[3] *The Wizard of Oz* itself has
always straddled the borders between science-fiction and fantasy; even Hearn's
introduction refers to the Land of Oz as a "gentle utopia," in which "the good
are rewarded and the bad forgiven."[4] Retelling *The Wizard of Oz* as a "Sci-Fi" text, *Tin Man* already suggests its own hybrid nature: it is at once a part
of the fantasy tradition of its past, and yet stands in that science-fictional
space of posited utopias, of gaps and hesitations, with a "sci-fi" name[5]; it is
also an adaptation, and thus shares an uneasy relationship with the text on
which it is based. From the start, *Tin Man* creates a world of imaginary space
that is not clearly one genre or another, but shifting, complex, and not precisely comfortable.

The very world of Oz — in *Tin Man*, now the O.Z. — reflects this lack
of comfort, along with a pervasive interest in the grotesque, a science-fictional
concept that Csicsery-Ronay sees as fundamental to the genre. The grotesque
"has to do with the struggle to accommodate mutable, unstable objects and
beings in the world"[6]; the invocation of grotesque, fluid, or destabilizing
objects in a science-fiction text reflects the difficulty of dealing with destabilizing, liminal, and disturbing objects in reality. "Grotesque objects," Csicsery-Ronay claims, "bring a fundamental principle of mythological thought
into rationalistic modes of perception ... the mythic imposes perpetual metamorphosis."[7] In other words, the twisted and warped landscape of *Tin Man*,
which DG (Dorothy) refers to as "a nightmare that couldn't get any weirder,"
is a mythic world, in which things are always changing, limitless, and fluid.
In fact, Glitch (the Scarecrow figure of *Tin Man*) makes this precise point
shortly after DG rescues him from the abuses of the Munchkins, who he refers
to as "anklebiters": "It used to be a piece of heaven, too," he says. "Before
[the Wicked Witch] Azkadellia got her claws into it." The Witch, in fact,

plans to effect even greater change, utilizing a machine called the Sun Seeder to cover the land in permanent darkness.[8] The world of the O.Z., complete with man-eating trees and brutal police, is a space capable of transformation and change; Glitch's use of the word *too* is important here, because it indicates that the O.Z. is in fact capable of being both heaven and nightmare at once. The "heavenly" part has been subsumed by the nightmare, but the land contains both aspects at once, and exists in a state of metamorphosis. As Jessica Zebrine Gray notes in her discussion of witchcraft in *Wicked*, the tension between the natural and the supernatural, that point of hesitation and fluidity, permeates Baum's work,[9] though Baum's original Oz reflects more of Glitch's "heavenly" aspect: "On the other side of the water they could see the road of yellow brick running through a beautiful country, with green meadows dotted with bright flowers and all the road bordered with trees hanging full of delicious fruits. They were greatly pleased to see this delightful country before them."[10] Dorothy, as Baum's audience is informed, is happy to be there: "The sun shone bright and the birds sung sweet and Dorothy did not feel nearly as bad as you might think a little girl would who had been suddenly whisked away from her own country and set down in the midst of a strange land."[11] This Oz, to which Dorothy Gale, "the original slipper" of the O.Z. and DG's ancestor,[12] first traveled, is shown by *Tin Man* to be a science-fictional space, able to change and shift and metamorphose into DG's nightmare. DG and her friends prevent the Witch's evil plans for further metamorphosis, but as the mini-series ends there quite abruptly, any return of the O.Z. to the Land of Oz is never shown. The O.Z. thus remains a complex, liminal, and hybrid space, possessing the capacity for both heaven and for nightmare.

The characters of *Tin Man*, like the land now reinscribed as hybrid figures, further support a reading of the world of Oz as a science-fictional space, and moreover, a space that requires such human–Other heroes for its very survival. Raw (the Cowardly Lion), Glitch (the Scarecrow), Cain (the Tin Man) and DG (Dorothy) herself all both simultaneously belong to the O.Z. and exist separately from it, set outside its society through various means, from Raw's empathic power to Glitch's missing brain, from Cain's tin suit to DG's otherworldly upbringing and robot parents. Csicsery-Ronay observes that "it is now a commonplace that contemporary 'global culture' is characterized by hybridity"[13]; *Tin Man*, which offers heroes who save the world but never quite return to it themselves, thus suggests a profound ambivalence about the figure of the hybrid in this contemporary science-fictional Oz.

The Cowardly Lion of Baum's Oz is comical, kindhearted, and ultimately rewarded by a functioning place in society, ruling the beasts of the forest. He is first introduced with the sound of his roar, which he himself labels his defining attribute: "There came from the forest a terrible roar, and the next moment a great Lion bounded into the road."[14] But the roar is all there is, as the Lion explains:

> I suppose I was born that way. All the other animals in the forest naturally expect me to be brave, for the Lion is everywhere thought to be the King of Beasts. I learned that if I roared very loudly every living thing was frightened and got out of my way. Whenever I've met a man I've been awfully scared, but I just roared at him, and he has always run away as fast as he could go.[15]

Baum's Lion, while cowardly, nevertheless has a place in the world of Oz, a role accepted and expected of him; he is concerned not because he has no place, but because he does not feel that he is performing well in the place he has. However, he demonstrates his bravery on a number of occasions while accompanying Dorothy on her quest, as the Wizard points out to him: "There is no living thing that is not afraid when it faces danger. True courage is in facing danger when you are afraid, and that kind of courage you have in plenty."[16] And the Lion, after lapping up the symbolic liquid courage the Wizard gives him, knows that he is brave. He is rewarded for this self-actualization by a reaffirmation of his place in Oz, after he kills a giant spider that is terrorizing the forest: "Then the beasts bowed down to the Lion as their King, and he promised to come back and rule over them as soon as Dorothy was safely on her way to Kansas."[17] This Lion is uncomplicatedly heroic, and he finds a satisfyingly proper destiny.

But Raw, the empathic lion enslaved by the Wicked Witch in *Tin Man*, is not quite so comfortably settled into the world of the O.Z. Raw, an escaped slave, is already a marginalized figure; he is also a "viewer," one of a race of telepaths who are used by Azkadellia for information-gathering and control over the O.Z. Raw's abilities, and the abuses of slavery, cause him to be somewhat unstable and quite timid; his speech is sometimes disjointed, further detaching him from the world around him. Like the Cowardly Lion, Raw discovers the need for courage at the climax of the mini-series, after being captured by the Witch's soldiers and forced to perform telepathically by her sadistic Alchemist. The Alchemist pokes him with a cattle prod, grumbling, "You never understand! All you people need is a little encouragement!" Raw, at this point, takes the cattle prod away from him, shouts, "Raw just need courage!" and turns the prod on his torturer. Raw's actions here indeed demonstrate heroic courage, as he stands up to the Witch's abusive regime, and he is freed to use his telepathic talents of his own free will, later helping Glitch reconnect with his brain. But, unlike Baum's Lion, he is not reestablished in society. In fact, the moment is potentially, if unintentionally, disturbing, as Raw turns his torture implement on his abuser, implying that he will use his courage alongside the O.Z.'s nightmare methods. While he is thus able to escape and rejoin DG and the others in order to foil the Witch's plans, Raw, like the other characters, is never shown fully reassimilated into even the newly liberated O.Z. He remains a liminal and Othered figure, an escaped slave, an otherworldly telepath, a figure with the potential for violence. His great act of courage places him into a hybrid space, both enabling him to act as a hero but also demonstrating his separation from the world around him.

Similarly, Baum's Scarecrow manages to successfully learn to use his brain and finds a home and a purpose in Oz, while *Tin Man's* Glitch can never quite recover the man he once was. Baum's Scarecrow is from the outset a product of Oz (specifically Munchkin) society:

> Dorothy leaned her chin upon her hand and gazed thoughtfully at the Scarecrow. Its head was a small sack stuffed with straw, with eyes, nose, and mouth painted on it to represent a face. An old, pointed blue hat, that had belonged to some Munchkin, was perched on its head, and the rest of the figure was a blue suit of clothes, worn and faded, which had also been stuffed with straw. On the feet were some old boots with blue tops, such as every man wore in this country, and the figure was raised above the stalks of corn by means of the pole stuck up its back.[18]

He wears Munchkin clothing, and, like a proper scarecrow, has a function. Moreover, he and others consider that he is "a proper man," as he tells Dorothy:

> I had the fun of watching them make my arms and legs, and when they fastened on my head, at last, I felt very proud, for I thought I was just as good a man as anyone. "This fellow will scare the crows fast enough," said the farmer, "he looks just like a man." "Why, he is a man," said the other, and I quite agreed with him.[19]

This Scarecrow desires a brain to be better at his job, in fact, as it is the crows who tell him that he is ineffective because he lacks brains.[20] From the outset, he exists as a product of and an actor in the world of Oz, as good a man as anyone. The Scarecrow, like Baum's Cowardly Lion, is given the opportunity to demonstrate his intelligence while accompanying Dorothy to the Emerald City, as Hearn observes in an editorial note: "The Scarecrow is the Divine Fool, a simpleton who makes good by his natural wits. He is the one who solves most of the problems encountered along the yellow brick road, but he relies on common sense rather than dubious theory."[21] Like the Lion, he is given a symbolic reward, of bran brains (with pins and needles mixed in to demonstrate his sharpness) by the Wizard, who tells him, "You don't need them. You are learning something new every day.... Experience is the only thing that brings knowledge, and the longer you are on earth the more experience you are sure to get."[22] Like the Lion, the Scarecrow only receives a tangible symbolic version of his already intrinsic quality, a verification and reassurance of his worth. The Scarecrow, of course, is rewarded by taking the Wizard's place as ruler of the Emerald City: "Although he was not a Wizard the people were proud of him. 'For,' they said, 'there is not another city in all the world that is ruled by a stuffed man.'"[23] Interestingly, here it is the Scarecrow's very uniqueness that makes his people proud; it is his Otherness that allows him to be welcomed and to find his place in Oz.

For *Tin Man*'s Glitch, Otherness is far more problematic, and homecoming decidedly problematic. Glitch's hybrid nature is foregrounded at his first meeting with DG, when she observes that the giant zipper that holds his head together has come undone, drawing attention to this prominent intrusion into an otherwise human body. To DG, he jokes, "Gotta be careful not to lose your marbles ... but ah, since the sorceress made her medicos take mine, well, you flick the abacus...." Glitch's brain, or most of it, has been removed, we discover, by Azkadellia's minions, "because of what I know. Or used to know. Whatever it was," he explains. During his travels with DG, he begins to recover some memories, and eventually (literally) reconnects with his brain, which is being kept in the Witch's tower and used to control the Sun Seeder device that will cover the O.Z. in perpetual darkness. Glitch, in his former life, had been a man named Ambrose, the advisor to the Queen of the O.Z., and a great scientist and inventor (one of his recurring lines being "I think I invented that..."); now he exists in a half-human liminal space, a man with no memories, no brain, and no purpose, wandering through the O.Z. His identity itself is constantly in flux, as he is continually subject to the perspectives of outsiders who judge that he must be a convict because of his punishment, as Cain does on their first meeting.[24] Glitch does, however, successfully reconnect with his brain, with the help of Raw's telepathic talents, and is able to shut down the Sun Seeder machine; here the two Othered figures of Raw and Glitch use their special natures to, literally, save the world. But the miniseries leaves Glitch, like Raw, without a clearly defined place in this brave new Oz. He may have been able to use his brain to save the O.Z., but his brain is not replaced; he can access his memories, but only while attached to his brain through prostheses (both material and telepathic). He is not the man who was once advisor to a queen, and at the close of the mini-series he is aware of how much he has lost. Glitch thus occupies that shifting space, both human and monstrously changed from human, of the hybrid; he has helped to save the world, but he, and viewers, are left unsure of his place in it, as he cannot return to the place he once held.

Wyatt Cain, the titular Tin Man of the mini-series,[25] is perhaps the character most drastically altered from Baum's original, and though like Baum's Tin Woodman he is motivated by his heart, unlike the Woodman he does not find a comfortable ending in the land of Oz. Dorothy first spots Baum's

Tin Woodman shining in the sun, rusted stiff: "His head and arms and legs were jointed upon his body, but he stood perfectly motionless, as if he could not stir at all."[26] Once she oils him and he can move again, "he thanked them again and again for his release, for he seemed a polite creature, and very grateful."[27] This Tin Woodman demonstrates emotion from the very first meeting, showing gratitude and concern for social niceties. Interestingly, he is possibly the most hybrid of the four protagonists to begin with, as Hearn comments in a note, calling him "The first bionic man" and quoting Paul Abrahm and Stuart Kenter: "The woodsman was, inside and out ... a veritable showcase of successful spare-parts surgery — the ultimate in cyborgs."[28] He is a man motivated by love; he had desired to marry a Munchkin girl, but an old woman wished to keep the girl living with her and so asked the Wicked Witch of the East for help. The Wicked Witch of the East devised a means of punishment for him: "[the Wicked Witch of the East] thought of a new way to kill my love for the beautiful Munchkin maiden, and made my axe slip again, so that it cut right through my body ... once more the tinner came to my rescue and made me a body of tin, fastening my tin arms and legs and head to it by means of joints, so that I could move around as well as ever. But alas! I now had no heart, so that I lost all my love for the Munchkin girl, and did not care whether I married her or not."[29] Like the Scarecrow, this Tin Man desires nothing more than societal bonds, in this case the bonds of marriage; he is the son of a woodcutter and a happy member of Munchkinland. He wishes for a heart from the Wizard so that he can return to that world: "While I was in love I was the happiest man on earth; but no one can love who has not a heart, and so I am resolved to ask Oz to give me one. If he does, I will go back to the Munchkin girl and marry her."[30] Like all Baum's characters, his quest involves a restoration to society, and demonstrates that he has in fact had the quality he sought all along. "The Tin Woodman had no heart," Baum tells us, "and therefore he took great care never to be cruel or unkind to anything."[31] Like the other characters, he is rewarded for his self-discovery, though his encounter with the Wizard is slightly different from the others. Instead of telling him that he has had a heart all along, the Wizard tries to dissuade the Tin Woodman from wanting one at all: "It makes most people unhappy. If you only knew it, you are in luck to not have a heart." The Tin Woodman replies, "For my part, I will bear all the unhappiness without a murmur, if you will give me the heart."[32] The Tin Woodman, while aware of the potential pain this gift will cause, chooses it unhesitatingly, and receives the reward of a red silk heart stuffed with sawdust to carry inside his chest. Of all the gifts, Baum chooses to draw attention to the painful potential of a heart, and this theme will be later explored to great effect in the story of Wyatt Cain in *Tin Man*. Baum's Tin Woodman, of course, finds his proper place in the world of Oz at the conclusion of the story: "The Winkies were very kind to me," he says, "and wanted me to rule over them after the Wicked Witch died. I am fond of the Winkies, and if I could get back to the country of the West I should like nothing better than to rule over them forever."[33] The Tin Woodman will be the ruler of the Winkies, but unlike the Witch, the indication is that he will be a benevolent one, as he couches his rule in terms of kindness and affection. Like Baum's other characters, he finds a home, along with his heart.

Wyatt Cain, though along with DG the most unadulteratedly human of *Tin Man*'s characters, nevertheless finds himself separated from his human family and aligned with the other hybrid heroes. A former "Tin Man," one of the law enforcers under the benevolent previous rule of the Mystic Man (the Wizard), Cain joined the resistance movement to fight against the Witch's takeover and was captured by her Longcoat enforcers. As punishment, he was locked inside an iron suit and forced to watch a hologram of his wife and son being tortured, played on a constant loop for him to view. Like Baum's Tin Woodman, Cain's tin-suited figure is thus inextricably intertwined with love, in this case for his family, who he believes to be dead. However, as a member of a marginalized group of resistance fighters, this Tin Man has already placed himself in opposition to society. Moreover, his ties to others have been systematically stripped away: he has lost his family, his home, and, because of his experiences in the suit, his solidarity with the rest of the resistance. After DG first frees him from the suit, he initially refuses to travel with her, or to help her, declaring, "much obliged for the help, but I don't travel with kids, or convicts." Cain is seeking only revenge at this point, determined to hunt down the leader of the Witch's Longcoats, Zero, and make him pay. Though he does decide to lead DG and Glitch to Central City, as he says himself, "heart's got nothing to do with it;" he has no affection for his traveling companions, but he does not want to leave them to be consumed by man-eating plants, as their path leads directly through the fields of the Papay, which can "gnaw people in half inside 30 seconds." Throughout the course of the mini-series, however, Cain does discover affection for DG, Raw, and Glitch, even to the point of promising the Mystic Man that he will choose to protect DG over pursuing Zero. But, like the companions he chooses to protect, Cain never quite regains his position in the newly freed O.Z. When he discovers that his son, Jeb, is still alive and leading the resistance, he seeks Jeb out for a reunion. But the possibility of reconstructing the family quickly dissolves. Jeb has become a brutal fighter, killing without mercy; Cain and his son fight over the best means of dealing with captured Longcoats, and Cain eventually leaves his son and the resistance to aid DG, choosing his bizarre and hybrid companions over his flesh and blood. For this Tin Man, the illusion that the family can be restored is only momentary; though Cain does help DG and the others dismantle the Sun Seeder device and defeat the Witch's plot, he is left at the end of the mini-series in a kind of limbo. He has no official allegiances, whether as the law-enforcing Tin Man he once was or as a determined resistance fighter, and he has given up his family. Though among the least visually hybridized of the characters, Cain exemplifies the uneasiness of a figure who no longer belongs in any of the worlds he once knew. Interestingly, his title of Tin Man provides the title for the mini-series, suggesting that this liminal and nebulous unaligned position can be read as the defining theme for this new Oz overall.

Finally, the character of Dorothy undergoes a similar and drastic rewriting in *Tin Man*, as DG must deal with the revelation that the world she thought she knew was never her home. Though she appears to find the most acceptance at the end of the mini-series, her self-doubt and obscured memories remain far removed from Baum's cheerful Dorothy, who makes friends wherever she goes and returns to Kansas and the welcoming arms of Auntie Em. Baum's Dorothy is an orphan, living with her aunt and uncle, who mainly receives affection from her dog, Toto, and is described as "an innocent, harmless little girl, who had been carried by a cyclone many miles from home; and she had never killed anything in all her life."[34] This Dorothy, throughout her travels, learns how best to connect to others, even when deposited in the otherworld of Oz: for example, she not only rescues the Scarecrow, Tin Woodman, and Cowardly Lion, but also befriends the Queen of the Mice, who promises assistance if she requires it,[35] and the Winkies, who "would be delighted to do all in their power for Dorothy, who had released them from bondage."[36] Throughout Baum's tale, the concept of home remains her guiding aim; as she tells the Scarecrow, "No matter how dreary and gray our homes are, we people of flesh and blood would rather live there than in any other country, be it ever so beautiful. There is no place like home."[37] This Dorothy, like her companions, is a character who inarguably has a sense of belonging. When she finally successfully returns to Kansas, her goal all along, the sense of home is overwhelming: Auntie Em hugs and kisses her, and Dorothy says, "I'm so glad to be at home again!"[38] Like the characters she has met on her journey through Oz, Dorothy has found her proper place, the place where she is content; as Hearn comments, "Oz may be prettier and far more exciting than Kansas, but it lacks the safety and security of being back home with the people Dorothy loves."[39] This Dorothy ends her story with love and acceptance.

The DG of *Tin Man* leads a very different life, in which she is always isolated and alienated to some degree. At the outset of the mini-series, she is working as a waitress, living on a farm in Kansas with her family, but she is already aware that she is different somehow, as she suffers from dreams of a strange and unfamiliar place (later, of course, revealed as the O.Z.) and of a lavender-eyed woman who tells her that "a storm is coming." The storm does come, caused by the Witch's sending of Longcoat enforcers across the worlds to kill DG (an event that clearly singles her out as more than a Kansas farm girl, even if she had not already suspected as much). DG, however, escapes from the Longcoats, and finds herself in the O.Z., a woman separated from the world she has, until now, known as home. DG spends much of the mini-series as the clearest outsider, having no knowledge of the world she is now in. In her first encounter with the Munchkins, she makes this plain: "Okay, how many times do I have to tell you that nothing you guys have said has made any sense to me?" DG, like her companion Raw, here exhibits isolation even at the level of communication; though she will learn that she, in fact, comes from the O.Z., she does not even comprehend what the Munchkins tell her. When DG sets out to discover the source of her dreams and recover her memories, and eventually to oppose the Witch, she learns that her Kansas family were robotic constructs, that Azkadellia (the girl, now woman, possessed by the Witch's spirit) is her sister, that she herself has a certain amount of magical talent, and that her real mother is the lavender-eyed woman (never named) and Queen of the O.Z. before the coming of the Witch; her mother had sent her to Kansas and created the robotic family to protect her. This information dislocates DG even more; the home that she had known was, in fact, unreal, and clearly, she did not belong in Kansas. However, with only scattered memories and no real understanding of her past, she does not quite belong in the O.Z. either. In fact, DG is a liminal figure not only because of her shattered pasts, but because she has, quite literally, returned from the dead: the Witch has already killed her once, when they were children, though DG was revived and then hidden by their mother. This Dorothy, with her abbreviated and atypical name, exists at the heart of several paradoxes: she has been dead and alive, she belongs (or doesn't) to both Kansas and the O.Z., she is a descendent of the original Kansas-dwelling Dorothy Gale but was born and raised in Oz, and she is a sister to the witch she must fight against to save the land from darkness. Of all of *Tin Man*'s altered characters, DG is perhaps the most hybrid, always the product of multiple colliding and contradictory aspects, always at once in the realm of both the familiar and unfamiliar. As the Dorothy analogue and heroine of the mini-series, she does successfully defeat the Witch, freeing her sister from the spirit that has possessed her for years; the good Queen is restored, and the O.Z. will be preserved from perpetual darkness. DG, unlike Cain, is apparently reunited with her family in her original home, even closing the mini-series with the comment, "That's the O.Z. I remember. I'm so glad to be home." But her fate is not as simple as this comment suggests. DG still has not reacquired her complete memories; she also still retains the memories of her life in Kansas, marking her as "otherworldly" in the realm of Oz. She has also learned that she was responsible for the disintegration of the O.Z., as she had panicked and abandoned Azkadellia to possession by the Witch when they both were children. DG thus must carry the knowledge that her actions have led to the last fifteen years of suffering and violence throughout the O.Z., a burden that sets her apart from the world she has inadvertently harmed. DG may be restored to her family, but she is not precisely restored to her home, nor is her home restored. Like the rest of *Tin Man*'s heroes, she may have saved the world, but she fits back into it uneasily.

In his introduction to *The Wonderful Wizard of Oz*, written in 1900, L. Frank Baum explains his goal in telling the story:

> The time has come for a series of newer "wonder tales" in which the stereotyped genie, dwarf, and fairy are eliminated, together with all the horrible and blood-curdling incident devised by their authors to point a fearsome moral to each tale ... [*The Wonderful Wizard of Oz*] aspires to being a modernized fairy tale, in which the wonderment and joy are retained and the heartaches and nightmares are left out.[40]

In Baum's Oz, every character finds a place to call home, and each receives precisely what he or she deserves, good or bad, as Martin Gardner and Russel Nye observe in *The Wizard of Oz and Who He Was*: "the theme of selflessness as the cardinal principle of love runs through all the Oz books, forming the thread that binds them together ... those who use power for selfish ends are Bad, and are punished in proportion to their crime."[41] In *Tin Man*, by contrast, even characters with good intentions are always complex, fluid entities, who partake more of Istvan Csicsery-Ronay's grotesque aesthetic in their hybrid and unbounded identities; grotesque subjects, after all, have at heart "the vertiginous destabilization of the sense of natural balance,"[42] and none of the characters of the mini-series are, in fact, able to achieve any sense of stabilization. *Tin Man* returns the heartaches and nightmares to Oz, suggesting that the "newer wonder tales" of the twenty-first century are concerned not with heroes who happily come home to the worlds they defend, but with heroes for whom such a homecoming becomes a grotesque impossibility.

Notes

1. Hearn, Michael Patrick. "Introduction to *The Annotated Wizard of Oz*," in *The Annotated Wizard of Oz*. ed. & annotated by Michael Patrick Hearn (New York: W.W. Norton & Co, 2000), xiii.

2. Stratyner, Leslie, and James R. Keller ."Introduction: Fantasy Fiction Into Film," in *Fantasy Fiction Into Film*, ed. Leslie Stratyner and James R. Keller (Jefferson: McFarland & Co., 2007), 1.

3. Csicsery-Ronay, Jr. Istvan. *The Seven Beauties of Science Fiction* (Middletown: Wesleyan University Press, 2008), 3.

4. Hearn, xcvi.

5. Of course, the extent to which the Sci-Fi channel's programming can be designated as "science fiction" may be debated; nonetheless, the labeling invokes popular conceptions of the genre.

6. Csicsery-Ronay, 182.

7. Csicsery-Ronay, 187.

8. The character of the Witch may require some explanation here. Most of the inhabitants of the O.Z. also refer to her by the name Azkadellia, and the two personas are often treated as interchangeable. However, they are not; Azkadellia has been, we later discover, possessed by the Witch since childhood, a distinction either not known or made by the general population of the O.Z. This essay will generally refer to the character as "the Witch," to separate her from the girl Azkadellia seen in flashbacks and retrieved at the end of the mini-series.

9. Gray, Jessica Zebrine, "From Witch to *Wicked*: A Mutable and Transformational Sign," in *Fantasy Fiction into Film*, ed. Leslie Stratyner and James R. Keller (Jefferson: McFarland & Co., 2007), 166.

10. Baum, L. Frank. *The Annotated Wizard of Oz*. ed. & annotated by Michael Patrick Hearn, New York: W.W. Norton & Co, 2000, (*The Wonderful Wizard of Oz* originally published by George M. Hill Company, 1900), 128.

11. Baum, 58.

12. While any direct influence from the later Baum books is not evident in the mini-series, it appears that the writers at least knew of Dorothy's eventual return to Oz and permanent residence there.

13. Csicsery-Ronay 213.

14. Baum, 106.

15. Baum, 109.

16. Baum, 272.

17. Baum, 335.

18. Baum, 65.

19. Baum, 79.

20. Baum, 80.

21. Hearn, 69, note 12.

22. Baum, 270.

23. Baum, 296.

24. Quite a lot about the nature of the new O.Z. is revealed in the fact that lobotomy seems to have become the standard punishment for transgression against the Witch. We are a long way from Baum's Oz.

25. Cain's name also reflects a fascinating duality of nature, suggesting as it does both the law-enforcer and the murderer. In fact, the names of Glitch/Ambrose, Raw, and DG herself all seem chosen for this purpose, drawing attention to their unique characteristics, though "Wyatt Cain" is perhaps the most obvious.

26. Baum, 89.

27. Baum, 92.

28. Hearn, 99, note 19. He cites the quotation as from Paul Abrahm and Stuart Kenter, "Tik-Tok and the Three Laws of Robotics," *Science Fiction Studies*, March 1978.

29. Baum, 100.

30. Baum, 102.

31. Baum, 115.

32. Baum, 272.

33. Baum, 349.

34. Baum, 36.
35. Baum, 157.
36. Baum, 232.
37. Baum, 76.
38. Baum, 357.
39. Hearn, 356, note 2.
40. Baum, 4.
41. Gardner, Martin and Russel Nye. *The Wizard of Oz and Who He Was.* East Lansing: Michigan State University Press, 1957, 11.
42. Csicsery-Ronay 211

Works Cited

Baum, L. Frank. *The Annotated Wizard of Oz.* ed. & annotated by Michael Patrick Hearn. New York: W.W. Norton & Co, 2000. (*The Wonderful Wizard of Oz* originally published by George M. Hill Company, 1900).

Csicsery-Ronay, Jr. Istvan. *The Seven Beauties of Science Fiction.* Middletown: Wesleyan University Press, 2008.

Gardner, Martin, and Russel Nye. *The Wizard of Oz and Who He Was.* East Lansing: Michigan State University Press, 1957.

Gray, Jessica Zebrine. "From Witch to Wicked: A Mutable and Transformational Sign." In *Fantasy Fiction Into Film*, ed. Leslie Stratyner and James R. Keller. Jefferson: McFarland & Co, 2007.

Hearn, Michael Patrick. "Introduction to *The Annotated Wizard of Oz*." In *The Annotated Wizard of Oz.* ed. & annotated by Michael Patrick Hearn. New York: W.W. Norton & Co, 2000.

Stratyner, Leslie, and James R. Keller. "Introduction: Fantasy Fiction Into Film." In *Fantasy Fiction Into Film*, ed. Leslie Stratyner and James R. Keller. Jefferson: McFarland & Co, 2007.

Tin Man. Dir. Nick Willing. Starring Zooey Deschanel, Alan Cumming, Neal McDonough. RHI Entertainment & The Sci-Fi Channel, 2007.

CHAPTER 7

The Wizard of Oz as a Modernist Work

CHARITY GIBSON

Upon thinking of the modernists and their work, many have not considered children's literature as fitting within the category. Some of this has been due to the often condescending attitude toward "kiddie lit" in the past. However, as strides have been made in the field of children's literature, so has the consideration of how it relates to the modernist movement. The *Children's Literature Association* has devoted an entire issue to the subject in 2007. Karin Westman's explanation for why children's literature has not usually been considered within a modernist framework stems from its often being categorized by genre rather than chronology, as is the case in the Norton Anthology of Children's Literature, although the British and American anthologies are categorized by chronology (283–284). Since the study of modernism is dependent on a specific time period, the consideration of works that are classified in terms of period naturally followed. Recently, some of the famous names associated with modernism that are being considered in relation to children's literature are Gertrude Stein, Virginia Woolf, James Joyce, and Graham Greene. Also, well-known children's writers, such as E. Nesbit and Hugh Lofting, are being looked at through a modernist lens. One writer who has not been typically considered as both a children's author and a modernist is L. Frank Baum. However, his novel *The Wizard of Oz*, as well as the MGM film adaptation, depict elements of modernism that provide an argument for placing him within this framework.

Of course, there are always debates regarding dates within a movement. Although there are some who claim that modernism did not begin until 1910 or even 1915, there are numerous others who argue its beginning to be in the 1890s or specifically 1900. Some simply consider it to be the first few decades of the 20th century. I point this out because Baum wrote *The Wizard of Oz* in 1899 and published it in 1900. Obviously, if Baum is going to be looked at as a modernist, as I propose to do, then he is certainly an early modernist. The mantra of the modernists followed Ezra Pound's admonition to "make it new." This autonomy through originality is something that all the modernists strove to achieve. Baum can be seen as following in this tradition through his creation of the American fantasy. Interestingly, he did this before Pound ever began advocating for it. Some of the ways in which Baum can be seen as modernist serve as a precursor for later key elements of the movement.

Also, modernism is known for its embracement of a master narrative. Baum's work is one which I will show to be depicting a world view, as is key in modernism. Fredric Jameson has devised a theory on modernism and the way in which it depicts a "master narrative," though he does not use this term: "The first thing one wants to say about the ideology of modernism is that it is an American invention, and that it has some very specific determinants" (165). According to Jameson, the culture in any time period influences an author's opinions. American culture at the time of early modernism certainly affected Baum's ideology. As Karl Marx has said, "It is not the consciousness of men that determines their existence, but their social existence that determines their consciousness." Thus, although modernists may have interpreted the world differently and, consequently, advocated for a specific master narrative, they were all influenced by their time period, and they all believed in an all-encompassing truth for society: "The high moderns as such were reflexive or self conscious about representation itself" (Jameson 198). In this paper, I will be explaining how Baum's personal and cultural influence affects the master narrative *The Wizard of Oz* portrays. Neil Earle also follows this line of thinking and claims in his own book, "I will be proceeding under the assumption that an artifact of culture — be it "high" or popular — reflects the era in which it is produced much like the invisible imprint of a soundtrack upon celluloid" (ix). I will advocate that the ideologies of the novel and film are distinct because of different cultural experiences occurring at the time, and I will, thus, deal with the two versions separately.

The groundbreaking American fantasy genre that Baum created and the master narrative it embraces are the two main ways that allow Baum to be looked at as a modernist. However, Baum's inclusion and fascination with technology, which also proves to be a key element of modernism, will also be addressed. I do realize that the elite modernists, usually referred to as the avant-garde, also stressed the creation of high art and unconventionality of form. As Baum's work soon became a bestseller (as seemed to be his hope), the dissection from high art and mass culture cannot be advocated for, and, since his prose is simple and childlike, neither is his form the level at which he "makes it new." I do not consider Baum to fall within the category of the avant-garde. However, just because he was doing something different from Eliot's *The Wasteland* and W.B. Yeats's "Sailing to Byzantium" does not mean that he was not still a modernist writer who, as time has told, would find for himself a place within the pages of history.

In looking at Baum's introduction to his novel, he seems to be aware of master narratives, his focus being stories centered upon morality. He writes, "Modern education includes morality; therefore the modern child seeks only entertainment in its wonder-tales and gladly dispenses with all disagreeable incident. Having this thought in mind, the story of 'The Wonderful Wizard of Oz' was written solely to pleasure children of today." Baum seemed to believe that an ideology promoting self-betterment was unnecessary in children's literature. However, it is unclear whether or not he realized that his time period was one in which some sort of ideology automatically came forth due to the embracement of a master narrative. Society was not yet fragmented into the idea of separate truths. Baum consciously appears to have wanted to simply write a pleasing tale, devoid of a moral. Yet, he certainly conveyed a message in the process, though his introduction seems to suggest that such was not his intention.

The ideology, or master narrative, that Baum portrays, due to the influence of his time period, is the need to escape reality and its loss of the American dream. Many critics have concluded that the period in which the frontier was closing and the focus on class inequity was widening proved to be a time in which Americans began to lose faith in the American dream; consequentially, the underlying force behind Baum's novel is the need to escape the crushing realization of the lost dream of what America was supposed to stand for and be able to offer its citizens. Baum's inclusion into modernism through his creation of something completely new, the American fantasy, occurred because of the cultural situation of the time. Selma Lanes explains that before the 1900s "[f]ew had time or need for the solace provided by fairy tales.... Long before the traditional fairy tale was frowned upon ... it was out of tune with the freshly minted optimism generated by the New World's promise" (93–94). Brian Attebury argues, "The successful creation and immediate acceptance of Oz indicates that Americans by 1900 had finally begun to feel the need of an ideal world apart from America itself, as it was believed to be or as it was expected to become" (88). Finally, adding to the conversation, Laura Barrett agrees,

> When that time [the time of fairy tales] passed, along with a concomitant loss of faith in the American dream itself, a space opened for the American fairy tale. That dream, constructed on realities as visceral as available frontier, westward

expansion, financial success, and technological know-how, could only be resurrected in fantasy.... One hundred years after the nation gained its independence,
and just a few decades after Horatio Alger published his rags-to-riches fantasies,
the fairy tale comes alive to chronicle the rise and fall of the American dream. [151].

As Lanes, Attebury, and Barrett all notice, Baum's fiction is a reaction trig-
gered by the time period. However, what I am pointing out is that the reaction is typical of the modernists' inclusion of a master narrative which is
reflexive of elements of the time. Furthermore, Baum's need to create an escape
through the introduction of American fantasy brings him into the originality and autonomy that the modernists strove for. It may be telling that in his
introduction Baum chides the need for morality. However, what is his own
tale if not a move toward the decency and principles he finds lacking in the
United States? T. S. Eliot claims that "All first-rate poetry is occupied with
morality" (157). Perhaps this statement can be extended to not only poetry
but literature in general. For, whether or not Baum realized it, his work does
deal with morality, in some respect, in its master narrative and critique of the
United States.

In addition to what was occurring at a national level, Baum's own personal struggles undoubtedly helped form his distrust in America's promise.
His multiple failed business ventures and his lack of ability to care for his
family as he desired certainly caused him to doubt the so-called land of plenty.
Barrett also says, "Baum's brief residence in South Dakota coincided with the
1890 census's conclusion that the frontier was closed, and his experiences no
doubt confirmed that the rumors of infinite riches in the west were unfounded"
(154).

One seemingly contradictory element in the novel is at the level of ideology. Baum seems to be presenting the fantastical land as a positive escape
from the reality of the United States. However, Dorothy's entire mission
throughout the story is to find a way to go home to Kansas. One initial reason for the contradiction may be Baum's own lack of awareness of the master narrative he was portraying. Of course, he seems to be purposefully creating
a land, as he states in his introduction, "in which the wonderment and joy
are retained and the heart-aches and nightmares are left out." Though it is
questionable whether or not he succeeded in leaving out heartache and nightmares, the fact that he was trying suggests that he was trying to eliminate the
harsh realities of American reality, which suggests a movement away from
"home" rather than toward it. While Dorothy desires to go home and eventually does, the novel as a whole does not present a unanimously positive view
of Kansas. Joel Chaston points out that "Baum presents a much more ambiva-
lent attitude toward 'home.' While it is true that, in the last chapter of *The
Wonderful Wizard of Oz* Dorothy exclaims, 'I'm so glad to be at home again!'

taken as a whole, Baum's 'Oz' series rejects traditional views of the value of home" (261, 209). Baum portrays Kansas as bleak indeed:

> Not a tree nor a house broke the broad sweep of flat country that reached the edge of the sky in all directions. The sun has baked the plowed land into a gray mass, with little cracks running through it. Even the grass was not green, for the sun had burned the tops of the long blades until they were the same gray color to be seen everywhere [3].

The scarecrow tells Dorothy he cannot understand why she would want to live in such a place (27). Although Dorothy responds that he only thinks this because he has no brains, it appears that Baum is himself questioning the value of home in the United States. Americans at the turn of the century remained faithful, like Dorothy, but outside circumstances seemed to depict the American dream to be paling in comparison to their hopes. Chaston also declares that "the novel and its sequels often include images and characters that subtly undercut the message that there is 'no place like home'" (211). Although I am only focusing on Baum's first book, it is certainly true that later in his series he becomes more secure in his doubt of the American dream and removal from "home."

While many agree that Baum's creation of fantasy occurred due to the loss of the American dream, there is much debate over what Oz represents. Some see it as a glorified America based on what they read as symbols or allusions to the United States. Others see it as a utopia completely separate from the U.S. I agree with the second mindset due to the fact that if Baum were trying to escape the United States, it would make the most sense to create something dissimilar to it. Any possible connections with Oz and the United States may be read as the basic points of reference every author must have even when creating fantasy. It is impossible to be creative without drawing to some extent on life experiences grounded within reality.

Oz as a utopia is imaginative and critical of the U.S., both of which are within modernism through Pound's mantra to "make it new" and the modernist's reflexivity of time period ideology. Jack Zipes firmly believes that critics who interpret Oz as a type of America are making a mistake, for it is "clearly another world." (introduction xxi). In another work he expands on this idea,

> Oz *is* a place and space in the American imagination, and as such it embodies that which is missing, lacking, absent in America. Oz is the counterpart to the reality of America, a possibility that has never been realized except in the imagination of writers such as Baum and his heirs [Fairy Tale 138].

I will briefly acknowledge three ways in which Oz is a utopia completely separate from the United States. First, as both Ray Bradbury and Russell B. Nye have noticed, there is no class consciousness in Oz. Dorothy, a lowly farm girl, is treated with a sense of equality by the rulers of the land. Her age and economic status are not hindrances. Baum's own inability to be able to come into the rags to riches experience (at least at the time he wrote the first Oz book) may be a reason he makes Oz such a land of opportunity. Baum's ability to create a land with hierarchical roles but devoid of hierarchical attitudes and limitations suggest that leaders are important even in utopias, but their function should be for the good of all.

In addition to a positive lack of class consciousness, neither is there oppression of the female sex. In 1900, the Angel in the House and Separate Sphere ideologies were only beginning to be absolved, and women were still certainly treated as inferior to men. The American dream, though perhaps an illusion, always held more opportunity for men than women. But, in Oz, the powerful witches, whether good or evil, are all female. Dorothy herself is able to experience agency in Oz and be deemed as an equal with her male companions. Stuart Culver writes that Baum offers young female readers "a promise, a way of growing into a proper young woman while yet regarding her gender as something other than an inescapable biological limit" (608).

Finally, Oz is a utopia due to its unconquered land. Throughout the story, the Scarecrow, Tin Woodman, and Cowardly Lion all acquire kingdoms to rule, the Scarecrow as ruler of the Emerald City, the Tin Woodman as ruler over the Winkies, and the Lion as the King of Beasts in the forest. While the United States declared that there were no more frontiers to be conquered, Oz not only contains wild lands but the opportunity to peacefully master them.

In addition to a moralizing master narrative which elucidates the United State's downfalls by creating Oz as superior, Baum also includes a theme of technology, which was one of the largest interests during the modernist movement. Russell Nye comments that Baum has "grafted twentieth-century technology to the fairy tale tradition" (168). The turn of the century brought the continual raising of factories and modern workers as well a movement toward urbanization. Lawrence Rainey explains, quoting Stephen Kern, that the "sweeping changes in technology and culture 'created distinctive new modes of thinking about and experiencing time and space" (xxii). The Gilded Age, with its electricity and movement away from agriculture, created an atmosphere in which Baum also became intrigued. His inclusion of technology in Oz does not appear to be so much a statement, be it positive or negative, regarding the United States. Rather, it seems to simply be a fascinating aspect of the time period that he incorporates, thus showing that the time period automatically influences writing, as it is impossible for authors to write without points of reference even within a fantastical world. I make the distinction of utopian Oz being a specific critique on America but Oz including technology as being a basic statement in general because technology was not an inherent part of the American dream. Also, the United States was not the only country experiencing technology, as well as the fact that technology was becoming as much a part of life as other basic essentials, such as food, clothing, and housing, which are basic points of reference.

Barett focuses on Baum's incorporation of technology saying, "Baum was enchanted by technology, considering it akin to magic." His work is "a fond farewell for a time when agrarianism was a cornerstone of American industry but also a pleased recognition that technology has come to stay and to rule" (156–157).

Baum does not reference technology in Kansas. Oz, however, does contain its share. The Emerald City, with its green spectacles and pavement, certainly seems to embody the most positive aspects of technology. The Wizard himself appears quite modern. No explanation is given as to how he appears in different forms to Dorothy and the others, but as Toto exposes him behind a "screen that stood in a corner," (127) one can assume he uses some sort of technological special effects. His hot air balloon is a further example of technology. Since the Wizard uses technology both in deceptive and benevolent ways, Baum does not seem to be making a moral statement about technology. He seems to simply be noting its current place in the world, as most modernists did, and, consequently, including it in his tale.

Elements of modernism are not, however, only found within the novel. The 1939 MGM film also falls within the modernist period and employs modernist tendencies. Yet, the events of the time were reasonably different from 1900, so, although a master narrative is still advocated, it is somewhat different from Baum's escape from America due to the loss of the American dream. As most are more familiar with the film than the novel, the ideology of the film is often taken as a standard to also be applied to the novel. But, this is actually not the case, as is seen when the influencing cultural aspects of the separate time periods are considered, which Marx would call the social existence. I believe some of the key influences relating to the film are World War I, the Great Depression, and the Roaring Twenties. The heartaches and successes that the nation experienced led for a movement back toward nationalism and homeland pride. Judy Garland's famous words "There's no place like home" is truly the master narrative of this film. Director Victor Fleming's statement, "I made the film because I wanted my two little girls to see a picture that searched for beauty and decency and sweetness and love in the world" (*The Wizard*) seems to reflect not only the film's plot but also the truth about the America which the film's ideology portrays.

Roland Marchand suggests that in this period the film industry was an extremely effective way to advertise mindsets to the public, often using an emotional appeal to do so (62). The film was effectual in this regard because it avoids doing what Baum so detested, blatant moralization. However, in a non-invasive, heart-warming way, the film depicts an ideology of the greatness of home and, consequently, the United States. Certainly the theme of the film is one that the nation truly needed on the brink of entering into World War II. Carol Billman comments that a "common denominator for the novel and the film is the pervasive moralizing" (93). Yet, these common denominators are simultaneously similar and different. Both the novel and film convey a similar story line, and both are modernist works, yet they suggest such different world views. Their similarity is not in the view that they present, but rather the fact that they do present an all-encompassing master narrative.

Geoffrey Wagner explains, in regard to adapting novels to films, that transition can occur in three ways. The novel is either transferred almost verbatim to film (transposition), kept basically the same but altered in some respects (commentary), or blatantly changed but kept within the nature of the novel (analogy) (222–226). I believe that *The Wizard of Oz* most closely employs transposition: "This is where an original is taken and either purposely or inadvertently altered in some respect. It could also be called a re-emphasis or restructure.... Film can make authentic reconstructions in the spirit of so many cinematic footnotes to the original" (223). While the film obviously condenses the story line and places more focus on Kansas and the Wicked Witch, overall the story line is the same. The largest change is a re-emphasis, which occurs at the level of ideology.

For instance, the film's beginning, the largest fabrication from the novel's plot, is meant to orient viewers within Kansas so that they understand why Dorothy desires to return. Baum never did this with Kansas, giving only a very brief, impersonal, and depressing description, which is why although Dorothy desires to and eventually does return home, the master narrative turns toward an escape rather than an embracement of the United States. Paul Nathanson pronounces, "Her attempts [to return to Kansas in the novel] are quite inadequately motivated. The movie, on the other hand, represents Kansas nostalgically as a cozy, turn-of-the-century farmhouse. Dorothy's family and friends are over-worked but not unloving. Her desire to return is, therefore, adequately motivated" (5). The writers of the film felt that it was necessary for audiences to relate to Dorothy in reality before they would be able to do so in the fantasy of Oz. This is the reason they focused their attention almost as much on Kansas as on Oz, according to Aljean Harmetz (27).

The opening in Kansas begins in conflict as Dorothy falls into a pig sty, Ms. Gulch takes Toto away, Dorothy runs away, a twister comes, and Dorothy is knocked unconscious. All of the chaos could be read to relate to the war and economic instability the country had recently gone through. Yet, even as Dorothy wishes for "a place where there isn't any trouble," the truth that such a place does not exist soon becomes apparent, as Oz still has its share of trouble. The same can be said for the United States. Perhaps the nation did realize that the American dream was not all that was expected, but that did not change the fact that it was still one of the best nations in which to live. Baum's Kansas is much more peaceful than the film's but still proves to be less inviting. Regarding Dorothy hitting her head, John Beebe says, "the film expresses a reaction to trauma itself" (70). Trauma is also a fitting word to describe the events of World War I and the Great Depression, from which the country was still dealing with the aftermath. The film depicts Kansas showing a sense of community even in times of trouble. Zeke comes to Dorothy's aid when she falls into the pig sty; Aunt Em openly stands up for Dorothy and criticizes Ms. Gluch for taking Toto away, and Professor Marvel talks Dorothy into returning home. The support is reinforced at the end of the film when everyone surrounds Dorothy in her bed once she wakes up. A sense of camaraderie is just as important to nationalism as an esteem of home, and all the aforesaid elements enhance the film's master narrative for the American people. Beverly Lyon Clark has commented that the film draws in a diverse audience in terms of age, gender, race, and sexual orientation due to film's ability in general to bridge more gaps in audiences than literature typically can, as well as the nature of the diverse group that makes up Dorothy's company in Oz (144–147). This encompassing aspect further lends to the sense of nationalism needed in the melting pot of the United States.

Oz also depicts the idea of a united country. While the novel's geography is split up into separate quadrants, the film consists of only one cohesive Oz; there are no separating colors or regional names. But, in many ways, the film's Oz can be interpreted as quite different from Baum's utopia. It certainly contains more violence. The Wicked Witch threatens Dorothy's life and gives only an hour glass length's time for her to live, while in the novel Dorothy simply has to perform household chores. Dorothy, the Scarecrow, the Lion, and the Tin Woodman are also more violent in their quest to kill the Witch; in addition to the Tin Woodman carrying his axe, which is consistent with the novel, the film adds the Scarecrow carrying a handgun and Dorothy a net. Also, the three have to fight off, and presumably kill, guards in order to rescue Dorothy. The very change of color in the slippers from silver to ruby, which is universally understood to represent danger, passion, and blood, alludes to the heightened sense of violence in the film. All these elements of violence in Oz certainly motivate Dorothy's longing for Kansas. For viewers, they can help represent the worse situation in other countries and, conversely, the somewhat imperfect haven of the United States. The violence in general in what would be considered a children's film, though certainly watched by adults as well, can be seen as an influence of the war and culture on modernist art.

Though the film's Oz may be considered less than utopian due its violence, it does still certainly contains pleasantries; thus, the main reason for Dorothy wanting to go home stems from what home represents rather than comparing ways in which Oz is better or worse than Kansas. Dorothy's loyalty to return home is based on the community aspects that were presented at the beginning of the film. The fact that Dorothy's journey is but a dream, even a nightmare in the film, suggests that Kansas is what is real and stable, rather than the ethereal Oz. This master narrative of the stability of the United States and the importance of loyalty portrays the modernist technique of reflecting ideology influenced by the time period. Dorothy's song "Over the Rainbow" is truly the song of dreams, and in the end she finds that home is still the most likely place for them to come to fruition, much like the United States in 1939. Dorothy, as well as the viewer, "finds new value in a home that provides continuity and purpose, remains, for the political feeling of the country, a hopeful irony in a bleak political landscape" (Beebe 79).

The master narrative is not the only modernist element that both the novel and film include. The film is also consistent with the modernist fascination with technology. The film itself seems to embody the use of technology by using many special effects quite daring and new for the time period. In this way, the film also follows Pound's admonition to "make it new." The twister whirling across the prairie, the house falling from the cyclone, the images appearing in the crystal ball, the Wicked Witch writing "Surrender Dorothy" across the sky, the monkeys grouped in flight, and the melting of the Wicked Witch are all very advanced technological effects for the day. The film using such cutting edge techniques perfectly embodies the modernist fascination and Baum's inclusion of technology throughout the novel. As is also the case with Baum's novel, the film does not seem to make a definite statement about the virtues or vices of technology. It simply presents them in the newest fashion as a way of emphasizing such an important cultural element and fascination.

The last cultural influence I will mention is that of the Twenties and ways the Flapper movement seems to have had influenced the film. Anne Goodwynn Jones explains that the time period between the two world wars brought about great advancement for women due to their newfound independence in entering the workforce while the men were away at war. This experience soon led to the suffragist movement and better female education, both thoroughly embraced by the modern "flapper" (43–49). In the film's beginning, Dorothy immediately displays her agency by running away, rather than allowing herself to be subjected to unpleasant circumstances. Viewers see that Oz does not suddenly bring out independence in Dorothy; rather, it has been an integral part of her character from the beginning. In Baum's Oz, Dorothy is treated as an equal due to the utopian setting, but she does not seem to see herself as an independent female as much as the Dorothy of the film. The Flapper movement seems to have transformed the film's Dorothy into a young woman willing to confront the Wizard for scaring the Cowardly Lion enough to faint. When in the Wizard's presence, both Dorothy characters introduce themselves as "the Small and Meek" (Baum 87). However, the novel's Dorothy goes on to call herself weak and "only a helpless little girl" (87), something the film's Dorothy never does. The obvious age difference from the novel's illustrated Dorothy to the film's sixteen-year-old Judy Garland provides a visual demonstration of autonomy found through age. The illustrations portray a very innocent, helpless girl, while Garland's image allows the authority brought with age to be transferred to the female. Beebe has even suggested that Garland's mature look can be seen as a symbol of America and its move toward maturity as a world power (65), which fits nicely with the ideology of nationalism the film can be read to reveal.

Finally, the film introduces additional strong female characters. While both the novel and film portray the witches as being powerful, the film extends some of this power to Aunt Em. She bosses the farm hands and even somewhat henpecks Uncle Henry, as he looks to her to do most of the talking. Also, Elvira Gulch is the most powerful woman in the county and is capable of exerting her authority over men and women alike. The heightening of female agency in the film is, I argue, undoubtedly attributed to the Flapper movement and the typical reflection in modernist art of ideologies of the time period.

In coming full circle, while *The Wizard of Oz* in both novel and film versions are not typically considered in terms of modernism, such is certainly the case. When looking at the novel and film separately, it is fascinating to see the ways in which the modernist quest for originality, as well as time period interests, such as technology and female agency, affect their work. When comparing both art forms with one another, it is even more captivating to see how the two works within the same movement can relay such different messages while still adhering to the consistent modernist format of portraying a master narrative. Baum's message of the need to escape reality and its loss of the American dream through fantasy is almost completely refuted in the MGM film's message of a renewed sense of nationalism and community amongst American citizens due to the struggles they have endured. However, both versions portray ideologies imperative to the time period, and both will continue to be revered for their creativity and imagination.

Works Cited

Barrett, Laura. "From Wonderland to Wasteland: The Wonderful Wizard of Oz, The Great Gatsby, and the New American Fairy Tale." *PLL* 42.2 (2006): 150–80.

Baum, L. Frank. *The Wonderful Wizard of Oz: The Kansas Centennial Edition*. Lawrence: The University Press of Kansas, 1999.

Beebe, John. "The Wizard of Oz: A Vision of Development in the American Political Psyche." *The Vision Thing: Myth, Politics and Psyche in the World*. Ed. Thomas Singer. New York: Routledge, Taylor and Francis Group, 2000.

Billman, Carol. "'I've seen the movie'": Oz Revisited." *Children's Novels and the Movies*. Ed. Douglas Street. New York: Frederick Ungar Publishing Co., Inc., 1983.

Chaston, Joel D. "If I Ever Go Looking for My Heart's Desire: Home in Baum's 'Oz'" Books." *Lion and the Unicorn* 18 (1994): 209–19.

Clark, Beverly Lyon. *Kiddie Lit: The Cultural Construction of Children's Literature in America*. Baltimore: The John Hopkins University Press, 2003.

Culver, Stuart. "Growing up in Oz." *American Literary History* 4.4 (1992): 607–28.

Earle, Neil. *The Wonderful Wizard of Oz in American Popular Culture: Uneasy in Eden*. Lewiston: The Edwin Mellen Press, 1993.

Eliot, T. S. "The Lesson of Baudelaire." *Modernism: An Anthology*. Ed. Lawrence Rainey. Malden: Blackwell Publishing Ltd, 2005.

Harmetz, Aljean. *The Making of the Wizard of Oz*. New York: Alfred A. Knopf Inc., 1977.

Jameson, Fredric. *A Singular Modernity*. New York: Verso, 2002.

Jones, Anne Goodwyn. "The Work of Gender in the Southern Renaissance." *Southern Writers and Their Worlds*. Ed. Christopher Morris and Steven G. Reinhardt. Arlington: University of Texas at Arlington, 1996.

Lanes, Selma. *Down the Rabbit Hole: Adventure and Misadventure in the Realm of Children's Literature*. Kingsport: Kingsport Press, Inc., 1971.

Marchand, Roland. *Advertising the American Dream: Making Way For Modernity, 1920–1940*. Berkeley and Los Angeles: University of California Press, 1985.

Marx, Karl. *A Contribution to the Critique of Political Economy*. With some notes by R. Rojas. Moscow: Progress Publishers, 1977.

Nathanson, Paul. *Over the Rainbow: The Wizard of Oz as a Secular Myth of America*. New York: State University of New York Press, 1991.

Nye, Russell B. "An Appreciation." *The Wizard of Oz* by L. Frank Baum. Ed Michael Patrick Hearn. New York: Schocken Books, 1983.

Rainey, Lawrence. "Introduction." *Modernism: An Anthology*. Ed. Lawrence Rainey. Malden: Blackwell Publishing Ltd, 2005.

St. John, Tom. "Lyman Frank Baum: Looking Back to the Promised Land." *Western Humanities Review* 36.4 (1982): 349–60.

Vidal, Gore. "On Rereading the Oz Books." *New York Review of Books* 24.15 (1977): 38–42.

Wagner, Geoffrey. *The Novel and the Cinema*. Cranbury: Associated University Presses, Inc., 1975.

Westman, Karin E. "Children's Literature and Modernism: The Space Between." *Children's Literature Association* 32.4 (2007): 283–286.

The Wizard of Oz. Dir. Victor Fleming. Perf. Judy Garland, Ray Bolger, Jack Haley, and Bert Lahr. 1939. DVD. Warner Brothers, 1999.

Zipes, Jack. *Fairy Tale as Myth*. Lexington: The University Press of Kentucky, 1994.

_____. "Introduction." *The Wonderful Wizard of Oz*. Ed. Jack Zipes. New York: Penguin, 1998.

PART TWO

Oz and Philosophy

CHAPTER 8

Ask the Clock of the Time Dragon

Oz *in the Past and the Future*

RANDALL AUXIER

"It takes all kinds to make a world."
— Mother Yackle, *A Lion among Men*

Questions, Questions, Questions

My question is simple to state but wickedly difficult to answer. Why does the Marvelous Land of Oz keep re-inventing itself in our culture? Lots of things get recycled, but Oz is at a completely different level, being remade in major new variations regularly, and with a significant number of those new versions having a huge impact on our culture. Individually and collectively, it seems that Oz is one fantasy world we just can't leave alone. People dream up fantasy worlds all the time, but rarely do they get such a foothold in our general lives. We grow and slough off new fantasy worlds in literature, film and stage like so many snake-skins, which is to say, most lands never go deeper than dermal. But somehow Oz got under our skin, and we all know that.

It would be foolish to attempt a full account of the relationship between Oz and the human imagination, or how even our social imagination might be captured by one world and not another. But if I can find just one road into the heart of the romance between us and Oz, perhaps I can also find a road back home. It's more of a journey than an explanation, or, perhaps, all explanations are journeys of some sort anyway, and this is just one more. Since I have spent the last two or three years thinking and writing about Oz, finding something new to say has been a bit of a challenge. Fortunately Gregory Maguire has facilitated my prospects for novelty by offering a new installment to *his* Oz writings, and I must say that I think he has really outdone

121

himself this time (and that isn't easy, since he's done so well before). I know
that not everyone follows Maguire's progress in elaborating his Oz, so a few
general remarks are needed.

Son of Oz

Gregory Maguire is the latest to *succeed* in altering Oz. His novel *Wicked*,
retelling Oz from the standpoint of the Wicked Witch of the West, reori-
ented the public's judgment about her and about Oz. Maguire's Oz is not the
innocent coloring book image that we carry with us from Baum's books, nor
the complex Freudian dream of the 1939 movie, nor is it the glitzy and sur-
real Manhattan of *The Wiz*. Maguire has a "new" Oz with more realistic politics, cloak and dagger intrigue, racism and sexism, and yet, somehow, it is
still just Oz, only more so. Maguire has finished three books and he now calls
all the Oz novels "The Wicked Years." It is clear from the configuration of
his latest book, *A Lion among Men*, that he is not finished with Oz. Whereas
the first two books looked as if they did not *demand* another installment, this
third book indicates a willingness on Maguire's part to devote his considerable talents to developing his Oz for at least one more book, and quite possibly more.

In each of his books, Maguire dips into the materials provided by Baum,
by the 1939 movie, and also draws from numerous other sources, to work his
magic. He has done similar work with other familiar stories, such as Snow
White and Cinderella. His approach isn't exactly formulaic, but there is a strategy in how he does what he does, and the pattern becomes increasingly rec-
ognizable as one reads more of his books. Basically, he shows us what was
"off-screen," so to speak, the untold side of the story. But Maguire also likes
to get at whatever was just beyond the edges of imagination, in our familiar
versions of the stories we know so well. He follows characters apart from the
main ones, and we learn to see the fantasy world from their perspectives. Of
course, with a change of perspective, there is a sense in which we always get
a new world, but it is a world which has been there all along, so we also recognize it.

Yackle Snarling

In *A Lion among Men*, Maguire provides the full back story on the Cowardly Lion, and some of his feline fortunes and misfortunes, before and after
the "Dorothy business." Very little actually *happens* in the new book. It covers a period of about one full day, using flashbacks to tell the history. The
Lion's life is revealed in a series of interviews with the mysterious Mother

Yackle, one of Maguire's original characters, who seems always to be hovering around the fringes of the life of Elphaba, the Wicked Witch of the West. Yackle's main occupation, we learn, is that of "oracle," which is very much in keeping with the matriarchal arrangement of Maguire's Oz — an order implicit in every Oz, which all by itself is plenty intriguing.[1] I will not trot out the full plot, but I need to mention some of its main features. The oracle Mother Yackle has no memory of her childhood and was born old. Not knowing her purpose in life, she followed her inklings and got along the best she could.

So Yackle became a sham fortune teller, until one day when Elphaba's Nanny came to call, asking for advice on elixirs, and Yackle had an actual vision, the content of which was, "You have to leave the way you came in." From that day forward, Yackle kept an eye on Elphaba, since she believed the revelation was connected with the green girl. In true oracular style, Yackle had no idea what her own prophecy meant, and we learn eventually that she misinterpreted it for fifty years, until the Lion, called Brrr, made a remark that helped her grasp its meaning.

SPOILER WARNING. *The next paragraph contains a spoiler,*
for those who have not yet read A Lion among Men.

The enigmatic saying applies to Yackle herself. We learn later that Yackle is a magical being, an angel, conjured from the mysterious book, the Grimmerie, and in the climactic scene of *A Lion among Men*, she reveals her wings, flies up and dives back into the book.[2]

The Clock of the Time Dragon

Mother Yackle is set in opposition to a different type of oracle called The Clock of the Time Dragon. It is described several ways, but this is the most telling:

> This thing was massive — mounted on a flatbed cart, three times as high as [the Lion] standing upright. From a distance, he guessed it would resemble a stupa of some sort, an ornately carved portable omphalos, but up close one could see the ticky-tacky aspect [LaM, 176].

In *Wicked*, Maguire says:

> The Clock of the Time Dragon is mounted on a wagon and stands as high as a giraffe. It is nothing more than a tottering, free standing theater, punched on all four sides with alcoves and proscenium arches. On the flat roof is a clockwork dragon, an invention of green painted leather, silvery claws, ruby jeweled eyes. Its skin is made of hundreds of overlapping discs of copper, bronze and iron. Beneath the flexible folds of its scales is an armature controlled by clockwork. The Time Dragon circles on its pedestal, flexes its narrow leathery wings ... and belches out sulfurous balls of flaming orange stink [W, 11].

The clock has a will and intentions of its own, but it is periodically rolled around Oz by a company of seven barely grown boys, led by an ageless dwarf, and accompanied sometimes by a celibate princess whose main function is to have "no future" because she does not believe what the time dragon says (see pages 112–113; 197, 203, 222). These bacchants create havoc wherever they go. We are supposed to perceive in the contraption a symbol of Tiamat, the dragon whose dismemberment creates the world in Babylonian mythology. Maguire mentions at one point the prehistoric Oz legend of the dragon that dreams the world (LaM, 88; W, 44). This mechanical Tiamat is having her revenge on *our* dreamworld of Oz, and she is enjoying it. Between her laps of Oz, the time dragon sits camouflaged for long periods, but calls her crew back when the time is ripe. As Maguire says, "the handmade masterpiece snapped right back into business. The play of its gears remained deft, the tension in its belts and chains keen. Its mechanical advantage was said· to have been augmented by a stubbornly adhesive magic" (13; see also page 109).

The mechanical dragon shows up at various crucial moments in Maguire's first novel. For example, Elphaba is born inside the dragon, due to a complex series of unlikely events — events we are tempted to see as meaningful, and that is where the magic of the Clock *really* begins, by tempting its audience (including the residents of Oz and the readers of Maguire) to *interpret* the meaning of the display. The whole contraption is sort of like a traveling Hamlet's mousetrap. The idea of the Clock has developed over the course of the three Maguire novels, but by the third book, the Clock creates puppet shows for its audiences that reveal the secrets of their own lives, depicting what *has* happened that they were unaware of, but which affected them. It really does not tell the future; rather, it is an oracle of the unknown forces of the past that are still in present operation — or at least, that is how its audiences *understand* the *puppet* shows. In the earlier novels, the Clock doesn't always tell the truth, but in *A Lion among Men* it is depicted as always and only representing what actually happened in the past.[3]

Dueling Oracles

So there are two oracles, Yackle and the Clock. They are in tension — mechanical time against the more traditional, magical oracle, and the sort of time *she* can see and foretell, which isn't mechanical but more cyclical, like the days and nights, the seasons, and the cycle of birth, growth, flourishing, decline, death and rebirth. The traditional oracle sings a song of what was, is, and will be again. I could spend a long time describing the sense in which a traditional oracle communicates, but in the case of Mother Yackle, it comes down to the statement of vague and generalized necessities that are supposed to have some particular application to those listening. The oracles of Yackle are not inherently futural because they are not linear in their temporal structure. But her listeners *take* the oracular utterances as having future portent, and *not* as the revelation of past truths of which they had been unaware. Tacitly, then, the listeners switch from the mode of receiving revelations of the concrete past from the Dragon, to receiving generalities with future portent. I say the switch is tacit because no character in any of the novels comments on how the two oracles are really charged with completely different types of knowing, and modes of communication. In fact, Mother Yackle does have one vision of the concrete past, relating to Brrr's capture as a cub, but as she puts it, "Just because I have had visions doesn't mean they're true" (LaM, 141).

The point is not whether the mechanical oracle and the human oracle dwell in different modes of time; rather, what is important is that the other characters will not take responsibility for their own acts of interpretation of either oracle: offered magical symbols, whether mute and mechanical or uttered in the ecstatic condition of the seer, the hearers insist upon externalizing the source of the meaning, attributing it to past or future, and ignoring the present. All the other characters recognize is that both Mother Yackle and the Clock *are* oracles, and that knowledge fills and also occludes the present moment, even the difference between the oracles (that one is a living being and the other is a mechanical device). So everyone is inclined to see them as being in competition for control of the future.

There is a profound difference between the two oracles, of course. Yackle really *is* interested in the future because she wants to know how to die. She can't die and she isn't sure why. But her vision of the future came in a short aphorism, and her real struggle is to learn its meaning. On the other hand, the Time Dragon is, apparently, able to show only the past in the form of re-enactment, not words. But here is the wrinkle: in Maguire's Oz, as in our own world, whether in the form of the unbidden word or the repeated action, the past is *active* in the present, in ways we do not perceive. Large parts of the past are hidden from us, but somehow there, just below our consciousness, and what we do not know *can* hurt us, or help us, or shock us. Whether the *future* is active in the present (or past) is *the* major question Maguire confronts in *A Lion among Men*, and he does so with great intellectual subtlety. He recognizes that *if* the future is active like the past is, then *fate* rules our days and we are justified in feeling demoralized and unfree. But Maguire toys with whether there might be some way to understand the future as active in the present, but not possessing the omnipotence we ascribe to fate. He calls this puzzle "A Question of Influence." He parses his characters in *A Lion among Men* according to how they see this difficult question about the active character of the future, and when all the characters finally meet, their first order of business is to have a philosophical argument about fate.

Maguire essentially argues, in this new book, that our struggle with the concept of fate is tied to our ignorance of the active presence of the *past*. We feel unfree because forces beyond our individual or collective *memories* are exerting pressures upon the present that seem sometimes to overwhelm or even cancel our free choosing. And yet, without the past, the present has no definition, no meaning, and we have no way of gnawing our way into the future. Maguire has his ideas quite worked out in this regard — he has thought about time a good deal, and also fate and free choice. His dominant philosophical influence in this book, as in the other two on Oz, is Nietzsche. He has read Friedrich Nietzsche (1844–1900) from early to late, and he puts into concrete narrative a number of the more provocative ideas we can associate with Nietzsche's thought. Let me offer you just a sample. Here are some passages from Maguire that are paraphrases and applications of Nietzsche:

> We start out in identical perfection: bright, reflective, full of sun. The accident of our lives bruises us into dirty individuality. We meet with grief. Our character dulls and tarnishes. We meet with guilt. We know, we know: the price of living is corruption. There isn't as much light as there once was. In the grave we lapse back into undifferentiated sameness [8; Maguire's reverie on the effects of war; compare with pages 58 and 197].

> Nothing in [Brrr's] own life was worth remembering, really. Every turn had promised reward, and delivered something less. So in truth, searching out the twists of someone else's life ... was a downright comfort. A welcome distraction. It was diverting to consider lives that had been as hobbled as his own troubled existence.... Brrr had nothing left to be, to become, but himself. How limited, even sour a prospect. One may, oh, cook poorly, or be socially graceless, or invest unwisely, or fail to achieve the best of personal hygiene. But one doesn't want to live wrong — from breath to breath, from start to finish, to get it wrong, so wrong, so fully wrong, that one has never had the glimmer of an idea that it might be better. Or does one? If you're going to get it that wrong, it's better to get it all wrong. The proverbial stupid ant crawling on the hat brim of the prophet, eager only for the shade behind the prophet's left ear, and ignorant of the civilization-altering sermon it is witnessing" [194–195].

About Nor's attempts to be no one, to escape time by effacing the "I":

> The *I*, the singular first-person pronoun, had to be eradicated in order to sustain the argument about justice's brash lack of interest in individual history — even as justice existed to champion the rights of such histories to exist. I and I and I and I, all the land over [197; compare with lines from pages 8, 58].

> "I'm coming," she announced, for it was her history to do so, and she could no more avoid her future than she could escape her past. However often she sat quietly apart, fretting over it [203; this is Nor's dilemma].

But Maguire does not simply give in to Nietzsche's eternal return, or to "become what you are," or to his insistence on *amor fati*. Rather, Maguire associates these ideas mainly with the two characters who seem least equipped to handle what *has* happened to them in the past, the Lion and Nor. These ideas are set against other ideas about time. In these other characters, Maguire is toying with process philosophy. Some of the ideas he suggests I would associate specifically with the philosophy of Alfred North Whitehead (1861–1947), although I do not go so far as to claim Maguire has read Whitehead (clearly he has read Nietzsche). Yet, Maguire's familiarity with writers such as Virginia Woolf place him in the general domain of non–Nietzschean process thought. Here are some representative passages from Maguire:

"Ghosts are nothing *but* pasts" [53, Cubbins to Brrr].

Was it [the clumping of ghosts] because once a creature became a ghost, it shirked off the differentiations of biological diversity and, uniqueness annihilated, became just shades of life? Footfalls of the past? "I have a feeling I'm not in Oz anymore," said Brrr [58, compare with pages 8 and 197; this is Whitehead's doctrine of perpetual perishing and objective immortality of the past].

The ghosts, the Ozmists in Cloud Swamp, speaking to Brrr:

We have no more experience of the future than the living do, they said ... "And you hunger for future history," said Brrr. *This day you live in today is the impossible future for us.... Is the Wizard still sitting upon the throne? We crave to know the future* [61; this is what a perpetually perishing actual entity might say to the present actual entity of whose world it is a part].

And this wash of recollections [Brrr shared with Yackle] had become a slick along which Brrr careered, like it or not. Brrr's recall of what had happened *before* seemed limited to apparent causes of what had happened *next*. The future reshapes the memory of the past in the way it recalibrates significance: some episodes are advanced, others lose purchase [56; this is like Whitehead's doctrine of prehension].

But the Whiteheadian moments in Maguire are outnumbered and overwhelmed by a slightly contrasting view of time, similar to that of another process philosopher, Henri Bergson (1859–1941). Whenever Maguire deals with the perception of time, and especially the powers of the mysterious Mother Yackle, he waxes Bergsonian. I also do not say that he read Bergson. Quite possibly he is assembling the ideas from his own imagination that simply resemble those of Bergson and Whitehead. Yet, if he continues working out this intellectual thread, he will end up with a philosophical view that is clearly a process view of time. Here are some of Maguire's Bergsonian moments.

"Even those whose memories are corrupted by illness still have their pasts pocketed somewhere. But I have nothing to remember — no childhood to flee from.

Don't you understand? I think that's why I can see the future — to the extent that I can. I suppose it's your principle of compensation. I can't remember the past, so I can remember the future" [96–97, Yackle to Brrr].

Here the idea is of the full active presence of the past along with the view that memory overtakes the future for a being with a long past, the converse of which is that the future is more perceivable to a being with a shorter history.

And, then, reminiscent of Bergson's image theory in *Matter and Memory*, we have on the vision: "You have to leave the way you came" on page 105:

"I had had my first vision, even if it was induced [by the elixir]. Something about possibility. All that misty apprehension, those swirls of image trying to form into something intelligible ... in all that, I perceived force and hope alike. And I saw that I would be a real oracle, whatever kind of oracle I could manage to be. My calling wasn't just a joke" [108, Yackle to Brrr].

After sex with the Ivory Tiger, Muhlama:

When he [Brrr] could think again in words — was it then, was it later, he didn't know — it was simply this: Now I fit in. His reverie was delicious. Eyes closed. He was partly conscious of the floating strings of the world, its selvages restitching themselves into a prettier apprehension. Some might call it afterglow.... For Brrr it was as if a new appetite was just beginning to stir out of his dreamy slumber [149; this is Bergsonian duration as it breaks through into spatialized time consciousness].

About Mister Mikko and Professor Lenx:

Their memories were stronger than the present moment [170; this is Bergson's theory of memory as applied to organic beings that are old].

The Bergsonian view is mainly in line with Whitehead's but there are just a few crucial differences.[4] Whitehead has a doctrine of perpetual perishing, which is to say that past events are taken up into present events only partially, by "prehension," and as such they are considered only objectively (as objects for a present experiencer. A "prehension" renders a past actuality more abstract, increasingly *less* present in each successive moment, and hence less active and less available. The prehension contains none of the subjective immediacy the past event originally held for itself. By contrast, Bergson holds to the *full presence* of the past. Nothing that happens is really lost, and all that has ever happened is *still happening*. Subjectivity is not an illusion, but it is an *ex post facto* effect of the reduction of external images to virtual spaces of action in which the common origin of action is the same collection of images called "the body."

A second crucial point of contrast with Whitehead has to do with Bergson's view of perception. I will not explain the subtle differences here, but I will employ Bergson's theory of the image in my subsequent remarks. The key points are that a central nervous system has two primary functions: the afferent nervous sustem and brain filter out most of what the senses actually take in and narrow the sensations into perceptions by a process of reduction. In short, most of what your body does is absorb and kill off what you might otherwise experience. What is allowed through to the sensorimotor system is only whatever portion of the image system can be acted upon. That collection of possible actions, *when not yet acted upon*, is perception. Action cancels present perception and memory floods in to replace it. The second function of the central nervous system is the communication between brain stem and spine which, in the presence of perception, amounts to the latter asking the former several times per second "what do you want to do?" Thus, if the brain withholds its impulse and impedes the signal to the spinal cord, a perception is the result. The result of this view is that *personality* is actually born and cultivated by *inaction*.[5] We become who we are in the space we can create between sensation and action, the world of many spaces, the world of perception. I find this view, and not Whitehead's, to be the intellectual thread Maguire pursues in the story.

At the climax of *A Lion among Men*, Mother Yackle declares that all the problems haunting the motley crew locked in the Mauntery could be solved if they just asked the clock of the time dragon, because, as she tells the Lion, "I know more than you do and it knows more than I do." In short, the trouble is that they create all their own woes and fears by inaction, by being a collective brain and con sciousness that will not answer the constant call to action. The Clock of the Time Dragon is, then, a mostly mechanical spinal cord with limited intention, and able to act only upon what is already happened, not upon what is now happening. In actying, it can replay or repeat a sort of puppet show that follows behind the completed and remembered intention of those who perceive.

Image and Time

• What is an image? How is it different from a symbol?
• Two views of the image: augmentation of perception and reduction to the virtual and functional surface.
• The space of action, the space of complementarity, and the space of compensation

Intellectual imagination is not moral or emotional or even aesthetic imagination. It moves along the tracks laid by ideas. Imagination moves in a space created by the absence of temporal duration — for every mode of temporal absence, there is a mode of active imagination. The past, the present and the future are absent in different ways. Thus, there are different sorts of images that show us what might be, what is but is out of view in the present (Sartre's four modes of annihilation), and what might have been.

The intellectually imagined idea has a different tonality or hue than does emotional imagination. Maguire's intellectual themes are independent, and yet, they invoke the same Oz in idea as we felt, loved, or morally judged. The relation between intentional modalities and the sorts of objects they discover must be taken seriously. When the characters finally do stop talking about fate and freedom, and ask the Clock, the past and future are brought into meaningful relation, first as a puppet show, but then, in the climactic moment, the Time Dragon reveals that it is not limited to re-enactment, but is also capable of affecting and effecting the future. Thus, the view of time Maguire offers is one that seeks to get beyond the old dualism of dueling oracles: life versus mechanism. Instead there is something like magic, even through the mechanical side of existence, and something like free will and also destiny, but not quite fate. Here are a couple of telling passages:

> "I wouldn't take on a [fortune telling] client unless she — it is nearly always a she who cares about the future, isn't it? — unless she promised not to call the authorities if my reading provoked some catastrophe or other" [99, Yackle to Brrr].

On fate:

> "Elphaba is condemned to nothing," I found myself saying. "Nothing is written for her, which means everything is possible" [102, Yackle to Brrr; this idea returns when Nor gives Brrr the nearly blank book at the end].

One could multiply examples, but I think the secret is to see how the tension between mechanical and living time is resolved without eliminating the reality of either, and without playing down our experience of either one. Maguire's resolution of the old dilemma is, as far as I can see, a literary version of Bergson's philosophical resolution. That is a good resolution in my view, since I also regard Bergson's account as the best I have discovered.

Books about Books about Books

Maguire's theme in *A Lion among Men* is not intellectual, however; it is moral. He is exploring, throughout the book, the shadowy border between, as he puts it, the world of *mystery* and the world of *war*. The image chosen for the cover of Maguire's book illustrates well enough that he is interested in how the *impending* character of war, the war that is about to happen but hasn't yet, *stretches out time and calls forth confessions about history*. The entire book unfolds in the day before a huge battle occurs. It is like all the characters are locked in a brain that must sooner or later send some signal to the converging mechanical necessities of opposing armies, armies arrayed against one another like mutually exclusive choices are presented to a single human being.

Eventually all our characters decide to evade the armies and live for another day. The Lion's last free act in the book is to bring in a harvest for an old couple (whose strong sons have been taken into the army), and to do so before the soldiers arrive and destroy the crop. That is the Lion's courageous act of charity, and it is an entirely free act, not necessitated b y anything but the perception of it as a possible (if unlikely) act that the Lion *can* perform.. Maguire's ruminations on war make his position clear. He opposes it and he is responding to *his* own time, our time, and the senseless slaughter that has characterized the last decade. That is his moral theme.

But Maguire's *philosophical* insight has to do with what happens to time in anticipation of a terrible judgment, the decision to act is irrevocable, and it annihilates both choice and personality. In short, the decision to *act* is *war on the future*, using all of the present as the gun and some portion of the past as its ammunition. Just as time seems to slow down as a car accident is occurring, we can imagine waiting for an army to arrive as an accident in extreme slow motion. But such is almost all action — with a few exceptions, such as the Lion's last act.

Thus, something about the impending battle, or the need to act, brings on a sense of urgency that is stretched and strained across many hours (or seconds), and in that extension, the realm of mystery, the problem of time, of fate, of freedom, comes into contact with our whole temporal sensibility — it is as if, in being forced to fear and to face an impending catastrophe, and being prevented from running, our awareness spreads itself before us for examination, and we must take advantage of the opportunity. Soon enough the soldiers arrive and we will be obliged to be so much confused by the present that we have no leisure for an durational span beyond a few seconds and our next few actions.

The impending arrival of an army, or mechanical action in the face of contrary choices, transforms a second into an hour, and a day into a lifetime. In short, mysteries *become* revelations in these moments, we become strangely self aware, and oddly *in charge* of our own interpretive powers. But being aware of our responsibilities as interpreters of our pasts, presents and futures, is not the same as knowing *what* these times really mean. This second question, what our lives, collectively and individually, mean, is the realm of mystery. For Maguire, the realm of mystery is that of the symbol, of the ethereal "watermark." When finally the Clock gives up its treasure and reveals that it, the Clock, is really a reliquary designed to protect and transport a magic *book*, the Lion sees in the book a "watermark" on a page. The watermark rises out of the book and dances in the air as a kind of portal, an efficacious portal. Here is how Maguire describes the climatic revelation:

> Then the watermark rose off the page. It did not flesh out like a suddenly luminous puppet or like a radioactive green parrot, but retained its drawn outline, its crude symbolic origin. It reared, it rose in a sweep of cape, it lifted like a green flower from a bed of words and red roses on a black fringed background. It was not Elphaba; she was not here. Her time was over and done. It was the mark, of Elphaba, vivid as ever. Their eyes stung, to see her again, or for the first time [LaM, 296].

The symbol is more than a word but less than the full past. It is the ghost of a meaning, and one not reducible to a course of present action. It is a lure for future acts of thinking, but not yet the demand for physical activity. The possibility of genuinely free action lies in reversing the order of experience. Instead of acting only upon the present space we perceive, we act instead upon the space we do not perceive, the space that comes to our awareness through the symbol, which is a *possible* rather than *actual* past strutting magically across the virtual space of our thinking as a beacon to a course of action un-presented by our perception. The symbol is the ground of charity, and it is not the actual, physical book before our eyes, but what the book might *mean* before our minds.

Why So Many Ozzes?

Now it is time to return to our initial question, to see whether we have learned anything. The first thing we need to notice is that our reduction of present images into meanings is a matter of filling in what is *relevant* to the past, present, and future, but is not quite actual in any of them. Action, past, present and future, is precisely that of which there is and can *be no image*, because action *is* time, while perceived image *is* spatial compensation for inaction. But there *can* be symbols of past actions, symbols which are not those actions themselves, but rather their meaning. More precisely, the symbols invite us to consider all the things they might have meant, had the images been acts rather than words.

Thus, when we tell stories about the past or the future, the easiest thing to forget, to overlook, is that the story can *be* a story precisely because its meaning, the space filled by symbols of the images it reduces, are *not* the events themselves, but are rather spatializations bearing a resemblance in many intentional modalities to the temporal events symbolized. Most importantly, the images the actual book provides are intentional objects which are perceptual analogues upon which we may act (by reading them), with a firm expectation that the perceptual results will usually come close to what we foresaw in initiating action of reading. But the image is not the whole thing (the book); it is a reduction of the thing by way of a refusal to let the light and sound and tactile possibilities pass through us unimpeded. We use our own physical torpor to arrest light, sound, smells, and to hold it for a moment. In that moment, what rises up from the book, dances before us, and invites us to dive in, to act not upon what is but upon what is not, is the symbol. In co-ordination, these momentary pauses before the actual book create a pre-sentational space in which the *togetherness* of all our sensation, called percep-tion, is experienceable not as actual, not as a realm of physical action, but as something suitable for thinking. We think not about what is, but about what is not and might be. We are freed when we reverse their order and attach our faith to what is not, but might be, and assign our doubt to what is and might not be. The symbol is the instrument of this reversal.

Having experienced the togetherness of our world in the wider domain of the possible, and having subordinated all that is actual in past, present and future to the meanings of those symbols, we are as *free* as we can reasonably expect to be; we may take the symbol of the past as an invitation to action on the invisible, as a complement to present, uncoordinated feelings that are being experience in the present durational span, but are left out of percep-tion. Or we may take this togetherness as compensation for what we did not do and now cannot do, but might have done. Such is the ground of both relief and regret. That is the functional range of images symbolized: invitation, completion, compensation. No matter how complex a system of images may become, the act of taking the image as a symbol requires a great deal of fancy mental activity on our part, and the act of treating the symbol as an invita-tion, a completion or a compensation requires further work.

Oz is a very complex system of symbols, experienceable in many modal-ities — we may read the books, watch the movies in a theater or on a televi-sion set, go see the stage plays, see videos of the stage plays, or we may even re-enact them ourselves. However we may go about perceiving the actual and perceivable Ozzes, we do bring this complex system of symbols back to the present moment, and all versions will fall under the general structures char-acteristic of images and the ways in which they bear meaning. In short, it doesn't matter whether we are offered these symbols from a Time Dragon, a clockwork device like a television, or from a magic book — and for Maguire, every book is magic. We can get the symbol system, in all its efficacy, by either means. There is a difference, however. Maguire suggests that a book is an angel and a witch; it is alive in its own way, and it doesn't know how to die. But television, movies, stage plays, are all clockwork in a certain sense. But that doesn't mean they are inferior or less true, it just means that in their presence you will be less aware of your own interpretive activity when you take in their images. You will tend to forget that they are symbols, since they seem like genuine actions.

Oz stands out among fantasy worlds, I think, because of something in the way all three temporal domains are continuously available, whether we are reading or watching — we love to remember Oz, we love to re-experience it, and we love to anticipate it, even while we are reading or watching. Oz. And this experience in Oz is unlike the experience of Tolkien's Middle Earth, which also invites everyone to become aware of his or her act of interpreting. We wish to be passive before Middle Earth, to abolish our own will to power and become submissive to the imagination of Tolkien. He is our master, and we do not want *his* imagination, not our own. But Oz is more fun than that. In fact, I will go so far as to suggest that there has never been a place that was more fun than Oz. It's more fun than Neverland and Wonderland and Gilligan's Island all rolled together. In Oz, we get a tremendously powerful sense of the relation of the "was," the "is" and the "will be," from an actual Kansas made into a symbol by its graying, until our mind are prepared to think about the symbols. Instead of Kansas, we move into the "might have been," the "not quite here and now": and the "almost might be." That is Oz. It is so balanced, temporally, among memory, perception and possible action, by the organic symbol system. Pieces of Oz crowd our actual pasts, and our actual present, and the future we hope for. We know we are in Oz at any moment that we feel we aren't in Kansas anymore.

I think Maguire gets this, even if he wouldn't describe it in just the way I have. My clue is that he is clearly aware when his tale is getting too much like Kansas, during this most recent book, and he has the Lion remark, "I've a feeling we're not in Oz anymore." The key to a good story is to keep your Ozzes fun, which means keeping them magical, which means following the logic of the symbols and their meanings, not bending under the harsh whip of the unsymbolized images. The symbols co-ordinate in surprising new ways your entire intentional life, and not just as a substitute for living your life, not as an escape — and that, dear reader, that is the importance of the ontology of "home" upon which all the Oz tales are based. Without the ontology of home, Oz is mere escape. With it, Oz is completing and compensatory. By showing us all we almost were, are, and will be, it provides a perspective upon that regarding which we can form no image at all: what we were, are, and will be.

Notes

1. I explored this in some detail in my essay, "In the Merry Old Matriarch of Oz," in *The Wizard of Oz and Philosophy*, eds. R. Auxier and P. Seng (LaSalle, IL: Open Court, 2008).

2. See the discussion of the nature and history of angels in Oz in *LaM* on pp. 234–235; and Yackle's theology and metaphysics on pp. 219–220.

3. I wondered about the origins of Maguire's idea for The Clock of the Time Dragon, but I could find nothing in Baum's Oz books or any others that might have provided a template for this clockwork oracle. Asking all the Oz scholars at the Henderson State Oz conference brought only shrugs, so I was stumped. But then, in July of 2009, Gregory Maguire spoke at the national conference of the American Library Association in Chicago, and my new friend Laura Keyes, the head librarian at the Limestone Township Library near Kankakee, IL, used her five minute opportunity to ask Maguire my question: whence The Clock of the Time Dragon? Maguire said it was modeled on a 16th century German clock described by Daniel Boostin in his famous trilogy on science and invention (*The Discoverers*, book one). I am grateful to Laura for using her limited time to help me!

4. For a fairly complete account of the similarities between Bergson and Whitehead, see my "Influence as Confluence: Bergson and Whitehead," *Process Studies*, in the special focus section on "Bergson and Whitehead," 28:3–4 (Fall/Winter 1999), 267; 301–338; 339–345.

5. See Henri Bergson, *Matter and Memory*, auth trans. N.M. Paul and W.S. Palmer (New York: Zone Books, 1988 [1908]), ch. 1, but especially pp. 14–15 (corresponds to pp. xii–xv in the Dover edition).

Works Cited

Auxier, Randall. "In the Merry Old Matriarch of Oz." *The Wizard of Oz and Philosophy*, eds. R. Auxier and P. Seng. Chicago, IL: Open Court, 2008.

_____. "Influence as Confluence: Bergson and Whitehead." *Process Studies*, 28: 3–4 (Fall/Winter 1999), 267; 301–338; 339–345.

Bergson, Henri. *Matter and Memory*. Auth. Trans. N.M. Paul and W.S. Palmer. New York, NY: Zone Books, 1988.

Maguire, Gregory. *A Lion Among Men*. New York: William Morrow, 2008.

_____. *Wicked: The Life and Times of the Wicked Witch of the West*. New York: Regan Books, 1995.

CHAPTER 9

Down the Yellow Brick Road

Good and Evil, Freewill, and
Generosity in The Wizard of Oz

GAIL LINSENBARD

Introduction

Among the many thorny philosophical and theological problems introduced to our students are those of the origin of natural and moral evil and the possibility of freewill in a universe strictly governed by God, or, alternatively, governed by the natural laws of the universe. Teaching these philosophical and theological problems, as many of us do, through the writings of a figure as commanding and weighty as St. Augustine, brings great intellectual and, for many, spiritual rewards as well. Because Augustine's ideas and arguments can be subtle, conceptually abstruse, and challenging, it is helpful to ask students to consider the problems he raises in relation to the film, *The Wizard of Oz*. This film, loved and viewed by students across generations, has brought levity, imagination and, less appreciated, I think, deep philosophical lessons to its audiences since it first appeared in 1939. In addition to the broader and more widely discussed themes of the three major dimensions of the American economy in the first half of the 20th century, to wit, mid–western agriculture and farming represented by the Scarecrow, the manufacturing and industrial hubs represented by the Tin Man, and the forestry/environmental sector represented by the Cowardly Lion, *The Wizard of Oz* also parodies the impenetrable bureaucracy of the United States government that promises much but delivers little, represented by the great and wonderful Wizard of Oz himself (who, as we know, turns out to be "nothing but a humbug"). But *The Wizard of Oz* also offers deeply moving ethical insights on freewill, authenticity, friendship, love and generosity. While nearly

136

all of these themes are present in Augustine's corpus, and most significantly in his autobiography, *Confessions*, I will specifically focus here on the Augustinian themes of good and evil and freewill in relation to *The Wizard of Oz*, before going on to offer an account of certain broader existential themes that emerge the moment the film takes a decided existential turn.

Augustine's Encounter with the Problem of Evil and the Manichean Solution

St. Augustine, the West's first existential hero, was both protagonist and narrator in his *Confessions*, the world's first autobiography. Throughout this deeply moving text, we see Augustine struggle with great passion and courage to discover who and what he is. Augustine's existential and spiritual odyssey is fraught with agonizing pain and suffering, the necessary by-products of a human life lived honestly and authentically. Through the course of his spiritual journey Augustine tells both of his obsession with sexual gratification and schoolboy mischief and, later, of his intrigue with the unorthodox religious sect, the Manicheans, later to become one of many early Christian heresies. Under the influence of the Manicheans, Augustine is hopeful to have discovered a possible solution to the seemingly intractable problem of evil: how do we square the existence of both moral and natural evil in the world with the existence of an omniscient, benevolent, and loving God? Mani, the Third century Babylonian and founder of the Manichean movement, combined the Persian religion Zoroastrianism, with the themes of opposed light (goodness) and dark (evil), and Christianity to account for the problem of evil by claiming that Good and Evil are co-eternal principles fighting for supremacy. Two supreme powers, then, both equally eternal, uncreated, and opposed, with one representing light and goodness and the other representing evil and darkness, explained for the Manicheans the existence of evil in the world. On this view, the solution to the problem of evil is to fight against it and extinguish it so that good can prevail. Moreover, the Manicheans held that the opposition of good and evil is also resident in each one of us since we are ourselves a battleground between good and evil; the good part of us resides in the soul and is all lightness, and the bad part resides in the body or material realm and is all darkness. Hence, on this view a human being is part divine and part demonic, and the entire earth is the province of an evil power (since evil resides in matter). We are essentially souls, and as souls, we experience ourselves as dominated by matter, the body, and the world; we must confront in our earthly existence the evil that is both within us and outside of us.

Augustine became, in due time, disenchanted with this view for two principle reasons. First, he noted that the God/Good/Soul and Evil/Matter equivalences adversely affect the interpretation of Scripture: God could not be the creator of the physical world if this world is dominated by matter and, since God created the world, He could not be opposed to it. Here, Augustine abandons both the ideas of dualism and opposition in the Manichean teachings, opting instead for a Neo-Platonic interpretation of God and the soul as immaterial realities. Second, Augustine found the Manichean view too passive with respect to the agency of the will. The Manichean view held that we could be saved from the domination of evil power if we come to know who we are and learn to identify ourselves with our souls, which, as immaterial substances, are all lightness and goodness. But it did not allow for genuine human choices that could alter the outcome of our lives and bring us closer to God. Augustine, then, finally came to defend existential choice, responsibility, and authenticity in place of the dualistic Manichean view with respect to both the problem of evil and to the broader theological questions concerning spiritual enlightenment.

To sum up, then, the Manichean view attempts to solve the problem of evil by positing two co-equal, opposing powers, Good and Evil, and the practical problem of evil by the doctrine that the soul is essentially good, despite being hampered by evil in the course of its life. Of critical importance to our salvation on this view, then, is that we come to identify ourselves with our soul, a process that will allow us to experience salvation from evil.

Augustinian Themes in *The Wizard of Oz*

The Wizard of Oz offers useful pedagogical guidance with respect to teaching Augustine's first encounter with the Manichean view as a possible solution to the problem of evil, his eventual rejection of it as inadequate and counter to the teachings of Scripture, and his discovery of a more defensible reply that would involve an existential account of freewill and human agency.

Following a tornado that hits the Kansas farmland, Dorothy finds herself, as we know, deep in a dream after having been struck by an imploding window from the force of the wind. Her house, caught in the twister's eye, lands suddenly in Munchkinland and Dorothy and Toto cautiously open the door to behold their magical and colorful surroundings. Soon, a luminous, large bubble arrives, and upon dissolving, Glinda, the Good Witch of North appears who, in all her beauty and majesty, asks Dorothy if she is a good witch or a bad witch. Dorothy replies rather incredulously and somewhat offended, "Who me? I'm no witch at all; I'm Dorothy Gale from Kansas." Glinda then asks in puzzlement, pointing her wand at Toto, "Oh, well then is *that* the witch?" after which Dorothy protectively replies, "Toto? No, that's my dog."

Then, Glinda, waving her wand and pointing it at the fallen house confesses in a rather confused tone that she is a little muddled because, she announces, "Here you are, and there's your house, and that's all that's left of the Wicked Witch of the East." And so, Glinda states, "What the Munchkins want to know is are you a good witch or a bad witch?" After some clarifications about what Munchkins are, exactly, and where Dorothy and Toto are, there is great revelry and celebration because Dorothy has killed, albeit unknowingly, the Wicked Witch of the East and, consequently, relieved the Munchkins (and Glinda) of a terrible menace. The party continues with regal and official visits from the Mayor of Munchkinland, the Coroner, the Lollipop Guild, and the Lullabies, who tell Dorothy how grateful they are for her auspicious visit. But, as we know, this is all too short-lived. A black and green cloud of smoke and fire suddenly explodes and spoils the celebration. Now Dorothy, Toto, and Glinda are facing the Witch of the East's sister, the angry and terrifying Wicked Witch of the West, dressed in black, with broomstick in hand, who asks in a threatening tone, "Who killed my sister? Who killed the Witch of the East?" As we know, all the Wicked Witch of the West wants are her dead sister's magic ruby slippers, but when she tries to retrieve them, her scary, long, green fingers are electrocuted by lightening bolts, and the dead witch's striped long stockings curl up underneath the house. The Wicked Witch is aghast and proclaims, "They're gone! What have you done with them?" Glinda, pointing her wand at Dorothy's feet, triumphantly replies, "There they are, and there they'll stay," whereupon the Witch states in a menacing voice, "Give me those slippers; they're of no use to you; I'm the only one who knows how to use them. Give them to me, give them to me or I'll..." at which point Glinda announces, "Oh rubbish, you have no power here, now be gone before someone drops a house on you, too." Glinda then ominously whispers to Dorothy, "Keep tight in them; their power must be great or she wouldn't want them so badly." After warning Dorothy and her "little dog too" that they would not see the last of her, the Wicked Witch disappears as fast as she arrived in a cloud of green and black smoke (Dorothy proclaims, "My, people come and go here so quickly!") and the Munchkins, who had fled from the Witch, cautiously creep out from their hiding places. Dorothy wants more than anything to go home, but it is a long journey and she didn't bring her broomstick, so Glinda tells her that she should visit the great, powerful, and mysterious Wizard of Oz in Emerald City (whereupon the Munchkins solemnly bow) who will help her get home. In order to get there it is always best, Glinda observes, to "Just follow the yellow brick road" and, before floating away in her luminous bubble, warns Dorothy again to "Never let those slippers off your feet, or you will be at the mercy of the Wicked Witch of the West." Dorothy and Toto proceed down the yellow brick road with the Munchkins' encouragement, as they sing, "You're off to see the Wizard, the wonderful Wizard of Oz."

At this juncture, we can readily appreciate how the film suggests certain distinctive Augustinian themes. Early in the film we are confronted with the positing of the Manichean view of opposing, coequal, uncreated powers of good and evil represented by Glinda, the Good Witch of light, and by the Wicked Witch of the West, the witch of darkness and evil. Both witches, as we know, follow Dorothy and her friends to the end of the yellow brick road and on to Oz: the Wicked Witch threatens Dorothy and her friends first by animating the apple trees in the grove with mean-spirited and covetous personalities in order to frighten and threaten them, and again in the poppy field by stirring up a potion to put them to sleep, and finally in Oz itself ("Surrender Dorothy!"). The Wicked Witch's interventions culminate in ordering her menacing army of winged monkeys to fly to the haunted forest, attack Dorothy's friends, and bring Dorothy and Toto back to her unharmed ("Do what you want with the others, but I want that girl and her dog alive and unharmed...now fly, fly, fly!").

And Glinda? She is there, too, angelically offering her own luminous magic and inspiration. Although Glinda doesn't actually appear again until she floats down in her bubble of light at the very end of the film when Dorothy is ready to go home, she intervenes at just the right times to assist Dorothy and her friends, never so critically as when she makes it snow on the poppy field where they have fallen asleep under the spell of the Wicked Witch of the West; the snowfall awakens them so they can continue their journey, now so close they can see it ("Look! Emerald City — it's as beautiful and wonderful as ever!! Let's run!"). Throughout the film, then, the two witches, the two powers of good and evil, are ever present doing their respective work and, as it were, fighting it out during Dorothy's and her friends' journey.

Notably, just as Augustine ultimately rejects the Manichean view, the film will also reject it. It could be argued at this juncture that the film, in point of fact, does not reject the Manichean view since, as we know, the Wicked Witch is ultimately vanquished and killed by liquidation; however, and this is crucial, the Witch is not intentionally killed, rather, Dorothy kills her by accident while trying to put out a fire the Witch has maliciously ignited on her beloved Scarecrow. And prior to this event, Dorothy and her friends had been instructed by the Wizard to bring back the Witch's broomstick, not to kill her.

For Augustine, the Manichean view will give way to a much more defensible and coherent view that does not contradict the teachings of Scripture. This view, influenced by the Neo-Platonists, will argue that the problem of evil may be explained by our freewill and agency. That is, we may most reasonably explain evil by our freely turning away from God, light, and goodness; similar to Plato's cave allegory in *The Republic*, in ignorance and, for Augustine but not for Plato, in our free and willful refusal to turn toward God, we allow evil into the world. Here, Augustine offers a metaphysical worldview wherein he accounts for evil as the absence of good; on this view, evil has no positive, material existence; it is simply the absence of good that persons have freely chosen in turning away from God. Evil is where God is not; evil is where Love is absent. Hence, through the defense of freewill, Augustine is able to abandon the Manichean view and adopt the much more plausible view that evil exists, not as an independent material reality, but as the absence of good.

What is the parallel narrative in *The Wizard of Oz*? Even though the good and bad witches intervene throughout the film as the plot advances, they become less and less important as the character development of Dorothy and her friends becomes more important. Rather than the Manichean opposition of good and evil dominating the film throughout, what unfolds is the cultivation among four characters of genuine friendship, love, and generosity. As we know, the friends Dorothy meets along her journey are all in search of a quality they perceive to be missing in their sense of themselves: the Scarecrow laments that he lacks a brain, the Tin Man a heart, and the Cowardly Lion courage. And Dorothy, of course, only wants to go home. What all characters have in common is that they are engaged in a search for something they perceive is missing, and, as the film advances, they learn that they need each other in fundamental ways in order to live genuinely authentic lives. Here, the lesson is that a certain vulnerability or fragility is required in the face of the other in order for us to become authentic and to be able to authentically love another person. But of course, the relational dynamic also requires that the other be vulnerable, too. And the way in which we handle the other's vulnerability — and they ours — will decide whether truly authentic relations are possible or not.

Along Dorothy's journey to Oz, each character she encounters is invited to join her to see if the Wizard can help them, too. But Dorothy ominously warns her friends that she has a mean, Wicked Witch in pursuit of her and that she wouldn't want them to be endangered. Each friend in turn (even the lion!) dismisses the threat of the Witch as a trivial distraction and promises Dorothy that *they* will see to it that she reaches Oz safely. As the film advances, we witness the genuine, caring, and compassionate friendship that develops between Dorothy and her friends. Each friend sings his own story of how he ended up the way he did when Dorothy found him, and each one listens attentively as Dorothy explains her own situation and the purpose of her journey down the yellow brick road. And they each vow, in heartfelt generosity, to help each other.

The Existential Turn

As the film proceeds we see Dorothy and her friends manifesting the very qualities they claim to lack. Here is where *The Wizard of Oz* takes a decided existential turn. Each character, in his or her way, expresses the very quality they perceive to be lacking in themselves in committed action, and, in some cases, more than once: the Scarecrow, for example, far from lacking a brain, shows great cunning and keen thinking in the Witch's castle when he takes the Tin Man's hatchet to sever a rope that suspends a chandelier that will fall on the Witch's henchmen, allowing Dorothy and her friends to escape, at least for the moment. The Tin Man shows deep sentiment and compassion when he thinks of Dorothy locked up in the Witch's castle, pleading, "We have got to get her out of there!" We know that there is the constant worry that he will rust again if he cries. And the Cowardly Lion, the most amusing character among them, is the first to emerge from a scuffle with the Witch's guards, in full regalia with his wiry tail exposed, having beaten the guards back and disguised himself in one of their uniforms. He also shows, despite second thoughts, uncommon valor when he pledges to rescue Dorothy as they advance toward the Witch's haunted castle: "Wicked Witch or no Wicked Witch, guards or no guards, I'm going in there for Dorothy ... grrrrrrufff ... grrrrrufff." Even jumping out of the window after the Wizard's thunderous voice instructed him and his friends "Now go. I said Go!!" is courageous because, as the Wizard observes at the end of the film when he bestows on him a badge of courage, the Lion has confused a lack of courage with wisdom: true courage, as Aristotle has also noted, is knowing when to flee and when to fight.

We can also appreciate the existentialist theme of the negative playing out in the character development of *The Wizard of Oz*, as emphasized in the work of both Jean-Paul Sartre and Simone de Beauvoir. Given Sartre's and Beauvoir's phenomenological description of the kind of beings we are, namely beings who are situated in the world among others, and beings who must act; the way the world goes depends fundamentally upon us. The existential and phenomenological description of Dorothy and her friends allows us to readily appreciate that, far from offering a deterministic account of a proper or missing "nature" in the film's characters, the film begins with negativity — with what the characters are *not*—and infers from this, what they may *become*: no one learns this more than Dorothy who, at the end of the film, discovers that she could not run away from her problems, but had to face them (problems going back to her farm in Kansas where the nasty Ms. Gulch arrives with a sheriff's order to take Toto away because he ran into her garden). When asked by the Tin Man what she has learned, Dorothy replies, "Well, it wasn't enough to want to see Uncle Henry and Auntie Em, and if I ever go searching for my heart's desire, I won't look any further than my own backyard, because if it isn't there, I never really lost it to begin with." And with this recognition, three clicks of her ruby slippers, and a little help from Glinda, Dorothy is able to go home. And, as Glinda tells her friends, Dorothy had to figure this lesson out for herself; they could not have helped her figure it out with the qualities they now have also learned they had all along. We are alone in the world with regard to choosing and acting, and we are without excuse, Sartre famously states; but, importantly and equally brought out in the film, we need each other in order to live genuinely.

Hence, Dorothy's authentic self, revealed to her in a dream is prophetic of who she has become, of who she has learned she is. The love, friendship, generosity, and vulnerability that was shared between Dorothy and her friends during their long, arduous journey to Oz was fraught with danger and uncertainty, and each of them needed the other in order to get through it and discover who they are; each friend's need became the other's and each friend's hope and longing was fought for by the other. "There's no place like home" because "home" is the Other, if the Other is authentic in their love, guidance, compassion, and generosity.

Each friend, then, and Dorothy too, manifests the Sartrean existential maxim, "Existence precedes Essence"—that we exist first and later define ourselves, or our essence. None of the characters possess an antecedent essence that will determine them once and for all; rather, each shows that they are nothing *other* than the sum total of their actions, and that they exist first in a world (albeit in a dream world) in relation to others and define themselves throughout their journey only by their actions. Of equal importance and also deeply existential, is the idea that we define or create our essence, in Sartre's famous formula, by not being what we are and by being what we are not. Thus, the Scarecrow shows that he indeed has a brain only by actively engaging and using it in situations that calls for cunning and ingenuity. And not only in these circumstances does the Scarecrow manifest intelligence; it is he who warns the Tin Man both in the poppy field and the haunted forest not to cry because he will rust, and they will lose time. The idea here is that it is not the mere possession of a brain that is relevant to thinking, but what we do with our ability to think and how we actively engage our thinking in the world and in relation to others. This observation is interesting particularly in light of recent philosophical work being done in cognitive science and neurobiology; for example, the view of eliminative materialism, advocated by Paul Churchland, argues that mental states are reducible to brain states and human behavior may be exhaustively explained by the findings of neurobiology. But, as *The Wizard of Oz* shows, the Scarecrow may be no more strictly identified with his brain states or lack of brain states than the Tin Man and Cowardly Lion may be identified with the presence or absence of a heart or courage, respectively. It is not in virtue of having or possessing a certain organ, attribute, or quality that makes us who we are. The Scarecrow humorously drives this home when he declares to Dorothy after she asks how he can talk if he doesn't have a brain: "I don't know. But some people without brains do an awful lot of talking, don't they?" *The Wizard of Oz*, then, underscores the existential teaching that we become who we are through our actions; it is only in acting that I am truly myself. Thus, each character, by the film's end, learns the important existential lesson that it is only in virtue of *not* antecedently possessing wisdom, compassion, and courage that he may truly act wisely, compassionately, and courageously. Hence, in the effort to become, there is a perpetual playing of the negative; the characters are first at a distance from themselves (as Beauvoir would say) and may only coincide with themselves by agreeing never to regain themselves. This is the sense in which moral action is also creative action and that ethics becomes meaningful only if there is a problem to solve — only if we are at first at a distance from ourselves. The ethical problem in *The Wizard of Oz* and, indeed, in our own world, is how ethics is possible in an unjust world and how we may exercise generosity and authenticity toward one another in a world of danger and uncertainty.

Authenticity and Generosity

Of equal significance we, as viewers, learn through the characters in *The Wizard of Oz* the existential meaning of generosity. Each of the characters discover who they are in relation to the others and because of the others, and each freely takes up the freedom of the other and, in solidarity, generously helps them in their existential self–discovery.

In *Notebook for an Ethics*,[1] a work that was published posthumously (1983) and is less well known among scholars and students, Sartre offers a sustained account of authentic relations between persons, over against the conflict and opposition that permeated his early philosophy, fiction, and plays. The general tenor of *Notebooks* is to move away from the notion of conflict as essential to human relations, and to show how, through generosity, we may overcome conflict and opposition that is initiated by "the look" (le regard) in *Being and Nothingness*.

Following a conversion to authenticity wherein freedom is accepted as the highest value in oneself and others, Sartre argues that we will extend ourselves in such a way that we reach the other's project or goal; we will, he says, "unveil" others in all of their finitude and vulnerability. To adopt the Other's project as a part of my own and to help the Other express her freedom is for

Sartre to affirm our genuine humanity. Hence, one adopts a way of being that is consistent with, and faithful to, the human condition in its finitude, contingency, ignorance and vulnerability. Of course, one may also choose to be inauthentic; the inauthentic choice is a choice that Sartre does — and must — allow for, given his claim that we are ontologically free.

Since, for Sartre, we always live in a "peopled world," we make choices in relationship to others. Hence, he says, "The being of the Other is *my affair*.[2] In *Notebooks* he attempts to deepen the "we-relation" that is established by cooperation and generosity. One of the ways in which we may forge the conditions for cooperation, he thinks, is by unveiling and valorizing our own freedom as situated and responsible projects that participate in what he refers to as the adventure and unveiling of the other's existence. In unveiling the Other, I make the Other exist and thematize her contingency while perpetually surpassing it: I enrich the Other and the world and give meaning to the Other's existence. In authenticity, I thematize, or bring into view, the Other's fragility and vulnerability and choose to unveil her in all her finitude. But how do we do this? To unconditionally accept the Other in all of her fragility and vulnerability is for Sartre to reveal her project and to love her authentically. To authentically reveal the Other is to take a genuine interest in, and to invest oneself in, the Other's project.

In authenticity, then, our acceptance of freedom as a fundamental value constitutes an ethical unity brought about by a contractual agreement with oneself. This contractual agreement refers, in Beauvoir's language, to "agree," to lose oneself in order to find oneself and to make oneself a "lack of being in order that there might be being."[3] Similarly, Beauvoir states, "To attain his truth, man must not attempt to dispel the ambiguity of his being, but on the contrary, accept the task of realizing it. He rejoins himself only to the extent that he agrees to remain at a distance from himself."[4] It is in authenticity, wherein we valorize our freedom and the freedom of others, Sartre notes, that we attain "solidarity with others."[5] It is in this sense that, for both Beauvoir and Sartre, ethics may be understood as "the triumph of freedom over facticity."[6]

The relationship between Dorothy and her friends dramatically express the existential account authenticity and generosity. Each character is genuinely concerned about the Other's well being and flourishing. Each character's own personal quest becomes a universal quest, and the universal project reflects back on the aims and goals of each character. Dorothy's friends desperately want to join her in her journey to see if the Wizard will help them, too, but they have an even stronger desire to help Dorothy reach the Wizard safely. At the end of the film, Dorothy calmly stands by as each of her friends triumphantly receives a university diploma, symbolic heart, and badge of courage, respectively, from the Wizard, and she is genuinely happy for them when they discover what they always had, not thinking of herself, except to note "Oh, I don't think there's anything in that little black bag for me," after which her friends demand that the Wizard attend to her need next. Each character, then, joins the Other in solidarity and each remains at a distance from himself or herself in freely acting to advance the freedom of the Other, transcending the facticity of the Wicked Witch, the danger of the haunted forest, the trickery and deception of the Wizard, and their own limitations. *The Wizard of Oz* forcefully reminds us, then, of something that is all too easily forgotten, namely, that we need each other in order to genuinely and fully exist. That is, we need each other in order to help each other decide who we are and how, in our vulnerability and fragility, we may come to authentically and generously love each other.

Notes

1. Jean-Paul Sartre, *Notebooks for an Ethics*, trans. David Pellauer (Chicago: University of Chicago Press, 1992).
2. Ibid., 506.
3. Simon de Beauvoir, *The Ethics of Ambiguity*, trans. Bernard Frechtman (New York: Carol Publishing, 1991), 12.
4. Ibid., 13.
5. Sartre, *Notebooks*, 479.
6. de Beauvoir, *The Ethics of Ambiguity*, 44.

Works Cited

de Beauvoir, Simone. *The Ethics of Ambiguity*. Trans. Bernard Frechtman. New York: Carol Publishing, 1991.
Sartre, Jean-Paul. *Notebooks for an Ethics*. Trans. David Pellauer. Chicago, IL: University of Chicago Press, 1992.

CHAPTER 10

The "Wonderful" Wizard of Oz and Other Lies

A Study of Inauthenticity in Wicked: A New Musical

Mary K. Leigh

A contemporary study of the world of *The Wizard of Oz* reveals many alternate readings of the text itself as well as many alternate versions of the story. Gregory Maguire's *Wicked* is an interesting study in perspective — what makes one wicked really? Is it possible for such designations to simply be a matter of perspective? The answer is rather simple; yes, perspective does indeed matter. Stephen Schwartz's *Wicked: A New Musical* agrees, although the musical form differs significantly from its literary counterpart. Schwartz's *Wicked* addresses many complex issues regarding the nature of good and evil as well as questions of perspective. This essay, however, deals with an aspect of human development that is a necessary part of living a full human life — authenticity.

Before we begin a discussion of the musical, it is important that we define what exactly is meant by authenticity. The concept of living authentically is an issue of primary concern to Existential philosopher Jean-Paul Sartre. In his work *Being and Nothingness*, Sartre addresses inauthenticity by what is known as the project of bad faith. Inauthenticity is bad faith because it involves self-deceit and inadequate representations of what one is. Authenticity is necessarily its opposite. To be authentic is to come to a complete understanding of one's own nature and embrace a full and accurate representation of everything that one is.

Wicked: A New Musical introduces its audience to many characters; each of which has varying levels of engagement with the world around them. Frex and Melena, relatively minor characters in the overall development of the musical, interact with the world to some degree. Galinda and Fiyero, two of the show's major characters, do not seem to interact in any way that is not to their own liking. And then there is the malicious type of people; the Wizard and Madame Morrible engage with the world insofar as they can manipulate those around them to their own benefit, regardless of causing harm to the individuals. What do all of these characters have in common? They are forced to become authentic individuals, ones who actively participate in the reality of the world in which they live, because of their respective relationships with Elphaba, better known as the Wicked Witch of the West. In these relationships, each character is able to come to the realization that the life that he or she is living is inauthentic and changes his or her view of the world. Whether that experience is pleasurable or painful for them, Elphaba is an authentic person in that she recognizes the world around her for what it is, and she is unable to tolerate the dual natures of so many in Oz. Thus, Elphaba, either by her own actions or simply by her nature, both gently and forcefully encourages those she comes in contact with to shed the skin of inauthenticity and embrace their true selves.

Elphaba's parents, Frex and Melena, are the first to experience the awakening from an inauthentic life on the occasion of the birth of their child. Frex and Melena's marriage is inauthentic from its first introduction to the audience. Frex, the governor of Munchkinland, is leaving his wife Melena to go on a trip, an event that causes him pain as he does not want to leave her. Melena, on the other hand, does not seem to mind at all that he is going. Neither of the pair willingly recognizes the opposite nature of their feelings for each other. Frex and Melena simply live their inauthentic charade as the song "No One Mourns the Wicked" demonstrates. Frex pines, seemingly quite serious that he does not want to leave her. Melena, in a dismissive tone, points out that it is just for only the one night, after all. Attempting to reassure her, Frex sings that even though he is gone, she will always be in his heart. Melena politely turns her head when he attempts to kiss her, a sign of the inauthenticity of their relationship which he ignores. Frex's presence is soon replaced by that of Melena's lover. He is a rather odd man, dressed all in green and offering Melena green elixir. All of these events create the atmosphere into which Elphaba is born. As Glinda describes Elphaba, from her birth, she was, "well, different." Frex anticipates the birth of the child, anxiously assisting the midwife in the delivery until Elphaba's peculiarity is revealed. With a scream, the midwives and Frex indicate that something, in their view, has gone badly wrong. Melena, unable to see the child, is panicked by their shouts and wants to know what's wrong. After many expressions of disgust, they tell Melena that the baby is "unnaturally green." Through

Elphaba's strange appearance and Melena's horrified yet somewhat knowing response, Frex is forced to become a more authentic individual, and the relationship between Frex and Melena reaches its authentic conclusion. Melena is last seen being rushed off-stage; Elphaba later relays to the audience the information of her mother's death during the birth of Nessarose. Melena's memory or his unwitting complicity in her death holds no sway over Frex. It seems that inauthenticity has shattered his ability to engage charitably and fairly with the world around him. While Elphaba could not be said to be the active cause in bringing about authenticity in this relationship, it is her very nature of being "unnaturally green" that makes her the catalyst of this change.

Her parents are not the only ones that Elphaba affects simply by being. She affects every student at Shiz University, particularly Glinda, or Galinda as she is known then, and Fiyero. The fact that Galinda's name is changed is given two explanations in the course of the tale. The intriguing facet of this change is that Galinda becomes Glinda only after she begins down the path of becoming a truly authentic individual. Hers is a slower transition, marked by an almost coming of age experience and an introduction into what it means to be powerless in the presence of a powerful lie.

Galinda, as we know her in her school days, is an arrogant girl, accustomed to the world approving of her and giving in to her every whim. Her initial reaction to Elphaba is a combination of jealousy, fueled by Madame Morrible's interest in Elphaba's talent, and disgust for someone who is so outside of the "normal" realm yet still refuses to see her, Galinda, as worthy of deference. Their reaction to each other is intense. The duet "What Is This Feeling?" describes the definite polarity of the pair's early relationship. Every feature of their characters, even the tiny ones, evince loathing on the part of the other. So powerful is the revulsion they feel, that they also feel curiously energized. The two girls are complete opposites in their outlook on the world. Elphaba, a more authentic individual because of society's treatment of her, cannot comprehend Galinda's rather vapid and self-centered view. As such, neither feels any desire to interact with each other or to change how they experience life.

The relationship develops into a more positive one, however, when Galinda and Elphaba move away from their respective world views at the Ozdust Ballroom. Galinda gives Elphaba a particularly ugly hat, encouraging her to wear it in the hope that she will acquiesce and thus give Galinda the opportunity to make Elphaba look foolish. For her part, Elphaba is somewhat grateful to Galinda for finding a date for Nessarose and making her sister extremely happy. Searching for some form of acceptance, she does indeed wear the ugly hat to the event. Further, Elphaba attempts to appeal to Galinda's authentic self by asking Madame Morrible to take on Galinda as a student, an act that Elphaba knows will help fulfill one of Galinda's dreams. When Elphaba appears in the hat and is mocked by the crowd, Galinda experiences remorse, a rather new feeling and an important one for the development of an authentic self. Fiyero blithely remarks that Elphaba must not care what others think of her, noting how Elphaba is attempting to ignore the crowd's jeers. Galinda recognizes the error in this; she tells Fiyero that Elphaba keenly feels these insults. She just refuses to show it. Galinda sees in this moment what her inauthenticity has done; she purposefully hurt a girl who not only had not caused her harm but had gone about trying to help her. Quickly, she reconciles Elphaba with the crowd of students. Galinda is certainly not yet an authentic individual, but she has, although perhaps not quite intentionally, moved toward a more reality-based concept of the world and of herself.

As if to underscore the fact that Galinda still has quite a distance to travel before she can be truly authentic, she and Elphaba next collaborate during a song entitled "Popular." The Galinda that just demonstrated that she can be caring and somewhat engaged regales Elphaba with her plan to make "Elphie" into a popular and socially accepted young woman, just as Galinda sees herself. She does not value the person that Elphaba actually is, offering a scathing criticism of her new friend and attempting to soften the critique by calling her comments a form of "personality dialysis." Elphaba calmly accepts the rather negative view as she recognizes that engagement in life is sometimes uncomfortable but necessary. This scene, with all of its over-the-top commentaries on the necessity of being popular, is actually an important component of both Elphaba's and Galinda's development. Elphaba allows Galinda the opportunity to mold her character and behavior, and Galinda experiences for the first time a level of responsibility to an individual outside of herself.

The young women soon find, however, that their moments of gradual relationship development are over when Elphaba leaves Shiz to meet the Wizard of Oz. Galinda, now Glinda as a result of an attempt to impress Fiyero, agrees to accompany her friend to the Emerald City, where inauthenticity is far more common than an authentic life. In fact, the girls' meeting with the Wizard begins and ends with his inauthenticity. He first frightens the pair with the Oz Mask, but relents. He explains that he rarely allows people to see anything other than the mask, but the girls' arrival is something special for which to make exceptions. Soon thereafter, he tricks Elphaba into using a spell to create spies for his mission of repression. Before she can recover from the duplicity of the Wizard's actions, he places her in a moral dilemma; she may have all of the things she has wanted, but she must not reveal the Wizard for what he is, and she must aid him in his plans. In essence, Elphaba may have all of the things that she has longed for, but she must live inauthentically. She does not hesitate in her decision-making; Elphaba refuses, the result of which is the creation of the Wicked Witch image. Madame Morrible, the Wizard's new Press Secretary, declares Elphaba's evil nature to all of Oz, citing her green skin as a visible sign of her perverted soul and claiming that Elphaba is solely responsible for mutilating the monkeys who now have wings at the Wizard's behest. Elphaba confirms her authenticity, yet it is a painful experience for her. She is now an outcast among those who do not mind inauthenticity particularly when it benefits them in some way.

Where Elphaba is able to refuse the Wizard and Morrible because of her strong, authentic self, Glinda struggles to choose between inauthenticity and the authentic life. Her authentic nature has just begun to develop under Elphaba's care, and she is now frightened and keenly feels her perceived powerlessness in this situation. As such, she is unable to leave the Emerald City with her friend. She does not contradict the Wizard or Madame Morrible and becomes a figurehead of their manipulations; however, because of Elphaba's friendship and courage, Glinda is no longer naïve and completely inauthentic. She questions the life she has chosen, attempting to develop some authenticity even in her teacher's absence.

Glinda is revealed at the beginning of Act II as being declared "Glinda the Good" by the Wizard, standing as the opposite of her friend, Elphaba, the supposed Wicked Witch of the West. Glinda attempts to be happy with her position; after all, the people of Oz love her, and just as before, almost all of her wishes are allowed. However, Glinda is unable to look past what has happened to bring her to this point. In the opening song of the second act, Glinda details her new view of the world, one that is characterized by a confusion of how to deal with being afraid to change and yet realizing that it is necessary. As she sings of her happiness — that she couldn't be happier — she notes that the happiness has a tinge; it isn't the feeling she anticipated it being. Further, rather than simply recognizing the complex nature of the authentic world, Glinda attempts to understand why she feels as she does and how to go about creating a change. Still singing that she couldn't be happier, she recognizes that one doesn't always get what one wishes for in the way one wishes it, and that the gift of "happiness" is not the naïve sort that her earlier self wished. Indeed, though she has gotten, in a sense, what she dreamed, it's, well, somewhat "complicated," after all. Glinda's first burst of true authenticity is revealed in the culmination of this questioning; she recognizes that she did not understand the consequences of some of her decisions until she was left with the binding results. Glinda's self is a fledgling but authentic one at this point, leaving her and her audience to wonder if happiness is really what one gets even if all of one's dreams are fulfilled.

The authentic self that Glinda has developed thus far is still fragile, and she depends on others for her confirmation of self. An anticipated argument against Glinda's being authentic is her advising the Wizard and Morrible in making Elphaba show herself after Fiyero, Glinda's fiancé, has run away with Elphaba. However, these actions are not taken in an inauthentic gesture to be what the Wizard and Morrible wish her to be; Glinda attempts to hurt Elphaba, and by extension, Fiyero, for causing her great emotional strife. Just as Aristotle points out that great tragedy can affect any person on the path to virtue, so too does great emotional turmoil affect the authenticity of self. Glinda wants revenge, not the approval of anyone; thus, while she chooses to do the wrong thing, she chooses to do it authentically. Glinda is no longer the puppet of the Wizard and Morrible; she is living her life and making her own choices. Authenticity in this sense is a matter of being self-directed. While Glinda's actions are consistent with the malicious pair's desires, her motivations are purely her own.

Glinda's vengeful feelings toward Elphaba and Fiyero subside with the passage of time and from the realization that betrayal cannot happen when there is nothing to betray. Glinda's inauthentic self allowed her to believe that Fiyero loved her, despite almost overwhelming evidence that he did not. In this she is an exact parallel to Nessarose, who believes Boq must love her despite all the evidence, and his claims, that he does not. Unlike Glinda, however, Nessarose never abandons inauthenticity, and Boq is irreparably altered as a result. With authenticity comes an acceptance of reality, which Glinda notes when Fiyero threatens her life to save Elphaba's. She tells the guards that Fiyero was not determined to harm her; he simply loves Elphaba. Once again, Elphaba has proven to be the catalyst for change. Glinda realizes, perhaps for the first time, that the life she had created to this point bears little resemblance to the truth of the world.

The two friends are ultimately reconciled in Glinda's attempt to save Elphaba from the Witch Hunters. Despite the risk that the move poses to Glinda's position as "Glinda the Good," she acts authentically, and in this instance, she acts from benevolence and love. She chooses to put in danger her comfortable, yet inauthentic, image to save her friend. However, Elphaba refuses the offer, knowing that Glinda will be necessary to guide Oz in the correct path after Elphaba is gone. It is in this moment of mutual respect that the pair straightforwardly acknowledges the impact they have had on one another. Elphaba claims, rightly, that Glinda is the only friend she has ever had. Glinda, still harkening back to her inauthentically "popular" past, responds that while she has had "friends" aplenty, Elphaba is the only friend who really mattered or made a difference in her life. Elphaba finds fulfillment in her relationship with Glinda, and in turn, Glinda finds in Elphaba a person who led her from the shadows of inauthenticity to the bright, full day of an authentic and engaged life. Glinda herself describes this process in the penultimate song of the musical, "For Good." She sings of the old notion that everything happens for a reason, some sort of teleological cause that shapes character. She concludes that Elphaba has changed her life, and while she is not sure it has been a change for the better, she nevertheless believes that it has. More than that belief, though, whether she has been changed for the better (where "better" can mean a plethora of things, material and transient or spiritual and eternal), she knows that she has been changed for good. "Good," here, does not carry the ambiguity of "better." "Good" has to do with the moral state, the authentic state that Glinda now has. She is now Glinda, the Good, and not Glinda, the "Good" of the propaganda of the Wizard and Madame Morrible.

Elphaba's ability to lead others to authenticity is not limited to those who are unwittingly inauthentic. Fiyero, the third major player in the show's cast, has a different rationale from Glinda; he understands the nature of authenticity, the pain that one may experience for example, and deliberately chooses to be inauthentic. Elphaba's presence in Fiyero's life must accomplish an appreciably more difficult task — she must convince him to embrace that which he has already rejected.

Fiyero arrives at Shiz University with a determination to live inauthentically. He states his view quite clearly in "Dancing through Life," a song that reveals much about his choices and his reasoning. He invites his fellow students to stop worrying about the difficult decisions to be made in the world and live an "unexamined life." Further, he entices his captivated audience by noting that it is difficult to look foolish if one never tries. In his assertions here, combined with his many affirmations that this type of life is painless, we are able to develop a better understanding of Fiyero's decision to live this unexamined life. By not truly engaging with the world, one cannot be hurt. Superficial interaction can only allow superficial wounds. It can certainly be inferred that the only way that Fiyero would understand the pain of life that he warns others of is to have experienced it himself. As we have noted previously, great pain can profoundly affect an individual, and Fiyero certainly seems to have experienced something in his past that has caused him to feign this persona of shallowness. His later relationship with Elphaba further elaborates his disguised ability to keenly feel and engage. The song finishes by gently reminding both him and us that our lives can still be changed, even while we're "dancing through."

It does not take long for Fiyero to cross paths with Elphaba; as he somewhat humorously asks her, "Why is it every time I see you, you are causing a commotion?" Her response demonstrates what we would guess of a girl with a powerful gift for magic and an unfortunate hue of green — "I don't cause commotions. I am one." Despite the fact that Fiyero has cultivated his inauthentic outlook for some time now, he proves to be somewhat unable to carry off this inauthenticity in Elphaba's presence. When she appears in class fresh from Galinda's makeover, Fiyero slips in his inauthentic façade. He watches her flip her hair in imitation of her mentor in social acceptability and ultimately offers his opinion that she doesn't really need to act that way. If Fiyero were truly inauthentic, why would he care to interfere with the development of Elphaba's life, especially when she is attempting the very inauthentic world view that he claims is the answer to all of life's troubles? Even more telling, Fiyero describes Elphaba as "Galinda-fied," which is obviously negative in this context. Galinda is the girl that Fiyero has just described as perfect and as one with whom he could forever "dance through life." By using her personality as a negative adjective for Elphaba, Fiyero reveals something rather interesting about himself. Perhaps he does not truly believe in the benefits of inauthenticity; after all, he just engaged with the world in trying to make Elphaba see that she should be her own person, or, in other words, authentic.

This classroom encounter goes much further than a moment of engagement, however. The pain and confusion of the authentic world is thrust in front of all of the students as Dr. Dillamond is forcibly removed from his teaching post and a new breed of caged, non-speaking animals is introduced. Elphaba recognizes that these actions are wrong and unjust and turns to the one person in the classroom that she suspects is not too self-involved to help her, Fiyero. Of his own accord, Fiyero grabs the caged animal and runs from the room, again demonstrating a level of authentic engagement with the world. Elphaba rushes along with him, cautioning him that they must find a safe place to release the animal. Fiyero's response gives Elphaba the chance for which she has been waiting; he lashes out, yelling that she must think he's stupid. Elphaba's reply reflects what we have already come to suspect, "No, not really stupid."

Fiyero pauses but quickly continues on; however, Elphaba is unwilling to let this moment of authenticity go unacknowledged. She points out that Fiyero could have been like the others; he did not have to try to help. She begins by suggesting that Fiyero may not be truly self-absorbed and shallow. Fiyero, a bit unnerved by Elphaba's rather quick deciphering of his attempt at self-deception, argues that he is not pretending; he is "genuinely self-absorbed." True to her own authentic nature, Elphaba's view is decisive — he cannot be those things or he wouldn't be "so unhappy." Fiyero's silence confirms Elphaba's words. He may have been unhappy with his previous experience of authenticity, but his current defense of inauthenticity brings him no fulfillment either. Stunned and contemplative, Fiyero rushes off.

Dissatisfaction with inauthenticity comes to Fiyero in a rush. Galinda describes his new behavior to Elphaba; he is "distant," and "he's been thinking." Thinking and caring are the hallmarks of authentic and engaged lives. In fact, Fiyero himself demonstrates to Elphaba that he is preoccupied with his self-development, admitting to her that he often thinks of the day they rescued the lion cub and "everything." While it is obvious that he is not yet ready to be fully authentic, he is certainly unable to continue on blithely unaware.

Where Glinda needed Elphaba's presence to confirm her attempts at authenticity, Fiyero is able to take inspiration from Elphaba's example of an authentic life. As the people of Oz extol Elphaba's status as the Wicked Witch of the West, he storms off, not willing to be inauthentic and pretend to believe all that they are saying. He fumes that he cannot stand before them "pretending to go along with this." Inauthenticity, at least on this issue, is something that Fiyero can no longer abide; thus, he is moving closer to authenticity with every decision.

However, there is one area in which Fiyero still cannot force authenticity—he cannot be fully authentic when it will cause another person pain. Glinda announces her engagement to Fiyero, a decision apparently made by the Wizard without Fiyero's input. Realizing that Glinda would be extraordinarily happy if he married her, he agrees, telling Glinda that if it will make her happy, of course he'll marry her. When she questions if he will be happy as well, Fiyero again falls back on inauthenticity: "I'm always happy." For the sake of Glinda's feelings, Fiyero forgoes authentic choices, but there is little doubt that this attempt will be feeble and half-hearted.

Fiyero's inauthenticity crumbles for good, however, when he is reunited with Elphaba. As all of his previous actions have demonstrated, he has found it difficult to convince her of his well-developed charade even when he was quite convinced of it himself. Now that he no longer believes it, he cannot hope to sustain the image in her powerful, authentic presence. He goes through the motions of capturing Elphaba only insofar as it is necessary to remove the other guards from the room. He confirms his own authenticity in three simple words: "I have changed." He leaves with Elphaba, taking his first fully authentic action. Despite the fact that this decision will cause Glinda pain and that he will no longer have the approval of the Wizard and all of Oz, he leaves anyway. He admits his love for Elphaba, and the pair begins to explore the only truly authentic love relationship in the musical. Fiyero proclaims the positive nature of the change from inauthentic to authentic living and the fulfillment it brings in "As Long as You're Mine." Fiyero sings that because of Elphaba and her love—the spell he's under—he has "fallen upward," or gained a more authentic view of both himself and his life. He, too, has been changed for good. He obviously sees his first truly authentic decision as an improvement upon his inauthentic life. Not only has he fallen in love, he has found what it is to be truly himself. He invites Elphaba to be who she truly is and enjoy the fulfillment they find in each other. Fiyero and Elphaba finally find the happiness both have been searching for in the mutual respect and unconditional love that is made possible by living authentically, even in the inauthentic Land of Oz.

To this point, we have taken for granted that Oz is an inauthentic place. Yet, we must ask ourselves, what kind of person could create a society so dedicated to spectacle that it is unconcerned with ideas of objective truth? The answer is found in the person of the Wonderful Wizard of Oz.

The Wizard's inauthenticity has been sketched previously in his first meeting with Elphaba and Glinda. He tells the girls then exactly what he is, though they only come to understand it fully toward the end of his reign. In reference to his frightening persona, he relates, "People expect this sort of thing. You have to give people what they want." First, it is unlikely that anyone would truly desire their leader to be inaccessible. Nevertheless, the interesting facet of this revelation is that he gives primacy to giving people what they want, or what he thinks they should want. His betrayal of Elphaba's trust further demonstrates this tendency; he manipulates people in order to maximize their usefulness to him. As his associate, Madame Morrible, attempts to quell Elphaba's horror, "Well, you benefit too, dearie. You benefit, too."

The Wizard's inauthenticity takes a track that is entirely different from the purposefully ignorant Frex and Melina and the benign misguided attitudes of Glinda and Fiyero. The Wizard argues that there is no objective truth; thus, authenticity is not an issue. In "Wonderful," he outlines his philosophy in the creation of Oz. Like the Prince of Machiavelli, it isn't reality that's important, it's the label that is attached to one. Thus, whether traitor or liberator, one is remembered, not for what one has done, but for the label that forms the lens through which ones actions are seen by others. He supposes that he can do as he wishes, so long as the labels are positive, and they are positive because of the spin he puts on them. Elphaba bluntly confronts this line of inauthentic thinking: "So, you lied to them?" Unmoved, the Wizard replies, "Only verbally; besides, they were the lies they wanted to hear." Sensing that Elphaba is casting a moral judgment, the Wizard attempts to manipulate her as he has manipulated all of Oz. He soothes her by pointing out that few people are comfortable with "moral ambiguities," so they simply pretend not to see them. In point of fact, the Wizard is excusing his own inauthenticity by offering a persuasive argument to Elphaba to stop fighting for an authenticity that perhaps does not exist. Ultimately, the Wizard's effort fails, but Elphaba is not successful in convincing the Wizard that authenticity is necessary either. At this juncture it becomes clear that it is far more productive to save the members of Oz from the harm of further inauthenticity than it is to try to change the maliciously unchangeable.

In an act of beautiful symmetry it is not Elphaba but Glinda, the Wizard's former puppet, that removes the Wizard and Morrible from power. Elphaba's supposed death shocks the Wizard; the revelation that he was her biological father weakens him. However, it is Glinda's authenticity learned from Elphaba that allows her to finally excise the cancerous effects of the Wizard's inauthenticity. She declares, "I want you to leave Oz. I'll make the pronouncement myself— the strains of wizardship have been too much for you, and you are taking an indefinite leave of absence! Did you hear what I said?!" When confronted by such powerful authenticity and the realization that his inauthenticity will not sustain him through this kind of attack, the Wizard gives up. "Yes, your goodness," he replies as he slinks off the stage escorted by his former guards. Morrible soon follows, and thus ends the Wizard's rule of inauthentic happiness and "wonderful" magic. Glinda steps into the role of leading her fellow Ozians, a task she can now be expected to execute wisely.

Stephen Schwartz's *Wicked* offers us an intriguing view of not only a beloved literary classic, but also the important philosophical and innately human ideal of authenticity. Elphaba serves as the musical's catalyst for authenticity, unwilling to let inauthenticity replace a full and rich representation of one's own identity. Despite the hardships that Elphaba faces, she never relents in her pursuit of bringing authenticity to the people of Oz. Ultimately, Elphaba accomplishes her goal; Oz is left in the capable hands of Glinda, a fully authentic and truly benevolent leader, while she and Fiyero are free to live out their authentic, loving relationship far from the insidious lies of the former Wizard of Oz.

CHAPTER 11

Memories Cloaked in Magic

Memory and Identity in Tin Man

ANNE COLLINS SMITH

Introduction

In *Replications: A Robotic History of the Science Fiction Film*, J. P. Telotte argues that "through its long history, one that dates back to the very origins of film, this genre (science fiction) has focused its attention on the problematic nature of human being and the difficult task of being human" (1–2). The thesis of the book, he states, is "relatively simple — that the image of human artifice ... is the single most important one in the genre. [...] Through this image of artifice, our films have sought to reframe the human image and reaffirm that sense of self about which we ... appear so anxious today" (5).

Substitute "magical" for "technological" — or at least, substitute a magically-infused steampunk form of technology — and Telotte's thesis applies as well to the SciFi channel's miniseries *Tin Man* as to any other science fiction work. In particular, *Tin Man* offers a varied and subtle exploration of the sense of self in terms of the issue of the relationship between memory and identity by offering us not one but three characters who must regain and acknowledge ownership of their memories in order to restore their true identities, restorations which are important not only to the characters on a personal level, but which are critical in the resolution of the plot.

Locke

The gold standard for beginning a discussion on self-identity in the modern age of Western intellectual history is the philosophy of John Locke. Best known in the United States for his *Second Treatise on Government,* which provided the philosophical underpinnings of the American Revolution, Locke also propounded a highly influential view on self-identity:

> Since consciousness always accompanies thinking, and it is that which makes every one to be what he calls self, and thereby distinguishes himself from all other thinking things, in this alone consists personal identity, i.e. the sameness of a rational being: and as far as this consciousness can be extended backwards to any past action or thought, so far reaches the identity of that person; it is the same self now as it was then; and it is by the same self with this present one that now reflects on it, that that action was done [*Essay Concerning Human Understanding*, Book II, Chapter 27, Paragraph 9].

Locke's position is often glossed as saying that memory is the key to self-identity, but he does not precisely say that; rather, he says that *consciousness of past actions* is the crucial element. This understanding can help us explore issues of memory and identity in *Tin Man*.

Prologue: The Mystic Man

While the character of the Wizard is splintered into several analogues in *Tin Man*,[1] the Mystic Man is the most obvious; the heroine and her three companions travel to Central City to find him, hoping that he can help them on their quests. Upon reaching him, they are disappointed to observe that he has become addicted to a substance known as the Vapors that causes disassociation and memory loss. A character who knew him in the past says, "That's not the Mystic Man I remember," clearly linking his willingness to recognize the Mystic Man's identity to the Mystic Man's ability to access his own memory. The Mystic Man's memory is magically restored shortly thereafter, and he is then able to provide assistance to the characters. The transition from his first amnesiac appearance to his magical cure takes only a few minutes; nevertheless, his case demonstrates in microcosm the more extensive problems of memory and identity that three of the characters face throughout the course of the entire program.

DG

DG (the analogue to Dorothy) is a princess of the O.Z. (the "Outer Zone," the analogue of Oz in *Tin Man*), the younger daughter of the Queen. Killed at the age of five by an evil Sorceress (whom we shall discuss later), DG was brought back to life by her mother, a powerful magic user, and sent to live on the Otherside, that is, in our world. Her memories of her life in the O.Z. were deliberately cloaked in magic by her mother to safeguard valuable information. As a result, DG does not know that she is originally from the O.Z. She does not know that she is a princess, nor does she know that she has inherited considerable magical ability. Her life as a waitress and part-time student in small-town Kansas is the only reality she knows. At the age of 20, she is brought back to the O.Z. when a tornado descends on her farm-house.

Aristotle says (Nicomachean Ethics III.1) that certain types of ignorance are very unlikely.

> (T)he term "involuntary" tends to be used not if a man is ignorant of what is to his advantage — for it is not mistaken purpose that causes involuntary action (it leads rather to wickedness), nor ignorance of the universal (for that men are blamed), but ignorance of particulars, i.e. of the circumstances of the action and the objects with which it is concerned. For it is on these that both pity and pardon depend, since the person who is ignorant of any of these acts involuntarily. [...] A man may be ignorant, then, of who he is, what he is doing, what or whom he is acting on, and sometimes also what (e.g. what instrument) he is doing it with, and to what end (e.g. he may think his act will conduce to someone's safety), and how he is doing it (e.g. whether gently or violently). Now of all of these no one could be ignorant unless he were mad, and evidently also he could not be ignorant of the agent; for how could he not know himself? [1110b15 — 1111a17].

On one interpretation, DG is in exactly this situation. When she says to her companions in the O.Z., "I've never been here before," Aristotle might say that she cannot be blamed for lying, for she is ignorant of who she is, and therefore doesn't know that she is actually from the O.Z. A more radical interpretation, however, and one more consonant with Locke's theory, is that the DG who utters these words is telling the truth because she is not the DG who lived in the O.Z. She has no access to those experiences in her memory and is thus not the same person. Although DG's physical substance is the same as that small child, her consciousness, that is, her true self, is not. The fact that her physical body is continuous is, to Locke, irrelevant.

> For, it being the same consciousness that makes a man be himself to himself, personal identity depends upon that only, whether it be annexed solely to one individual substance, or can be continued in a succession of several substances [II.27.10].

Locke argues that when a being has been "wholly stripp'd of all the consciousness of its past existence" it is not the same self as the earlier being (II.27.14). Insofar as DG is not conscious of her past experiences, she is not the same person who had them.

Although DG's memories of her early life have been suppressed, she has three sources of information about the O.Z. that come to her before she travels there.

1. She frequently sketches scenes from the O.Z. as if they are fantasies from her own imagination.

2. As the miniseries begins, DG has just begun to have dreams featuring both memories from her life in the O.Z. and a vision of the Queen (her real mother, whom she does not recognize); these dreams were apparently sent by the Queen as a signal that it was time for DG to return to the O.Z.

3. Finally, DG's adoptive father Hank has been telling her stories and sayings since childhood, making sure that she has them memorized word-for-word. Because of her lack of memories about the O.Z., she does not understand the significance of these stories and sayings while she is on the Otherside. Only when she travels to the O.Z. does she realize that they provide clues to her quest. Her adoptive mother Em explains that "our deeper purpose was to tell you the stories of our world, stories that would prepare you for your return."

DG is initially guided in her adventures by these sources of information; she gradually recovers information on her own, recognizing places she has been but without recalling the experiences that she had there. Not until Part II does she have an actual memory in which she is conscious of having experienced events in the O.Z.

A close reading of Locke such as that proposed in John Sutton's *Philosophy and Memory Traces: Descartes to Connectionism* (Cambridge: Cambridge University Press, 1998) strengthens this understanding of DG's position of discontinuity. Sutton observes that Locke explicitly moves away from an definition of memory common in earlier philosophers as a straightforward repository of information and toward the idea of memory as the power to revive at will perceptions that a person once experienced (167–168). While DG has access to information about the O.Z., it is quite another matter for her to revive the perceptions that she once experienced.

Nonetheless, we must observe an important difference between DG and Locke's theoretical being who has been "wholly stripp'd of all the consciousness of its past existence." Locke only insists on a loss of identity when that consciousness has been lost "beyond the power of ever retrieving again" (167–168). Since DG's memories have been cloaked in magic — a reversible process — she is able to regain consciousness of her previous existence. Beginning in Part II, she begins to recover actual memories, depicted as flashbacks, in which she is conscious of having experienced events from her childhood in the O.Z.

DG's magical abilities, a significant element of her identity, are tied to her memories. Unlike Harry Potter, her childhood in Kansas was not sprinkled with accidental mysterious incidents; there is no mention of her banishment from the reptile house at the local zoo. DG only evinces magical powers in tandem with her recovering memory. Her first actual use of magic coincides with her first actual memory of the O.Z. that is not a piece of disconnected information, a dream, a sketch, or one of Hank's stories: she recognizes a spinning doll that her old tutor carries with him and is able to make it spin, then remembers in a flashback the first time she made it spin as a child. Her subsequent uses of magic are also accompanied by flashbacks to her early childhood, and she demonstrates increasingly powerful magical abilities as she acquires more of her memories and further integrates them into her identity. It is a struggle for her to reintegrate this new awareness of her past experiences into her present self and one of the themes of the miniseries is DG's transition from denial to acceptance.

Part of what makes the transition especially difficult is that DG's suppressed memories include an experience, which she vividly relives, of her abandonment of her sister Azkadellia during an attack by an evil Witch. DG feels tremendous guilt as she realizes that everything that has happened since the Witch took possession of Azkadellia is at least partly her fault. Once this transition is accomplished, however, the DG we see at the end of the miniseries is continuous in identity both with the little princess of the flashbacks and with the frustrated waitress of small-town Kansas.

When the miniseries begins, it appears that DG's identity is discontinuous; although her physical substance is the same as that small child, her consciousness, that is, her true self, is not. The fact that her physical body is continuous is, to Locke, irrelevant:

> For, it being the same consciousness that makes a man be himself to himself, personal identity depends upon that only, whether it be annexed solely to one individual substance, or can be continued in a succession of several substances [II.27.10].

Locke argues that when a being has been "wholly stripp'd of all the consciousness of its past existence" it is not the same self as the earlier being (II.27.14).

DG has acquired information about the O.Z. from dreams, sketches, and stories while on the Otherside, but she does not have consciousness of her self as having experienced her own life as a young child in the O.Z. Insofar as DG is not conscious of her past experiences, she is not the same person who had them. This is why she does not feel a sense of identity with the DG who grew up with the Queen and Ahamo as her parents, the DG who studied magic with Tutor, the DG who played with Azkadellia. At this point she is not, in fact, the same person.

A close reading of Locke such as that proposed in John Sutton's *Philosophy and Memory Traces: Descartes to Connectionism* strengthens this understanding of DG's position of discontinuity. Sutton observes that Locke explicitly moves away from a definition of memory common in earlier philosophers as a straightforward repository of information and toward the idea of memory as the power to revive at will perceptions that a person once experienced (167–168). It is one thing for DG to have access to information about the O.Z.; it is quite another for her to revive the perceptions that she once experienced.

Nonetheless, we must observe an important difference between DG and Locke's theoretical being who has been "wholly stripp'd of all the consciousness of its past existence." Locke only insists on a loss of identity when that consciousness has been lost "beyond the power of ever retrieving again." Since DG's memories have been cloaked in magic — a reversible process — she is able to regain consciousness of her previous existence. It is a struggle for her to reintegrate this new awareness of her past experiences into her present self, and one of the themes of the miniseries is DG's transition from denial to acceptance.

Part of what makes the transition especially difficult is that DG's suppressed memories include an experience, which she vividly relives, of her abandonment of her sister Azkadellia during an attack by an evil Witch. DG feels tremendous guilt as she realizes that everything that has happened since the Witch took possession of Azkadellia is at least partly her fault.

Once this transition is accomplished, however, the DG we see at the end of the miniseries is continuous in identity both with the little princess of the flashbacks and with the frustrated waitress of small-town Kansas.

Early in the miniseries, DG is possessed of a vague sense, similar to Neo's at the beginning of *The Matrix*, that something about reality is not quite right. In Part I she tells her adoptive parents, "This isn't my life!" and "I just don't feel at home here." Possibly because of her sense of dislocation, DG rejects the socially-constructed identity that is imposed upon her in Kansas. Resisting the expectations that would normally be placed on a pretty young woman in a rural community, she dressed like a tomboy, racks up speeding tickets on her motorcycle, and helps her adoptive father fix farm equipment. In addition, she seeks escape metaphorically through artwork, drawing pictures of her dreams and daydreams, and more literally by poring over travel brochures for exotic places like Australia.[2] Although she clearly rejects social norms, they nevertheless play a role in her self-construction; her choice of jeans and sneakers is directed by her decision not to conform to more feminine garb, while her tomboyish behavior is directed by her decision not to adopt more ladylike hobbies. As feminist philosopher Sally Haslanger observes, "Whether or not I accept [social] norms, negotiating them was the process by which I became a woman" (Haslanger 2008).

Once in the O.Z., DG's social identity is entirely reconstructed, as she learns that she is a princess who is expected to save her people by wielding magical power. She resists this new imposition, curiously enough, by taking refuge in the identity she had previously striven so hard to escape. When her mother appears to her in a vision to urge her on, DG protests, "I'm a waitress. And a part-time student. I don't think I can do this." As she gradually recovers her identity in terms of her memory, however, she also becomes more and more capable of taking on the social identity of a world-saving princess. She never lets go of the behaviors she has developed in resistance to social expectations in our world; active and brave, she repeatedly rescues herself and comes to the aid of her companions in a refreshingly nonstereotypical manner.

Glitch

Glitch (the analogue to the Scarecrow) has lost his memory in a different way than DG. He was a royal adviser and inventor who had designed but not yet built a machine (partly technological, partly magical) to extend the growing season by altering the position of the suns, called the Sun Seeder. He refused to cooperate with the Sorceress' plan to build the machine in an altered, evil form intended to cast the O.Z. into perpetual darkness; as a result, she had a portion of his brain removed by alchemists, keeping it in a life-support mechanism and extracting from it the information required. Although this is not in fact how the human brain works — at least, not in our universe — the miniseries appears to propose a computer analogy, as if the portion of his brain removed was the filled memory storage, while the portion remaining to Glitch included the operating system, other software, and enough blank storage space to form new memories. The audience, along with DG, learns from Cain (the analogue to the Tin Woodman), that brain removal is a normally a punishment used to "re-educate" criminals.

Glitch has inconsistent access to his long-term memory. He does not know his real name or the Queen's. He does not recognize most of the people he once knew. He clings fiercely, however, to what little he does remember, particularly his status as an adviser to the Queen and his occupation as an intellectual; he has a strong sense of consciousness of himself as having experienced his life in the O.Z. prior to the removal of part of his brain. This explains why he retains such a strong sense of identity and even pride in his previous accomplishments.

Glitch makes a number of statements that indicate his attachment to his identity, beginning with his statement in Part I that part of his brain was removed "because of what I know, or used to know." Unlike DG, who initially insists that she is a waitress, not a princess, he consistently refers to his previous self as "I" and retains a strong sense of continuity between his former and present selves.

He cannot, at will, revive all of the perceptions that he once experienced; in this respect, his long-term memory is severely damaged by the removal of part of his brain. On several occasions, however, he does appear capable of reviving those perceptions in a partial and disjointed manner. On another occasion, an empathic healer is able to retrieve memories to which Glitch himself did not previously have access, which suggests that the ability to revive further perceptions may still exist in a latent fashion. Sutton observes (170–171) that Locke is reluctant to discuss in detail the effects upon the continuity of identity of ordinary forgetfulness and the normal tendency of memories to fade over time; while Glitch's loss of memory is not ordinary or normal, some inability to revive distinct perceptions is not incompatible with continuity of identity within Locke's theory.

Locke also acknowledges the phenomenon that our memories are sometimes activated without our conscious control, reviving earlier perceptions that we did not particularly seek to reactivate (II.10.7; discussed in Sutton 173); we see this on several occasions when Glitch unexpectedly pops up with chunks of technical detail concerning the identification of a holographic projector or the characteristics of a rare chemical element.

Glitch's situation is thrown into sharp relief by contrast with the backstory of Cain, the Tin Woodman analogue. Cain had joined the resistance against the Sorceress, and as punishment his family was dragged away before his eyes while he was imprisoned in a tin suit, held captive there until DG and Glitch let him out. While in the suit, he was subjected to a holographic projection replaying his own capture and the seizure of his family, over and over. Thus, he was not able to rely on the normal tendency of memories to fade over time to soften the blow of what was done to him and the ones he loved; rather, he was forced to re-experience those perceptions repeatedly during his imprisonment. If we take memory in Locke's sense of a power to revive perceptions, Cain's was artificially enhanced, while Glitch's was artificially damaged; both forms of alteration were harmful.

In a scene that strongly echoes the Wizard's conversation with the Scarecrow, Tin Man, and Cowardly Lion in the 1939 movie, DG assures each of her companions at a critical moment that he already possesses the quality he seeks. She tells Glitch, "Glitch, you're the smartest guy I know. You helped me remember my past, and that's probably the most important weapon I have now." In addition to explicitly linking Glitch's situation to her own,[3] DG's speech appears to affirm that Glitch has a complete identity of his own, whether or not he is ever reunited with the missing portion of his brain.

When Glitch is reconnected with the missing portion of his brain toward the end of the miniseries, he is able to retrieve the information needed to shut down the machine. He also uses his newly recovered memory to strengthen his identity; the first thing he says is, "My name isn't Glitch. It's Ambrose." The connection, however, lasts only long enough to achieve the desired goal of shutting down the machine, after which Glitch is once again disconnected. The miniseries ends very shortly thereafter and we never learn whether he will be reconnected permanently to the missing portion of his brain. DG's earlier speech, however, suggests that he does not need to be.

Glitch's case enables us to apply some of Locke's more outlandish thought experiments, which otherwise might go unexplored, particularly by the squeamish. For Locke, if part of the body is removed, and consciousness does not go along with that part of the body, and in fact, the self loses sensation and awareness of that part of the body (for example, if a hand is cut off), then that part of the body ceases to be part of the person. We may compare this to Glitch's missing half-a-brain, of which (except for one brief period near the end of the third episode) he has no sensation or direct awareness. Conversely, for Locke, if part of the body is removed and consciousness does go along with that part of the body — he considers the possibility that a little finger is removed and that the person's self-consciousness is contained within that little finger — then that part of the body is the person. This again would seem to apply to Glitch's body, with its remaining half-a-brain, as being the part of him in which his consciousness is contained.

There is one difficulty with this interpretation, which results from a lacuna within the script. We are never told whether Glitch's missing half-a-brain has its own consciousness or not. If so, we have identity problems that go far beyond even Locke's weirdest thought experiments. I prefer to believe that it doesn't, if only to keep from multiplying hypotheses unnecessarily.[4]

Glitch experiences another complication with regard to his identity, well known to contemporary thinkers such as Haslanger, and also foreshadowed by Locke. Locke proposes yet another thought experiment to examine elements of identity; this one concerns a prince and a cobbler who swap bodies, so that the prince's consciousness now resides in the body of the cobbler. Locke observes that identity has a social and contextual component, so that the prince's consciousness, transferred into the body of the cobbler, will appear to those around him to be the cobbler, even though it will still appear to the prince to be the prince himself. Shabbily dressed in the rags of his former finery, marked as a "headcase" by the obvious zipper down the middle of his head, Glitch looks like a vagabond and a criminal; no one initially believes his claim to be an inventor and royal adviser. He receives no reinforcement from society for his identity; in fact, quite the opposite. In addition to struggling internally to maintain his own identity, Glitch must also resist the erroneous socially-constructed identity that is constantly forced upon him.

The Sorceress

The character of the Sorceress (the Wicked Witch analogue) is a complicated one. At first, the audience is led to believe that she is DG's older sister Azkadellia; later we learn that she is a fusion creature, made up of Azkadellia herself and an evil, unnamed Witch who has taken possession of her. Although the term "good witch" is not used in the miniseries, the Witch is always qualified as evil; the term "witch" alone is apparently not sufficient to indicate automatically that someone is a "bad witch."

The Witch and Azkadellia never blend into a single being like the Companion in the classic *Star Trek* episode "Metamorphosis" or the learned gentleman and Rekh-mara in the novel *The Story of the Amulet*. The Sorceress is depicted on multiple occasions having conversations with herself, which the audience comes to realize are conversations between Azkadellia and the Witch, who retain their individual personalities. Outside of these conversations, when the Sorceress speaks as "I," the Witch is clearly in control.

The Sorceress sometimes speaks as if she is relying solely on Azkadellia's memories, as when she tells DG that they were friends as children, sometimes as if she is relying solely on the Witch's memories, as when she rejoices that her plan is coming to fruition, "and this time I'll get it right." The Witch appears to be in primary control even when the Sorceress is relating information based on Azkadellia's memories. This is reflected in the reactions of Azkadellia's family members. At various times the Queen tells her, "You are not my daughter," and "I am not your mother." DG says "You're not my sister." The Sorceress herself tells Azkadellia's father that his daughter is gone.

We are shown that Azkadellia has possession of her own memories and is able to revive her previous perceptions, but we also see the Witch constantly re-interpreting their significance for her. During an internal conversation when the Sorceress has returned to Azkadellia's childhood home, which DG has magically restored, Azkadellia sighs, "We were so happy here." The Witch sharply reminds her that her family abandoned her, while the Witch will never abandon her.

While the Witch occasionally prods Azkadellia's memory to gain advantage,[5] Azkadellia's mother and sister believe that her memories are the key to her ability to fight the Witch and re-assert her own identity. The Queen says to her in Part II, "And what about you, Azkadellia? Perhaps DG isn't the only one who needs to unlock her memories." DG helps her sister to reassert her own identity and escape from the Witch's control by reminding her of specific events that DG has remembered from their shared past, causing Azkadellia to revive her own perceptions of those events (depicted in flashbacks from Azkadellia's point of view). During this conversation, both DG and Azkadellia are represented as their childhood selves, representing a return to the unambiguous identities that each once possessed.

Locke's philosophy is both helpful and problematic in the case of the Sorceress. The thought experiment of the prince and the cobbler and its discussion of contextual identity helps to explain why the Sorceress is frequently called Azkadellia even though the dominant personality within her is that of the Witch. She has the body and, therefore, the physical appearance of Azkadellia, which determines her apparent identity to others.

Locke's discussion of bodyswapping, however, is also problematic for this case; he appears to assume that only one consciousness governs each substance at any given time; the cobbler's body is "deserted by his own soul" (presumably the cobbler's consciousness takes up residence in the prince's body). While Locke considers the possibility that more than one consciousness could inhabit the same substance, he is referring to the theory of metempsychosis; the separate consciousnesses would inhabit the substance sequentially, and his point is that there is very little sense in which one such individual is the same as the one who lived a past life with the same soul. He does not address the possibility of two consciousnesses inhabiting the same body.

Furthermore, Locke's claim that "whatever has the consciousness of present and past actions, is the same person to whom they both belong" appears to raise a problem for the conclusion of the miniseries. We know that the compound being known as the Sorceress has access to the memories of both the Witch and Azkadellia. It is not clear to what extent the individual persons within the Sorceress have access to one another's memories; the most obvious interpretation, I believe, is that the Witch had some kind of access to Azkadellia's, while Azkadellia may or may not have had access to the Witch's.

If Azkadellia did have access to the Witch's memories, then the miniseries might not have ended the way we are meant to think it did. After Azkadellia re-asserts her own identity and separates herself from the Witch, the Witch reappears in her own physical form and is destroyed. (She is, in fact, melted.) At this point, we are meant to believe that the Witch is, in fact, really most sincerely dead. If, however, Azkadellia possesses her memories, then it is possible that the Witch still lives on in Azkadellia. Although Azkadellia tells her parents, "It's over. The Witch is gone," that's also exactly what the Witch would say under those circumstances.

However, I believe this terrifying prospect may be averted by paying close attention once again to Locke's theory. While Azkadellia may possess the information that was stored in the Witch's memory, she would not have the consciousness of having experienced events in the Witch's past herself and thus does not have the capability of reviving the Witch's perceptions. Since she does not possess this consciousness or capability, she is not, and does not possess the identity of, the Witch. This also explains why, even when they are combined into the Sorceress, the Witch must prompt Azkadellia to revive the perception of her past experiences at her childhood home; since memory is not merely a repository of stored information, only Azkadellia herself has the power to bring her past experiences to the fore. Thus, we can say that the two persons within the Sorceress, who clearly differ in personality and will, are also distinguished by their consciousness of past experiences.

Conclusion

While concepts such as the constructedness of the self and the anxiety attendant upon our realization thereof may appear peculiarly postmodern, in fact they are supported by a close reading of Locke's classic theory of self identity. Whether we are considering ourselves as bearing the responsibility to create ourselves, or whether we are concerned about the social norms that we must negotiate in order to claim our identities, Locke appears to foreshadow these contemporary concerns.

For Locke, our continued identity through time is not merely a matter of the static possession of a warehouse of information (a common misunderstanding of his position). Rather, it is a function of the power we have to revive perceptions that we have experienced. This power, Locke admits, is subject to some normal loss over time owing to ordinary wear and tear; we have to come to terms with the fact that we can never wholly revive all of our perceptions, and thus the self-identity that we have the potential to build will always be incomplete.

Three major characters in *Tin Man* also demonstrate possible ways in which this power to revive our perceptions and thereby construct our identities can be damaged from without: in DG's case, by the complete though benevolent blockage of access to her experiences, including traumatic and guilt-inducing events that are painful for her to recover; in Glitch's case, by the partial removal of portions of his brain in which some of his memories were stored; in Azkadellia's case, by the constant exploitation and re-interpretation of her memories. These cases may reflect our contemporary anxieties about reports of recovered memories of trauma, the curious problems of people with severe brain damage, and the effects of brainwashing. Or they may reflect in an exaggerated way our simple awareness that, as described by Locke, the construction of our self-identity is a difficult ongoing task in which we can never completely succeed, a realization that threatens our common-sense desire to believe in a stable self.

Telotte also argues that science fiction products not only depict our anxieties metaphorically, but enable us to work through them. DG is able to recover and successfully reintegrate her childhood experiences into her adult self; Glitch, despite his situation, never loses his strong self of identity; Azkadellia is able to break out of her conditioning and reassert her independent self. If these characters can emerge intact despite these obstacles, then surely we can cope with the imperfections of our own mechanisms of self-construction.

Notes

1. DG's father Ahamo is the Othersider from Nebraska who comes to the O.Z. by accident in a State Fair balloon; as happens to the Wizard in the book series, his name apparently derives from a misreading of the balloon's lettering, and like the Wizard in the movie, he acts as his own gatekeeper. DG is the one who assures her companions near the end that each already possesses the quality he seeks. Two minor characters — a shady fortuneteller and a traveling entrepreneur — appear to reflect the 1939 movie's Professor Marvel.

2. A veiled reference to the original; Australia, of course, bears the nickname "Oz."

3. Like DG's other companions, Glitch doubles and highlights an element of DG's quest.

4. We actually know very little about Glitch's missing half-a-brain. It is unambiguously described as a half-a-brain (on three separate occasions), but if you look closely into the very cool steampunk tank, it is in fact an entire brain. (This may, however, simply be a matter of the props department not reading the script.) Code-named "Ambrose" by the resistance, it not only contains the knowledge of how to build the Sun Seeder, which was mysteriously extracted from it, but it helps to control the machine as well. When Glitch is reconnected to the half-a-brain and helps Cain begin shutting down the machine, one of the alchemists reports from a separate control room that there is "power surging in the brain cortex — some kind of synapse interference." In context, he speaks of it as if it was simply a part of the machine. Further reinforcing the idea that the brain is part of the machine, when the reconnected Glitch cannot remember the final code to shut the machine down, Cain seriously considers destroying the half-a-brain, without which the machine cannot run. None of these details indicate that the half-a-brain has any consciousness of its own. Glitch's sudden change of personality when he is reconnected may be explained as the effect of the reintegration of the information contained in the half-a-brain into Glitch's consciousness, rather than as evidence of an independent consciousness or personality in that half-a-brain.

5. "DG's not the only one who can remember, is she?" the Witch says at one point in Part II, which prompts Azkadellia to remember a clue that helps the Sorceress to hunt down the long-lost Ahamo. Azkadellia's memory is depicted as a flashback, not simply a point of information but a perception revived and relived.

Works Cited

Aristotle. *Nicomachean Ethics*. Trans. Richard McKeon. New York: Random House, 1941.

Locke. *An Essay Concerning Human Understanding*. http://oregonstate.edu/instruct/phl302/texts/locke/locke1/Book2c.html.

Solomon, Robert. *Introducing Philosophy: A Text with Integrated Readings*. 7th Edition. Fort Worth: Harcourt College Publishers, 2001.

Sutton, John. *Philosophy and Memory Traces: Descartes to Connectionism*. Cambridge: Cambridge University Press, 1998.

Telotte, J.P. *Replications: A Robotic History of the Science Fiction Film*. Urbana and Chicago: University of Illinois Press, 1995.

Tin Man. Dir. Nick Willing. Screenplay by Craig Van Sickle and Steven Long Mitchell, based on *The Wonderful Wizard of Oz* by L. Frank Baum. Sci Fi Channel, December 2007.

CHAPTER 12

The Wicked Wizard of Oz

KEVIN K. DURAND

DOROTHY: You're a bad man.
THE WIZARD: No, no, my dear. I'm a very good man. I'm just a bad
wizard.

(The Wizard of Oz)

BOQ: People who claim to be evil are usually no worse than the rest
of us. It's people who claim that they're good, or anyway better than
the rest of us, that you have to be wary of.

(Wicked)

It wasn't Gregory Maguire's brilliant reimagining of the world of *The Wonderful Wizard of Oz* or Schwartz's catching musical reimagining of the world of *The Wizard of Oz*, that suggested to me that maybe the Wizard wasn't quite so wonderful. It was the Wizard, himself. Looking back, I would like to say it was some precocious philosophical reflection and rumination that made me hear his proclamation of goodness ring somewhat false that inspired my "not wonderful" view. It was not, however. It was, rather, a deep empathy with the Cowardly Lion. Or, perhaps, rather than empathy, it was understanding. I suspect that I, too, would have turned tail and fled, when faced with the huge disembodied head bellowing first at my compatriots and, finally, at me. It would be nice if I could claim that, like the good quasi–Aristotelian/Whiteheadian virtue ethicist that I have since become, fleeing such a menace was the right thing to do at precisely the right time, if perhaps not in the right way (surely, an exit less ignominious than an emerald green stained-glass window was available), and for the right reasons. But, alas, such a claim as this would also ring false. The reaction of a five- or six-year-old child to the Wizard as he presents himself to the intrepid band of travelers is likely consistent with the reaction of the Cowardly Lion — fear.

To be sure, Maguire has inspired several scholarly reflections on the Wizard and his character. In *Wicked*, he is a megalomaniacal despot who argues that the rules of polite Ozian society do not apply to him as he is an outsider. He is willing to use whichever means happen to be at his disposal, even a group of supplicants completely incapable of the task, to advance his power. He is simply a terror. As I argued, however briefly, in another essay ("Wicked? It's Not Easy Being Green," *Wizard of Oz and Philosophy*), the Wizard is seen in quite a different light than popularly received as one inhabits the world of Maguire's imagination.

In a similar way, Schwartz's musical provides another reimagination. The Wizard of *Wicked: A New Musical* is at some intermediate point between the Wizard of *The Wizard of Oz* and *Wicked*. As I argued in "An Emerald Canon," the musical *Wicked* is much more of a reimagination of *The Wizard of Oz* than it is a dramatization of Maguire's *Wicked*. The Wizard of the musical is rather a bumbling man, incapable of exercising the sort of Machiavellian power of the Wizard of the text. In this way, he is very much like the character of Professor Marvel that Frank Morgan portrays and whom the audience is expected to identify later as the Wizard, himself. However, there is a sinister undertone in the Wizard of the musical. He is a man perfectly willing to let Dr. Dillamond transform from Goat to goat, to use the propaganda machine to blame Elphaba for the plight of the flying monkeys, and to use Galinda to front his public relations campaign as little more than a puppet. However, he is unable to actually exercise his power to suppress Glinda's successful attempt to expel him.

As a matter of staging, the Wizard of the musical differs from the Wizard of Oz, also. The disembodied head of the musical is elongated and much more sinister in look. For all that the movie's disembodied head is a fright, it is still relatively human. So, the musical seems to give us a wizard intermediate between the movie and the book. However, I argue here that my younger self was not so far wrong, and neither was the Cowardly Lion. Indeed, it seems very much the case that the Wizard of Oz gets off very lightly in the reflections on the movie. Perhaps it is the fact that Morgan plays Professor Marvel and the guard at the gate (who has an Auntie Em, too) that deflects some of the impact of the Wizard. Perhaps it is the bumbling Marvel-like character who boards the balloon at the end, only to have no particular idea of how to make it turn around or to steer the thing. Whatever the case, the general reaction to the Wizard seems to have been that for all his bluster, the man behind the curtain is just a bad wizard, not a bad man. Perhaps another viewing is in order.

When Dorothy very memorably arrives in Oz and the Wicked Witch of the East suffers her architectural mishap, Dorothy is vexed with a number of problems. To be sure, there is the threatening, "I'll get you, my pretty, and your little dog, too." However, the more pressing dilemma is the return home. Nobody knows how this journey might happen (except, that in retrospect, it certainly seems that Glinda has some insights that she has neglected to share), but the consensus, quickly reached, is that the Wizard is the man with the plan. Indeed, Glinda says in what turns out to be a rather disingenuous plot device, "The only person who might know is the great and wonderful Wizard of Oz, himself." And, then, of course, they commence with the singing.

What's clear from the musical send-off is the view that the Wizard is, in point of fact, most wonderful. While one might wonder if too much protestation has gone into this ascription, nevertheless, the claim is before us: "The Wizard of Oz is a wonderful wizard," which leaves us with a question to ponder as we set off down the road with Dorothy. What sorts of conditions might we have for calling something "good," much less, "wonderful"?

What we find in Dorothy's naïve song, sung at the beginning in hopeful anticipation and sung again and again with an increasing sense of foreboding, is that the Wizard of Oz is a wonderful wizard because of "the wonderful things he does." We can take this at face value, as I think ultimately, we must, but first, it seems reasonable to concern ourselves with the possible reasons for labeling something "good."

Turning to the field of ethical theory, there tend to be three major divisions into which all foundational ethical theorizing takes place — deontology (or Kantian ethics), utilitarian (or consequentialist ethics), and virtue ethics. A very brief take on the "good" claim about the Wizard from each of these perspectives might well be helpful. The deontologists will argue that something is good insofar as it is the product of the good will and conforms to an expression of the Moral Law called the Categorical Imperative. The Categorical Imperative (or the moral maxim of action) is the moral imperative because it contains within it the notions of universality and causality that one would expect from something called a moral imperative. As a minor digression, it should be noted that the word of "imperative" has fallen out of common usage. However, I well remember my grandmother using the word commonly. She would say things like, "It is imperative that you finish your work before turning on the television." In this sense, an "imperative" is something that one must do, that one should or ought to do. Thus, an imperative can carry moral *should* as well. The Categorical Imperative is the moral *should*.

Kant argues in the *Groundwork of the Metaphysics of Morals* that there is a distinction between those imperatives (or *shoulds*) that are moral and those that are non-moral. Thus, the Categorical Imperative is distinguished from, for example, a Hypothetical Imperative. A hypothetical imperative would be of the following form: "If I want to pass my astrophysics class, then I should study for my final exam." Thus, there are certain things that I should do, but only provided that I want a certain sort of outcome. If, for example, I am not taking an astrophysics class, then it may well be the case that I need not study for such an exam. So, hypothetical imperatives apply only in those situations where they are necessary for some other goal that I have. The Categorical Imperative, however, is of the following form: "One should always act toward humanity, whether in oneself or another, as if it were an end in itself and not as a means only." This second form of Kant's Categorical Imperative is helpful in our Ozian quest. One would perhaps call the Wizard a good man if, for example, his actions, whatever their immediate consequences, grew from a will that was in accord with this maxim.

The virtue ethicist would argue that the Wizard was a good man (and a good wizard) if, and only if, his character exemplified human excellence. That is, if his actions were in accord with excellence in human reason. Virtue, then, is a state of character. It describes the whole of a person, intentions, will, and desires, *and* actions and their consequences. A virtuous action could be described as the right thing, done at the right time, done in the right way, and done for the right reasons. So, if as a matter of habit, or from *second nature*, the Wizard behaved admirably, exemplifying excellence in reasoning and action, then he would properly be called "good."

However, neither the view of the deontologist nor that of the virtue ethicist are embodied in either Dorothy's song or the Wizard's claim after his unveiling that while he is a bad wizard, he is a very good man. Instead, these seem to embody a consequentialist approach to goodness. That is, it is because of the good actions that the Wizard is called good or wonderful.

While it is mainly in keeping with the consequentialist approach to ask whether the Wizard's claim is true, I think it is also helpful to employ a version of a virtue model to the question as well. In the first case, we would straightforwardly take the Munchkins' lyric, that "the Wizard is a wonderful wiz, if ever a wiz there was," as the condition that makes the Wizard a good one. If we do that, then we have the following conditional. A wizard is a good wizard if he does what a wizard should do; or, in other words, if he is excellent at his craft, performing those magical feats that are appropriate for a wizard with those consequences of his actions that tend to promote the highest good for the greatest number. All but that last clause is consistent with a virtue view as well.

However, it seems that a consequentialist model really doesn't get everything we need, especially in light of the Wizard's own claim that he is not a good wizard, but is instead good man. If this is the case, then we would have the following set of conditions. He is a good wizard if he is excellent at his craft *and* if he is a good man. Here the consequentialist model fails. It doesn't fail because the Wizard fails to be an exceptional, or even mediocre, wizard; or, at least, that is not the important reason for which it fails. It is true that the Wizard fails at good actions. His actions, even if thought to embody good intentions (taking Dorothy back to Kansas and out of Oz) fail. However, even with this as a given, it seems more likely that a virtue view is to be preferred. For example, generally, when we call a person good, we do not do so because she does things that result in good consequences, more or less. Rather, we call a person good because he or she has the sort of character that answers to that label. This is a matter not only of actions, but also of intentions; this is a matter of the whole of a person. If the Wizard is to be believed that he is a good man, albeit a poor wizard, then his character must be one that embodies intentions that are good and the product of excellence in reasoning, not merely those that succeed through some sort of outrageous good luck.

However, both fail. With this background, we can look carefully at the Wizard of the text. I argue that we find not only a poor wizard, but a man who also fails at what a reasonable person might call "goodness," as well. Indeed, rather than a wonderful wizard, he is the Wicked Wizard of Oz. Consider the following examples.

When the gang arrives in Oz, they are driven around through town in a horse of a different color, they all get the spa treatment, and the lovely sing-around the town. When the Witch makes her appearance and demands a surrendering of Dorothy, the people all run to the Wizard's keep, completely assured that the Wizard will be able to solve whatever problem has manifested itself in the sky-writing above their town. Upon their arrival, the Wizard's mouthpiece stumbles over the assurances that the Wizard has everything well under control. He stammers, "Every... It's all right. Everything is all right! The Great and Powerful Oz has got matters well in hand... I hope... So, you can all go...." It's not the most ringing endorsement from the Wizard's spokesman, and one that suggests to the viewer that perhaps all is not right in the Emerald City.

Ultimately, Dorothy and her companions do get past the doorman, and when we first actually meet the Wizard, we only meet the face he shows to the world. Our intrepid band of travelers has traversed a long hallway (with threatening music in the background) utterly alone as they approach a sort of throne room. The careful viewer notes a disturbing lack of a king. In a structure that is clearly part of a fairy-tale kingdom, Merlin has supplanted Arthur from the throne; the Wizard is ruler and king. In this way, one might already anticipate the sort of despot that populates Maguire's *Wicked*, but whether the absent king is troubling or not to the little band, the sense of foreboding is clearly felt by them.

Finally arriving at the Wizard's door, they are summoned into his presence and met with an intimidating light show. The Wizard, having clearly written the script for his spokesman, thunders, "I am Oz, the Great and Powerful." Here, the Wizard is not only claiming greatness, but he is also claiming that he, himself, is Oz. Not the city. Not the land. Not the people. *He* is Oz. Ignoring that vainglorious, self-aggrandizing claim, the travelers soldier on. Yet, they cannot even get out a story of why they have come. "Silence! The Great and Powerful Oz knows why you have come." Leaving aside the intimidation, he moves straight to insults. To the Tin Man, he rails, "You dare to come to me for a heart, do you? You clinking, clanking, clattering collection of caliginous junk!" Not satisfied with berating the Tin Man, the Wizard turns to the Scarecrow: "You, Scarecrow, have the effrontery to ask for a brain? You billowing bale of bovine fodder!" Having asserted his "authority," he turns to the Lion — to, oddly enough, the king of the forest, who, just before the trip down the hall to the Wizard's chamber had been singing about not only what makes a king, but why he would be a good one. In this sense, it is perhaps the Lion that is the greatest threat to the Wizard. After all, if Merlin has supplanted Arthur, it would be quite problematic for the Wizard if the true king returned. Unfortunately for the Lion, his timid nature gets the better of him and before he can be insulted, he turns and sprints. Even after Dorothy's rebuke of the Wizard, he does not relent. In fact, he takes the step that may most clearly identify him not as the heroic, good man (if poor wizard), but indeed, as the villain of the picture.

With the full grasp of the incapacities of the group before him in mind, he sets conditions on offering help. He will not help (even as we later learn he is *impotent* to help) without a great deed done in return. He turns the little band into a completely incompetent team of assassins. It cannot be argued that he doesn't know what is in store for them or what he asks of them. The Scarecrow tells him that they must kill the Witch to get her broom, and the Wizard sends them anyway. Rhetorically speaking, what sort of person creates a death squad of a band as rag-tag and utterly incapable as this? Sending them out against a Witch, surrounded by well armed and efficiently trained guards and an army of winged monkeys does not seem so much like a mission of assassination as it does a suicide mission. Perhaps, the Wizard, knowing his own impotence and yet fully concerned with remaining in power, figures the Witch will do some of his dirty work for him. Indeed, when they do return, broom in hand and assassination complete, he seems utterly surprised. And, when Toto famously reveals the "man behind the curtain," the illusion is completely dissolved. Again, Dorothy finds her voice and says that the Wizard is a very bad man. He is shocked and quickly recovers: "Oh, no, my dear — I'm — a very good man. I'm just a very bad wizard."

Let us return to our criteria. To be a "wonderful wizard" is not only about having the capabilities of a wizard, nor is it even about doing wizardly things when they are called for. If this were all that were at stake, then the Wizard fails, even by his own lights. He is a fraud and a "humbug." Yet, still we have his own claim that he is a "very good man." Is it consistent with being a very good man to isolate oneself from the ones that think of him as their protector (and who even have some doubts about him even as they read from the "great and powerful" script)? Is it consistent with being a very good man to intimidate the powerless? Is it consistent with being a very good man to try to assassinate a rival, especially while demonstrating no courage at all on one's own part, and hiding behind the gingham skirt of a young girl? Is it consistent with being a very good man to put that girl and her companions, no more capable than she, on a path toward their sure destruction? Clearly, none of these seem consistent with the claim of being a very good man. We are left, at the end, with the giving of meaningless trinkets to the Tin Man, the Scarecrow, and the Lion, and failing to supply even the barest trinket, apart from false hope, to Dorothy. These are not the actions of a very good man. These are not the actions of an even fairly mediocre man. Indeed, in aiming at power, isolation, intimidation, assassination, and, when those fail, obfuscation, the Wizard is far from wonderful. More like Wicked.

CHAPTER 13

A Feminist Stroll Down the Yellow Brick Road

Dorothy's Heroine's Adventure

PAULA KENT

While researching feminist perspectives of *The Wonderful Wizard of Oz*, it became painfully clear that not much has been written specifically about L. Frank Baum's Dorothy Gale from a feminist standpoint. It appears that most critics, feminist and otherwise, prefer to study and write about the more popular 1939 film version. That is not to say that no critic has attempted to explore the original 1900 novel. Laura Raidonis Bates explores Baum's Dorothy, as well as other fictitious female characters, in her article "'Sweet Sorrow': The Universal Theme of Separation in Folklore and Children's Literature." She makes some valuable points when it comes to considering Dorothy as a stronger female figure in Oz, and this provides a good place to start when looking for some feminist perspectives to apply to Dorothy's story.

Additionally, some particularly thought-provoking comments have recently been made about Dorothy in the realm of feminist popular culture. In the Spring 2007 issue of *Bitch Magazine*, Briar Levit compiled an interesting list of what is dubbed "The Bitch List." One of the characters included in this list is Dorothy Gale. The entry specifically states:

> Most of us associate Dorothy Gale with Judy Garland's sweet but weepy portrayal in the 1939 film version of the Wizard of Oz. But long before Dorothy made her screen debut, she was the heroine of L. Frank Baum's popular book series at the early part of the 20th century. Baum's Dorothy was strong, curious, and clever. She took on everyone from the Wicked Witch of the West to the Nome King, and she led expeditions to save friends and stop wars among different nations within the Land of Oz [68].

Though this list introduces two versions of thought when it comes to Dorothy Gale, this entry was certainly a source of inspiration when considering how to apply a feminist critique to Baum's novel and the character Dorothy Gale.

The idea of Dorothy's strength is quite appealing, especially when considering Joseph Campbell's work, *The Hero with a Thousand Faces*. As Eva M. Thury and Margaret K. Devinney state, Campbell's idea shows us "the underlying structure of [the hero] myth and [...] help[s] us understand why humans have kept telling versions of that myth, over and over, in culture after culture" (135). This myth is certainly present in Baum's novel, particularly when considering Dorothy Gale. As Edward W Hudlin notes: "*The Wonderful Wizard of Oz* follows very closely the structure of the heroic myth as defined by Joseph Campbell" (443). Though he specifically seeks to apply the "heroic myth" to Baum's novel, I want to establish that Dorothy's adventure is, in fact, worthy of feminist criticism and establish her strengths as a heroine. As Richard Tuerk states, "To see *The Wonderful Wizard of Oz* simply as Dorothy's quest for a way to return to Kansas is to miss many of the sources of the book's strength, for like most quest hero's, Dorothy achieves far more than simply finding a way home" (22). This is certainly true, for Dorothy finds the strength she never knew she had but always did. It is important to note at this time that the focus of the paper will be limited to Baum's first novel in the *Oz Series* and will not consider any additional Oz book when exploring Dorothy's initial adventure through Oz. Nevertheless, when applying Campbell's "Adventure of the Hero" to Baum's main character, one can begin to see how Dorothy does in fact embark on the hero's, or in this case the heroine's, adventure that Campbell establishes.

The Hero's (or Heroine's) Adventure

The "Adventure of the Hero," or heroine in Dorothy's case, is a formula that can be applied to a variety of works. It can work for male or female characters, and it is generally accessible to several genres. This adventure is one that readers want to go on with the character(s) and can range anywhere from a small voyage to an epic journey. According to Campbell, "The wonder is that the characteristic efficacy to touch and inspire deep creative centers dwells in the smallest nursery fairy tale — as the flavor of the ocean is contained in a droplet or the whole mystery of life within the egg of a flea" (4). Dorothy's journey certainly falls within the scope of Campbell's "wonder," as readers, both young and old and male and female, continue to embark on the adventure with her even today.

Though the method for Campbell's "Adventure of the Hero" seems strict and formulaic, there are ways to adapt it, and some elements may not always be included. This is true for Dorothy's adventure, despite the fact that there are only minor adjustments. As Thury and Devinney note, Campbell "believes that the hero myth is really written about every human being: *each of us* is the hero struggling to accomplish his [or her] adventure" (135). Because of this, it should be expected that different adventures require different elements of Campbell's formula, depending on the character and the situation, and it is no different in Dorothy's case. The specifics of Dorothy's "Heroine's Adventure" will be specifically explored, but first, I will outline the basis of Campbell's original "Adventure of the Hero" to establish how this formula can be applied to Baum's heroine.

The first stage of the "Adventure of the Hero" is the *Departure*. Under this heading, there are five parts that the hero can follow: Call to Adventure, Refusal of the Call, Supernatural Aid, Crossing the First Threshold, and In the Belly of the Whale (Campbell ix). The order of this section will be altered to fit Dorothy's experience, but she does undergo each task.

The second stage of the adventure is the *Initiation*. Here, the six parts are: The Road of Trials, The Meeting with the Goddess, Woman as the Temptress, Atonement with the Father, Apotheosis, and The Ultimate Boon (ix). In Dorothy's case, this section will be reorganized and some tasks will even be omitted.

The final stage of Campbell's formula is the *Return*. Here, there are six parts once again, but it is already understood that the hero or heroine will likely not participate in each one. The specific parts are: Refusal of the Return, The Magic Flight, Rescue from Without, The Crossing of the Return Threshold, Master of the Two Worlds, and Freedom to Live (ix–x). Dorothy will not be a part of all of these situations, but she does have an opportunity to participate in some.

The following section will explore each stage of Campbell's "Adventure of the Hero," or heroine in our case, and its sub-parts will be further explored as to how they relate to Dorothy's "Heroine's Adventure" in Baum's premier *Oz Series* novel. What this application will ultimately show is that Dorothy is one of many "young female characters who make a transition from timorous to heroic, taking care not only of themselves but also of their male friends" (Bates 50). From this, feminist critics can begin to explore Baum's Dorothy, as opposed to the Hollywood version, as a strong-willed young woman who may ultimately surprise everyone, even herself.

Dorothy's Adventure

First, Dorothy must depart from her original world, specifically the "great gray prairie" of Kansas (Baum 12). It is in this stage where Dorothy will leave home and begin her adventure in Oz. Her "Call to Adventure" is what Camp-

bell says "signifies that destiny has summoned the hero [or heroine] and transferred his [or her] spiritual center of gravity from within the pale of his [or
her] society to a zone unknown" (58). It is her current situation at home with
Aunt Em and Uncle Henry that causes Dorothy to yearn for more. When
Baum writes that her dog, Toto, "saved her from growing as gray as her other
surroundings," he makes it clear that Dorothy wants more from life (13). The
only thing she is unaware of at this point is the fact that she is about to enter
a much more colorful world.

The next experience Dorothy has is being "In the Belly of the Whale,"
or in this case, a cyclone. Though this is out of order in Campbell's original
formula, the cyclone is what takes Dorothy into the Land of Oz at the beginning of the story. At this point, Dorothy has been reborn in a sense and is
now ready to accept her adventure, even if she is not aware of it yet.
Specifically, Campbell states: "The idea that the passage of the magical threshold is a transit into a sphere of rebirth is symbolized in the worldwide womb
image of the belly of the whale" (90). Her "rebirth" is reiterated in the fact
that her time in the cyclone is quite peaceful, and during that time, "[i]n spite
of the swaying of the house and the wailing of the wind, Dorothy soon closed
her eyes and fell fast asleep" (Baum 16). She begins her adventure in a drab,
gray world, and is transported in the belly of the cyclone to what Baum
describes as "a country of marvelous beauty" (20). Dorothy is now one step
closer to beginning her adventure, if she accepts her call.

Initially, Dorothy does refuse her call, because she cannot accept the fact
that she has killed the Wicked Witch of the East. When Dorothy encounters
the Munchkins and the good Witch of the North, she thinks to herself: "What
could the little woman possibly mean by calling her a sorceress, and saying
she had killed the wicked Witch of the East? [She] was an innocent harmless
little girl, who had been carried by a cyclone many miles from home; and she
had never killed anything in all her life" (21). It is at this point that Dorothy
becomes a character that Campbell says "loses the power of significant affirmative action and becomes a victim to be saved" (59). Dorothy must be convinced that her house did land on the Wicked Witch of the East and that she
has saved the Munchkins from an evil ruler. Once she is assured of this,
Dorothy realizes that she must now try to get back home.

Now that Dorothy accepts her call, she is given some help to start her
journey home. She must go to Oz to seek the help of a great wizard. However, this is not going to be an easy journey, and the Good Witch of the North
gives Dorothy some "Supernatural Aid" to help her along the way and acts
as the "protective figure [...] who provides the adventurer with amulets against
the dragon forces he [or she] is about to pass" (Campbell 69). Dorothy is given
the silver shoes of the Wicked Witch of the East, even though no one is really

aware of the powers they posses, and the Witch also kisses Dorothy on the forehead, an act that "left a round, shining mark" (Baum 25–27). This protective kiss will allow Dorothy safe passage through Oz. Specifically, it "becomes a visible halo on Dorothy's forehead and acts as an amulet against all evil" (Hudlin 450–451). Since she is protected by the Witch's magic, Dorothy can now face the first step of her adventure.

Before taking off on her "Heroine's Adventure," Dorothy packs some food in her basket, changes clothes (into her blue and white gingham dress), and puts on the silver shoes that formerly belonged to the Wicked Witch of the East (Baum 31–32). As she begins to walk, she comes up on "several roads" but quickly finds the "one paved with yellow brick" (33). Though she does not take long to find the yellow brick road and begin her adventure, this act does symbolize the "Crossing of the First Threshold," which is the final act of *Departure* and the first stage of Campbell's formula. It is this decision to follow the path of the yellow brick road that takes Dorothy into "darkness, the unknown and danger" (Campbell 77). Dorothy is sure to waste no time and instantly finds herself on the path that will lead her home.

The second stage of Dorothy's heroine's adventure is the *Initiation* where "the hero [or heroine] proves his [or her] merit, is tempted by evil, and learns the secrets of the gods" (Whomsley qtd. in Thury and Devinney 137). It is here where Dorothy meets and learns the stories of her three companions: the Scarecrow, the Tin Woodman, and the Cowardly Lion. Now that she is "[a]ccompanied by these protectors, Dorothy proceeds with confidence to the Emerald city" (Hudlin 455). Once these relationships are established, the "Road of Trials" begins.

First, the companions face the daunting task of outrunning the Kalidahs. According to the Cowardly Lion, these are "monstrous beasts with bodies like bears and heads like tigers" (Baum 79). When they cross a gulch by walking over a tree trunk, the Scarecrow instructs the Tin Woodman to cut the trunk at the end, and the Kalidahs fall to the bottom allowing the group to be safe once again (81). Once this trial has been concluded, the companions soon face another one.

As they come to a poppy field, they are impressed by its beauty, but the poison in the flowers causes Dorothy and the Cowardly Lion to fall into a deadly sleep. The Scarecrow and Tin Woodman must carry Dorothy to safety and call upon the help of a family of field mice and their queen to save the Cowardly Lion. After the Tin Woodman constructs a device with which to carry the Cowardly Lion, the field mice band together and pull the cart out of the poppy field while the Scarecrow and Tin Woodman push from behind (Baum 103–106). With everyone safe and awake again, the companions move on to face their next trial.

Once in the Emerald City of Oz, each member of the group sees the great wizard individually. In order to have their wishes granted, the Wizard tells each of them that they must kill the Wicked Witch of the West. With no other choice, the companions agree to find the Witch in the Land of the Winkies and kill her in order to get what they want. During this part of the adventure, the Wicked Witch of the West places many obstacles in their path, hoping that they will either not reach her or become her slaves. First, she sends a pack of wolves that the Tin Woodman slays; then, she sends a flock of crows that the Scarecrow faces and chokes; then, she sends a swarm of bees, and the Scarecrow instructs the Tin Woodman to spread his straw over Dorothy, Toto, and the Cowardly Lion, so the bees cannot see them and will sting the Tin Woodman instead, causing their stingers to break (Baum 142–144). When the Witch sees that these tactics will not work, she calls upon the golden cap that calls the winged monkeys to do her bidding. She uses her third and final command to send them to go and pick up the companions and bring them back to her castle to become her slaves.

Once the winged monkeys reach they companions, they drop the Tin Woodman over a "country thickly covered with sharp rocks," they find the Scarecrow and remove "all of the straw out of his clothes and head," they tie up the Cowardly Lion to where "he [is] unable to bite or scratch" in order to fly him to the witch's castle, and finally, they carry Dorothy to the castle unharmed because "she is protected by the Power of Good," which is the kiss from the Good Witch of the North (Baum 148). Now that Dorothy has been taken to the land of the Wicked Witch of the West with the Cowardly Lion, she has the opportunity to do what the Wizard of Oz asked of them. Dorothy becomes a slave to the Witch and is required to do housework around the castle. When the Witch trips Dorothy while she is mopping and gets one of the silver shoes from her, Dorothy becomes very angry. Her retaliation is to douse the Witch with the water she was using to mop, which ultimately leads to the death of the Wicked Witch of the West. Although Dorothy did not know this would in fact kill the Witch, she achieves what the Wizard asked of her nonetheless, and she and the Cowardly Lion can now go try to save their lost companions (153–155). By standing up to her nemesis, Dorothy becomes stronger and can now reunite with her companions and lead them back to the Wizard to have their wishes granted. Tuerk views this killing of the Witch as "a sign of her [Dorothy's] growth. In killing the Wicked Witch of the West, she is killing something infantile in herself so that she can be reborn not as an adult but as a more mature, more responsible child" (26). This growth allows Dorothy the strength to continue the journey and help her friends and herself find their way home. Once the Winkies repair the Scarecrow and Tin Woodman, the companions return to the Emerald City with the help of the winged monkeys to tell the Wizard that the Wicked Witch of the West is dead. Thus, the "Road of the Trials" concludes, and Dorothy and her companions must now face the Wizard to get what that for which they came. It is here that Dorothy comes face to face with the real Wizard of Oz.

Now, Dorothy must face her "Atonement with the Father" who, in this instance, is the Wizard of Oz. He is the character who will "test the hero [or heroine] to ascertain his [or her] worthiness" (Whomsley qtd. in Thury and Devinney 140). The Wizard sent Dorothy and her companions to kill the Wicked Witch of the West, and when she does kill her, she expects the Wizard to keep his promises. However, now that Dorothy has succeeded, the Wizard's "position and authority" is lost and "his impotence [is] apparent to everyone" (Hudlin 457). Dorothy's bravery to stand up to the Wicked Witch of the West has led to the demise of the Wizard because he knew all along that he would not be able to grant the companions' wishes. Dorothy's bravery allows her to become the strong-willed character that feminist critics can appreciate, especially since it directly leads to the Wizard's end in Oz.

When the Wizard's balloon takes off without Dorothy, all hope seems lost for her to get back home to Kansas. However, the "Meeting with the Goddess" will ultimately lead Dorothy back home and to the end of her adventure. Campbell notes that the "meeting with the goddess [...] is the final test of the talent of the hero [or heroine]" (118). When Dorothy and her companions are sent to the Land of the Quadlings to meet Glinda, the Good Witch of the South, Dorothy learns how she can get home and how she had the strength and ability to do it all along. The companions meet some interesting characters during this part of the journey, such as the fighting trees, the country of china people, and the forest of beasts, but they ultimately arrive at the Land of the Quadlings and meet Glinda. When the companions meet Glinda, she tells Dorothy: "Your Silver Shoes will carry you over the desert [...] If you had known their power you could have gone back to your Aunt Em the very first day you came to this country" (Baum 257). Though this news could have easily been frustrating, Dorothy is grateful for the adventure she had with her friends and is ready to go home to Kansas.

Before her *Return*, Dorothy experiences the "Apotheosis" or "achieves illumination" and comes to understand what her "Ultimate Boon" or her "final blessed gift" has been throughout her adventure (Whomsley qtd. in Thury and Devinney 141). Dorothy's illumination comes from learning that she had the ability to return home all along but appreciating the "Heroine's Adventure" she had to embark on and expressing gratitude for the friendships she has made. She is now aware of other worlds like Oz, but still feels the need to be in her own world. Her final gift is the silver shoes that allow her to go home, but she does lose them on her journey back over the desert. Nevertheless, the gift of the silver shoes proves to be of great importance since she would not be able to leave Oz without them.

The final stage, the *Return*, brings Dorothy back to Kansas and to her family and allows her to reintegrate with society (Whomsley qtd. in Thury and Devinney 137). There is no "Refusal of the Return" in Dorothy's case because she clearly wants to return home to Kansas throughout her "Heroine's Adventure," and her feelings do not change as she arrives at the end of the adventure. Of all the methods a hero (or heroine) has to come home, Dorothy's return comes as she "Crosses the Return Threshold" by using the silver shoes that were given to her. Dorothy's return is described by Campbell as a "coming back out of that yonder zone" which, in this novel, is Oz (217). Interestingly enough, she returns to Kansas in the same manner she was brought to Oz. Baum writes, "She was whirling though the air, so swiftly that all she could see or feel was the wind whistling past her ears" (258). Just as she was calm when she left Kansas in the cyclone, Dorothy is unafraid as she journeys back home through the whirlwind. By the end of this novel, it is not established that Dorothy will be able to become "Master of the Two Worlds," but she does acknowledge the "Freedom to Live." After all, as Campbell notes, the "goal [...] is to dispel the need for such life ignorance by effecting a reconciliation of the individual consciousness with the universal will" (238). Dorothy now understands that she came from the Land of Oz and her companions still remain there, but she goes back to life as it is in Kansas, a stronger young woman because of her adventure.

Adventure of a Feminist?

Applying a feminist critique to Baum's Dorothy Gale may not be done as often as the film version, but the strength she gains from undergoing a "Heroine's Adventure" like Campbell's cannot be ignored. As Bates asserts, "In the so-called real world, girls and women, often find themselves alone, abandoned, or separated from loved ones upon whom they had previously depended — upon whom, they perhaps assumed, their own survival depended" (48). This is the case for Dorothy, and she ultimately decides to go on the necessary adventure to get back home to the family she still needs and loves. Her story also translates to the readers who may go on her adventure with her. If young girls or women in the "real world" come across Dorothy's adventure, they can see that she was able to make it home, and she is stronger because of what she had to endure. When this allegory is applied to reality, it can become a source of inspiration for anyone who may be facing hard times because Dorothy shows them that they can do anything they put their minds to, even if it seems frightening at the time. Tuerk asserts that "Baum makes Dorothy's quest universal and timeless and makes *The Wonderful Wizard of Oz* an object of enduring interest," (34) and it is the universality of Dorothy's journey that feminist critics alike can appreciate and continue to learn from.

Works Cited

Bates, Laura Raidonis. "'Sweet Sorrow': The Universal Theme of Separation in Folklore and Children's Literature." *The Lion and the Unicorn* 31 (2007): 48–64. JSTOR. Texas Woman's University Library, Denton, TX. 12 Apr. 2008 <www.jstor.org>.

Baum, L. Frank. *The Wonderful Wizard of Oz: 100th Anniversary Edition.* New York: Harper Collins, 2003.

Campbell, Joseph. *The Hero with a Thousand Faces.* Princeton, NJ: Princeton University Press, 1972.

Hudlin, Edward W. "The Mythology of *Oz*: An Interpretation." *Papers on Language and Literature* 25.4 (Fall 1989): 443–462.

Levit, Briar. "The Bitch List." *Bitch Magazine: Feminist Response to Pop Culture* 35 (2007): 68.

Thury, Eva M., and Margaret K. Devinney. "The Hero with a Thousand Faces: The Book by Joseph Campbell, Discussed by Dave Whomsley." *Introduction to Mythology: Contemporary Approaches to Classical and World Myths.* Eds. Eva M. Thury and Margaret K. Devinney. New York: Oxford University Press, 2005.

Tuerk, Richard. "The Wonderful Wizard of Oz: Dorothy's Timeless Adventure." *Oz in Perspective: Magic and Myth in the L. Frank Baum Books.* Jefferson, NC: McFarland and Company Inc., 2007.

PART THREE

Oz and Social Critique

CHAPTER 14

The Wiz

American Culture at Its Best

RHONDA WILLIAMS

The production of *The Wiz* (1978) by Sidney Lumet is the grandest take on L. Frank Baum's classic tale *The Wonderful Wizard of Oz*. To date, *The Wiz* is often titled the "largest and musical adaptation" ever made (IMDb). The production team created sets with a sense of urban magic and spectacle: a New York subway station literally comes to life, and the massive plaza between the World Trade Center towers is transformed into the Emerald City, featuring nearly 400 dancers with three costume changes. Despite its grandeur, critics from 1978 to the present have denounced the film as a "romanticization of urban rubble" (IMDb). At the time of its release, movie critic David Kehr felt the original *The Wizard of Oz* theme "there's no place like home" is deserted and a new "learning-to-love-yourself" theme prevails (Chicago Reader). For Kehr, Lumet's *The Wiz* was "a lot to look at, little to contemplate, and nothing to hum" (Chicago Reader). A recent critic claims Lumet did not make a "single intelligent directorial decision" (IMDb). This critic cites the gloomy lighting, awkward camera placement, and clumsy editing as major downfalls in comparison to the 1939 adaptation of the text (IMDb). Unable to see past Baum's text of *The Wonderful Wizard of Oz* and Victor Leming's adaptation (1939) starring Judy Garland, Lumet's underlying theme and hidden messages of the adaptation are overlooked or dismissed without account for the reasons behind his decisions. His use of stereotypical images and typecast characters point to a greater political statement; however, all of this was dismissed and overlooked by critics. This dismissal by the critics is precisely the problem that the film addresses: mainstream America and Hollywood's refusal to come to grips with the issues and obstacles concerning Black people in the United States. Lumet shows that the salvation of the Black family and community lies with the Black woman.

Lumet, the father of two children from an interracial marriage (to Gail Jones, the daughter of singer Lena Horne), takes a civil libertarian's approach to politics rather than an ideological one. He is one of fifty charter members of the Performing Arts Committee for Civil Liberties, an organization designed to combat threats to free expression (Boyer 23). Many of his movies that actively engage in social commentary — *The Pawnbroker, Fail Safe,* the documentary *King,* and *The Wiz* — reflect this admirable, if rather unadventurous, political stance (Boyer 38). Known for his technical knowledge and his skill to get first-rate performances from his actors, Sidney Lumet is nevertheless a master of cinema, who has made over 40 movies. His films are often emotional, but seldom overly sentimental. Lumet often tells intelligent, complex stories (IMDb). He is politically left-leaning and often treats socially relevant themes in his films, but he claims "not [to] want to make political movies" in the first place (Boyer 41). Reflecting on Lumet's vitae and willingness to address political hot-button issues, the adaptation of Baum's *The Wizard of Oz* with an all-black cast is no surprise.

In the introduction of this classic text, L. Frank Baum purposely and clearly states the meaning for his text as "solely to pleasure children" in 1899 and 1900. Despite this clear effort to avoid speculation of underlying political themes or religious meanings, the literary criticism and analysis of Baum's text still finds that it could be viewed as a political allegory with religious messages, and critics search for political theories and hidden meanings and messages tied to American culture. In 1963, Henry Littlefield used Baum's book to educate his class of history students about the turn-of-the-century Populist Movement, giving one of the most popular and controversial interpretations of the text, termed the "Parable on Populism" (5). Littlefield alleged that Baum used to march in torch-light parades for William Jennings Bryan, a Democratic/Populist candidate in 1896. Littlefield states that when Baum went on to write his classic fairytale in 1900, he dressed it up as a Populist allegory. Littlefield makes the following comparisons between Baum's book and the Populist Movement: the stark opening of the book depicts the rural worker's despair and blasted hopes; the Wicked Witch of the East, who kept the Munchkins in bondage, stands for Eastern financial interests; Dorothy stands for everyman, i.e. a naive and innocent citizen; the Tin Woodman represents dehumanized machine-like labor in the factories; the Scarecrow represents the farmers; the Cowardly Lion represents William Jennings Bryan, with lots of roar, but not much accomplished; the Wizard of Oz represents William McKinley, the Republican president who upheld the gold standard; the Emerald City represents the national capital; the silver shoes were the silver standard; and the yellow brick road was the gold standard; and Oz is the popular abbreviation for how gold is measured. David Parker argues that since Littlefield's article, adults and scholars no longer read Baum's true text, but rather "read between Frank L. Baum's lines and see various images of the United States at the turn of the century" (49).

Parker himself also had a theory about the hidden meanings in Baum's text. Unlike Littlefields's political messages, Parker argues the narrative had a relationship between certain themes, episodes, and characters in the Oz stories and Baum's theosophical beliefs. Theosophy was a sort of New Age occult religion that was popular among certain groups of people a hundred years ago; Baum was a theosophist. Parker explains that the basic tenets of theosophical thought are relatively simple and include such notions as cosmic unity, planetary chains, human evolution within seven planes of existence, and reincarnation. It was re-reading Baum's *The Wonderful Wizard of Oz* that led Parker to discover the relationship between Baum's *Oz* writings and his theosophical beliefs. Parker gives some specific examples to illustrate how Baum's belief in theosophy could have several other implications for his writings: 1) Many early theosophists were feminists, and theosophy stressed a basic equality of the sexes. And, most of the major characters in the *Oz* series were female; 2) One can see a similar possible theosophical reflection in Baum's anti-intellectualism. For example, as Parker explains, the Scarecrow, who mistakenly thinks he needs brains ("head-learning"), actually gets by very well without brains, and is, in fact, the "smartest" of the travelers on the yellow brick road; 3) The theosophical belief in reincarnation can be seen in how Baum's characters sometimes change identities as seen in the other books in the Oz series; and 4) Colors were also important to early theosophists. Charles M. Leadbetter, an important shaper of early theosophical thought, came up with a list of colors and their correspondences with the astral body. Yellow meant "intellect," while emerald green stood for "versatility, ingenuity and resourcefulness." So, as Parker explains, Dorothy on her quest, follows the yellow brick road (intellect) and discovers, at the end, only a Wizard—"head-learning" alone is useless. Only after Dorothy applies the lessons of the Emerald City—"versatility, ingenuity and resourcefulness, applied unselfishly"—does Glinda tell Dorothy that she always had the power to return home. These intertextual studies of Baum's text require film adaptations to take notice of these aspects and connections. Arguably, there seems to be a link to Lumet's adaptation and its need to adapt the political mood of the country at the time. For Lumet, the political climate of 1970s centered on Civil Rights and equality of the races. The issue of racism and its associated stereotypes needed to be addressed and countered.

The Women's Rights Movement and the Civil Rights Movement of the late 1960s and early 1970s are closely aligned in defining the feminist and Black feminist tradition. The call to the first Women's Rights Convention came about, according to feminist Betty Friedan in her book *Feminist Mystique,* because "an educated woman, who had already participated in shaping society as an abolitionist, came face to face with the realities of a housewife's drudgery and isolation in a small town (Bell 239). According to Bell's research, most of the leading voices, faces, and ideas "were and are" for the benefit and betterment of upper-middle class white women (239). The question is how relevant are the "experiences, truths, and priorities" of upper-middle class white woman's to Black women without the middle class status facing racism and sexism? (Bell 239). The differences between the experiences, truths, and priorities made a world of difference where the question of women's rights and representation were concerned. As these and other problems were raised, Black women began to align and formulate definitions and categories about how and where they fit in the feminist movement. The duality of the Black woman made her unique but also raised several issues. Typically, the "experiences, truths, and priorities" of Black women were drastically glossed over and forgotten when looking at Blacks or women as a group. The only other people concerned about these issues were other Black women.

In order to better understand the placement of Black women within the feminist movement, there had to be a gap analysis done to understand the characteristics of traditional white feminism in order to figure out whether Black women could define themselves within that tradition or outside of it. Andres Benton Rushing convincingly determined that "Eurocentric" or white feminist qualities and categories of stereotypical white women were "passivity, compliancy, the submissive wife, and woman on a pedestal," which are inappropriately applied in analysis of Black women (Bell 241). Barbara Smith and Deborah McDowell joined the conversation and outlined the following signs and structures to categorize the Black women novelists falling within the Black feminist movement, separate and different than the white feminist movement (Bell 242):

- Motifs of interlocking racism, sexism, and classism oppression
- Black feminist protagonist
- Spiritual journeys from victimization to the realization of personal autonomy or creativity
- Centrality of female bonding and networking
- Sharp focus on personal relationships in the female realm or community
- Deeper, more detailed exploration and validation of epistemological power or emotions
- Iconography of women's clothing
- Black feminist language

At the same time that Smith and McDowell were creating the Black feminist signs and structures, Alice Walker added to the conversation with her text *In Search of Our Mother's Gardens*. Walker reclassified and renamed the Black feminist or feminist of color (non-white) as a "womanist" (xi). Her philosophical and multi-layered definition of womanism consisted of "black women's concrete history in racial and gender oppression," Black women as "traditionally universalist," and Black women that were specifically "committed to the survival and wholeness of entire people, male and female" (xi). Namely, Walker was interested in finding way to "foster cooperation among black women" and "foster stronger relationships between black women and black men" (xi). In an analysis of Black feminist tradition, Patricia Collins notes how Walker, along with "most black women" viewed feminism as a movement that, at best, is exclusively for upper-middle class white women and, at worst, dedicated to attacking or eliminating men (3). Collins goes on to note that womanism "seemingly supplies a way for black women to address gender oppression without attacking black men, but rather building them up to take their place as head of the black family and community" (3).

In adapting Baum's *The Wonderful Wizard of Oz* in 1978, given America's politically and socially heightened sensitivities to gender and race, I argue that Lumet's adaptation reflects and aligns with the Black feminist, or womanist, movement and coincides with the womanist film theory. The film highlights Dorothy's position of power within the Black family unit and community as the giver, nurturer, and taker of life for Black men and women. I assert that Lumet's Dorothy, unlike Baum's, has to rescue, re-educate, support, encourage, and uplift the Black man in order to reestablish the Black family unit and community. Dorothy and her life coaches, Auntie Em and Glinda the Good Witch, are responsible for the re-building of the Black community and the destroying of opposing forces, specifically female, that jeopardize or aim to work in opposition of the goal of Black unity.

In her work, *Rethinking the Novel/Film Debate*, Kamilla Elliot outlines six concepts of adaptation of text to film. Lumet's *The Wiz* exemplifies three of Elliot's concepts at play: genetic, ventriloquist, and de(re)composing. The "genetic" concept illustrates the film's compliance with the deep structure of the novel; this typically refers to the characters, actions, and settings. Aligning with the idea of a ventriloquist and his or her dummy, the "ventriloquist" concept of film adaptation uses the trappings and appearance of the text, but makes a different argument than the text does. In Elliot's de(re)composing, the original literary work is broken down into its basic elements, and the filmmaker fishes through the parts and recomposes the text in a new way for his adaptation.

Although the critics dismiss Lumet's *The Wiz* as a poor replica of Baum's text, the genetic, or deep, structure is still undeniably present. As in Baum's text, a person (female) is swept away from home by a natural wonder into the Land of Oz. *The Wiz* has the same characters, character flaws, and names as the Baum's narrative: Dorothy, the lost female; the Cowardly Lion; the Tin Man with no heart; the Scarecrow who seeks a brain; and a fake Wiz. The Land of Oz has the same plights of a Wicked Witch terrifying and abusing Munchkins and people in general. Just as in the literary version, Dorothy journeys through Oz to find the Wizard to send her home; likewise, the Wizard demands that she destroy the Wicked Witch before she can return home. Therefore, in both media, the protagonist, Dorothy, sets out to get home with her new friends. After the alignment on basic genetic structure, the text and film then depart from one another drastically.

Although similar in fashion, the dialogue, verbal/visual cues, and the prevailing purpose of *The Wiz* gets at the heart of the ventriloquist and de(re)composing concepts. Unlike the Dorothy in the original novel, Lumet's Dorothy is Black 20-something sheltered elementary school teacher from Harlem. Dorothy, played by the 30-year-old Motown icon Diana Ross, is at a crossroads in her life between being a responsible black woman who is working to rebuild the moral fiber of the Black family and community by getting out on her own and starting a family or by simply living isolated without hope to establish a place for herself. This is where the de(re)composing of the text is at play. While Baum's Dorothy is six-year-old child at a crossroads of being a "good girl" who obeys her Aunt and Uncle and stays "out of mischief," (21) Lumet's character is dealing with a dilemma that threatens to destroy the Black family unit, in turn destroying the Black community without her taking accountability for her place in the family. This twist on the genetic structure goes much further and deeper than Dorothy. Lumet uses stereotypical dressings to display the urgency for change in regard to the Black man in America; Dorothy has to help correct these flaws for the benefit of "saving" the Black family unit and community. Dorothy serves as a role model for the appropriate and necessary behavior that all of the Black, female moviegoers should emulate with the Black men in their lives. This passing of the torch from Dorothy to the black female moviegoer is set-up in the film as Dorothy's elders pass the torch to her. The film begins with a collage of Black women of the older generations working with the next generation to provide for the nurturing of future generations. This is done with a Thanksgiving scene in which the women rally around one another and the female children in order to guide them. The ventriloquist approach is seen throughout the recomposing of the text, and it is made clear through the musical selections in the film. Looking closer at Dorothy as the nurturer and the film's soundtrack, the recomposing of Black feminist model is evident.

Viewing Dorothy as a redeemer and savior requires a closer look at the Black men she saves. In order of appearance in the film, the Scarecrow (Michael Jackson) is the first that Dorothy rescues and resurrects. The Scarecrow, stuck on a pole and unable to escape, is subject to the constant cruelty and criticism of four crows. Ironically, the crows instill the spirit of worthlessness and failure into the Scarecrow for a number of years to the point that he believes he is a "dummy." They give him "Crow Commandments" that forbid him from asking questions, thinking, and especially, attempting to get off the pole. To drive his subjugation home, Lumet and musical directors Charlie Smalls and Quincy Jones insert a "Crow Anthem" for the Scarecrow to recite frequently when breaking one of the commandments called "You Can't Win." The intertextuality of the lyrics point to the oppression of uneducated, young Black men trying to "get out of the game" to no avail. Dorothy saves the Scarecrow from total destruction and a lifetime of oppression. Dorothy physically gets him off the pole, teaches him to walk, and teaches him of his worth by countering his frequent self-destructive attacks by explaining that he is the "product of negative thinking" and a "destructive environment." These phrases again point to the racist rhetoric heard during the 1960s and 1970s. After some philosophical quotes and walking lessons, Dorothy teaches the Scarecrow how to "ease on down the road" and overcome oppression. This song, "Ease on Down," serves as the chorus for Dorothy's education of the men in their renewal process.

Here, the Scarecrow symbolizes the Black man/child. He is naïve and youthful, but he has been robbed of his innocence and education by his environment and other negative forces. Dorothy's relationship to him seems to serve as mother to child as she teaches him to love himself. He is picked up first to see the entire journey in order to give him a well-rounded view of the world. In the Black feminist argument for the "betterment" and "unity of the black family," the Scarecrow represents the future for Black men; therefore, it is imperative that he is reformed, educated, and rebuilt at an early age because he has to carry out the tradition and role within the family and community (Collins 10).

Keeping in line with the thought of the growth and progression in relation to the Black family, the Tin Man represents a father/husband figure, who should be the head of the black family element. Again, as is the genetic structure of Baum's novel, Lumet's Tin Man (Nipsey Russell) seeks a heart. The film, in its ventriloquist adaptation, has the Tin Man is speaking a different language. Socially, the stereotype for Black men is their fast-talking and womanizing ways. Lumet's Tin Man is all of that: "Why I am just an ole flimflammer ... crushed in my youth by my third wife, Teeny." It is not until Dorothy teaches him to love that he actually feels his inadequacy. Dorothy frees him from him "postural prison, " oils his joints, and dances to his music, encouraging his song. In the recomposing of the text, Lumet's Tin Man, unlike Baum's, cries over Dorothy to bring her out of her poisoned, poppy-induced state. This is the recomposing of the text in its adaptation to point to a Black feminist reading, one in which Black men and woman are able to connect with one another for the benefit of the family. The musical direction is also at work here as the Tin Man belts out two songs, "What Would I Do?" and "Slide Some Oil to Me." Both songs show a more mature man than the Scarecrow, which signifies and adult relationship between a man and a woman. This ties in with the idea that the Tin Man is a husband figure for the Black family unit. Again, the rebuilding process of the Tin Man is supported and encouraged, and then it (the rebuilding) is fortified with another verse of the chorus of the "Ease on Down the Road" by Dorothy.

With the necessary components of the Black family intact, (Scarecrow as child, Tin Man as husband, and Dorothy as wife), the cowardly Lion (Ted Ross) enters the scene as a third male in need of reclassification. This time, the musical selection leads the assessment. The Lion bursts from a statue, attempting to scare off the crew of three plus Toto, roaring, "I'm a Mean Ole Lion." The song implies the external tough facade portrayed by Black men to scare off people before they can discover any hurt and sensitivity, which is demonstrated by the "King of Beasts." This stereotype could be seen in the movies produced and published in the years immediately preceding this film. All of these Black films encourage the masking of the Black man in the ultra cool, ultra tough image, which the American culture found delightful: *Superfly* (1972), *The Mack* (1973), *Claudine* (1974), *Cooley High* (1975), *Car Wash* (1976), and *Roots* (1977). These films portray the image of the Black man as needing to be tough and wear a mask in order to survive and combat discrimination and interracial pressures. Lumet's Lion aligns with this ideal; however, it is Dorothy, who is able to see through this facade to reach in and pull out the true Lion, the one who is a natural protector of his family and community. As a Lion, there is no need for him to fake the image of strength, for he naturally embodies the badge of honor and strength. Dorothy provides a support system of her family (husband and child) to back-up his understanding of his strength and courage. Again through song, Dorothy swoops in and soothes his bruised ego with the "Ease on Down" chorus designed specifically for him.

Fragmenting the chorus throughout the film gives Dorothy the power to strengthen and support all the characters in a unique, yet unified, way. The beauty is found in the fact that the other characters also get the message that support and encouragement revives a broken spirit. This message is especially important for the Scarecrow as the youth figure and future of Black men. He serves as a leader or role model for other young Black men in his family and community.

The men serve as proof of the need for and responsibility of Black women to serve as nurturers and builders of Black men in order to build the Black family and community. Dorothy almost single-handedly re-builds all the males in the film, and in doing so, she destroys any females who do not align with this agenda.

The recomposing and ventriloquist concept of adaptation in this film serves as a call to action for Black women in America. Demonstrating a political agenda of the Black Feminist movement, Lumet uses Dorothy as a model for all Black women to follow. This film is not about making a Black *The Wizard of Oz*, but rather about a handbook for Black women for the rebuilding of the Black family and community. The soundtrack only supports this message. The goal is for the audience to watch and emulate Dorothy's actions in the Black community, which is why its message is timeless and why *The Wiz* continues to generate video sales in the millions per year.

Works Cited

Baum, L. Frank. *The Wonderful Wizard of Oz*. Chicago: Harper Collins Pub, 1900.

Bell, Bernard W. *The Afro-American Novel and Its Tradition*. Amherst: University of Massachusetts Press, 1987.

Boyer, Jay. *Sidney Lumet*. New York: MacMilliam Publishing, 1993.

Collins, Patricia H. "What's in a Name: Womanism, Black Feminism, and Beyond." *The Black Scholar* 26.1 (1996): 9–17.

Internet Movie Database Inc (IMDb). Accessed 14 Nov 2004. http://www.imdb.com/. Elliot, Kamilla. *Rethinking the Novel/Film Debate*. New York: Cambridge Press.

Kehr, David. "Review of Lumet's *The Wiz*." *Chicago Reader* (1978).

King, Deborah K. "Multiple Jeopardy, Multiple Consciousness: The Context of a Black Feminist Ideology." *Words of Fire: An Anthology of African American Feminist Thought*. Ed. Beverly Guy-Sheftall. New York: The New Press, 1995.

Littlefield, Henry M. *The Wizard of Oz: Parable on Populism*. Ed. Michael Patrick. New York: Schocken Books, 1983.

Parker, David B. "Oz: L. Frank Baum's Theosophical Utopia." Faculty Colloquium Speech. Kennesaw State University, 1996.

The Wiz. Dir. Sidney Lumet. Videocassette. Universal Pictures. Universal City, 1978.

CHAPTER 15

The Wiz as the Seventies' Version of *The Wizard of Oz*

An Analysis

CLAUDIA A. BEACH

The 1975 Broadway musical production, *The Wiz*, has been described as the black version of the classic children's story, *The Wizard of Oz*. If this is the case, William F. Brown and Charlie Smalls' interpretation, as compared to the acclaimed 1939 film version, omits an essential element of the original story — its message. The production, directed by Geoffrey Holder, is unquestionably an entertainment success. It won seven Tony Awards, including Best Direction of a Musical (Geoffrey Holder), Best Choreography (George Faison), Best Costume Design (Geoffrey Holder), Best Featured Actress in a Musical (Dee Dee Bridgewater [Glinda]), Best Featured Actor in a Musical (Ted Ross [Lion]), Best Original Score (Charlie Smalls), and Best Musical ("Tony Legacy"). The familiar Oz characters are given delightful new interpretations. The well-known story is handled with outstanding originality and imagination. Production numbers sweep the stage with brilliant costumes, kaleidoscopic lighting effects, and contemporary music. However, beneath all the gloss and glitter of the production, the message of the play is almost indiscernible.

The story of *The Wizard of Oz* does have a very important message, particularly for children. The plot works to prove the message that the protagonist, Dorothy, actually states at the climax of the movie — "There's no place like home. There's no place like home." Although the character of Dorothy in *The Wiz* makes a similar statement, the production as a whole fails to prove it.

In order for the plot to convey the message of the story, three important facts must be established. First, from the very beginning, the audience needs to realize that Dorothy is loved and her place in Auntie Em's home is secure. Dorothy cannot realize this herself at the time because she is upset over the fate of her dog, Toto, but the audience must realize it. Dorothy's decision to run away from home, which serves as the inciting action of the play, then, may be seen as a childish and unjustified choice that begins the conflict and places Dorothy in the position of having to begin her quest to find home. The tornado is not the cause of Dorothy's travails. If she had not *chosen* to run away, she would be safe and sound in the storm cellar with the others.

The second fact that must be established concerns Oz. No matter how fascinating the Land of Oz may seem on the surface, it needs to be viewed as lacking in fulfilling the needs of a little girl from Kansas. Dorothy's happiness and well-being must be threatened. The audience must believe in Dorothy's desire to return home and, throughout the adventures in Oz, share this desire with her. Last, there must be a sense of relief at the end when Dorothy finally does return home. The audience should realize that Dorothy is safe, secure, and loved as she could never be in any other place. This last requirement is really an outgrowth of the establishment of the previous two. It is because these three basic facts — the security of home, the threat of Oz, and the relief of returning home — are not clearly established in *The Wiz* that the production fails to convey the intended message.

The security of home is not established from the very beginning, due largely to the interpretation of the character of Auntie Em (*The Wiz*). Rather than conveying the idea of being unintentionally neglectful of Dorothy, Auntie Em actually seemed to be resentful toward the girl. Whether this is the fault of the actress, Tasha Thomas, or simply the fact that the scene takes place so quickly that development is impossible, is difficult to tell. In the extremely short scene that precedes the tornado, Dorothy attempts to apologize for not helping Aunt Em hang out the clothes to dry:

DOROTHY: I'm sorry, Aunt Em. I didn't ...

AUNT EM: ... *think*. No, you never do, child. Now we're fixin' for a twister, an' you're playin' games with that dog! And in your Sunday dress, too! Serve you right if you *both* blew away!

DOROTHY: I imagine it would.

AUNT EM: What was that?

DOROTHY: Aw, I'm not much help around here for you and Uncle Henry. Always daydreamin' an' stuff. I bet it'd be a big load off your back if I *did* blow away, wouldn't it?

AUNT EM: I imagine it would.

Whatever the reason for Aunt Em's coldness, the fact remains that home does not seem like a happy place for Dorothy to be. When the tornado sweeps her away, it comes as a welcomed escape — and, significantly, as a totally random accident. As all three characters — Uncle Henry, Aunt Em, and Dorothy — are fighting the wind to enter the cellar, Dorothy just happens to be the one the wind sweeps up. There is no decision to run away from home here.

The staging of the tornado itself begins the dream/Oz sequence on a somewhat weak note thematically. The number is technically fascinating, a colorful and energetic production number, but it somehow lacks a sense of danger. The tornado evokes more of a pleasant sensation than a fearful one.

However, it is the fact that Dorothy never seems threatened in Oz that makes the conveyance of the message impossible. This lack of a threat is due primarily to the interpretations of several of the main characters. Although they are highly entertaining and original, it is this same originality that destroys their ability to appear as threats to Dorothy.

The first unusual character interpretation to present itself is that of the Good Witch of the North, Addaperle (Clarice Taylor). Rather than being characterized as a beautiful, awe-inspiring princess, worthy of imitation and reverence, she is a loveable but bungling ugly duckling. She immediately establishes herself as a friend to Dorothy, but just how helpful she could be is questionable. The fact that this character is not presented as being perfect removes her ability to heighten the evilness of the other characters by contrast.

The first potentially threatening character Dorothy meets is that of the Wiz (Andre De Shields). However, only at the very first does he seem truly threatening. Arriving in a puff of smoke on six-inch platform heels, the Wiz sweeps open his long black cape to reveal a beautifully proportioned human body clothed in a solid white, rhinestone jumpsuit. The subsequent song and dance sequence almost always receives the most vocal audience reaction. However, the reaction is one of admiration, not fear. The Wizard, after all, is only human. Just how threatening can Elvis Presley be? Later, when the real "Wiz" is discovered bedecked in pink sponge hair rollers, bathrobe, and fuzzy house shoes, he is not even worthy of pity, but appears merely silly.

The major threat for Dorothy should come from the character of the Wicked Witch, the most frightening character in the original *The Wizard of Oz*. The interpretation of this character, Evillene (Mabel King), however, also fails to achieve that goal. The Witch is given amusing comic qualities that soften the evil image. Characterized as a gaudily jeweled, heavily made-up, streetwalker-type, she barks orders to her followers and pounds them over the head with her scepter. Add to this the fact that she can scarcely stand up without help due to her extreme obesity and the temptation for slapstick comedy is overpowering. The temptation is not avoided, resulting in the removal of any potentially threatening capacity the Witch possesses.

The remaining characters in Oz — the Scarecrow, Tin Man, and Lion — are so loveable and fun that it is impossible to understand why Dorothy would ever want to return home. Her adventure in Oz has been delightfully entertaining. She has made several close friends and has not been seriously threatened by anyone.

When Dorothy finally does discover the way to return home, it is almost a disappointment — and it is not a particularly difficult choice either, as the Scarecrow points out that as long as she retains her "silver" slippers she can return for a visit whenever she chooses. Therefore, even though Dorothy sings the equivalent of "There's no place like home," it is difficult to believe her sincerity. Nothing that happens in Oz motivates her change of attitude.

Thus, we can see that in the 1975 Broadway version of *The Wiz*, Dorothy has no reason to feel relief at returning home. Home has not been proven to be superior. In fact, Dorothy's fantasy world of Oz seems preferable to the real one. It is also appropriate to note that, in fact, we never see how Dorothy actually responds to being at home. *The Wiz* ends as Dorothy closes her eyes and clicks her heels together.

The unique interpretation of the play is extremely successful in providing entertainment. The imaginative characters are delightful to watch, and the music and dancing are sensationally appealing. The concept of the production itself is fascinating, but somehow, in the midst of all the originality and sparkle, the message is ultimately lost.

Works Cited

Smalls, Charlie. "The Wiz." *Great Rock Musicals.* Ed. Stanley Richards. New York: Stein and Day, 1979.

"Tony Legacy: Search Past Winners." *Tony Awards: Official Website of the American Theatre Wing's Tony Awards.* 26 June 2009.

The Wiz. Dir. Geoffrey Holder. Prod. Ken Harper. Majestic Theatre, New York, 23 July 1975.

The Wizard of Oz. Dir. Victor Fleming. Metro-Goldwyn-Mayer, 1939.

CHAPTER 16

The Wonderful Wizard of Oz

Religious Populism and Spiritual Capitalism

KEVIN TANNER

The Wonderful Wizard of Oz had instant success upon being published in 1900, and allowed popular children's novelist L. Frank Baum to retire from the mercantile trade — never to travel the roads of America's Midwest selling chinaware again. As a full-time author, Baum wrote thirteen more novels set in the Land of Oz. In 1902, he turned *The Wonderful Wizard of Oz* into a musical for the stage production called *The Wizard of Oz*. After moving to Hollywood, California, Baum became interested in turning his Oz books into films and began the Oz Film Manufacturing Company. Though his silent Oz films and stage adaptations were largely unsuccessful, Baum spent nineteen years — from the publishing of *The Wonderful Wizard of Oz* to his death from a stroke in 1919 — as a prolific writer of plays, short stories, poetry, and novels for both children and adults. None of Baum's other works ever matched the success of his Oz books, especially the great success of *The Wonderful Wizard of Oz*, which is now one of the most beloved children's books in American history.

Today, *The Wonderful Wizard of Oz* remains the single most famous work of L. Frank Baum; however, the novel has been supplanted by MGM's *The Wizard of Oz* as the means by which most people get to know Baum's creation. This 1939 musical starring Judy Garland as Dorothy and Margaret Hamilton as the Wicked Witch of the West was not a commercial success, but with the advance of television, it became an annual treat for viewers beginning in the late 1950s on CBS, and like Frank Capra's *It's a Wonderful Life*, *The Wizard of Oz* became a television hit. The familiarity and popularity of the MGM film have overshadowed the fact that Oz books were a commercial success even after Baum's death. Upon Baum's death, his publisher

Reilly and Lee turned to Ruth Plumly Thompson to keep the Oz series alive, and Thompson did so by writing nineteen Oz books, which was five more than Baum wrote. Upon Thompson's retirement, the Oz series continued through the writings of John R. Neill, Jack Snow, Rachel R. Cosgrove, Eloise Jarvis McGraw, and Lauren Lynn McGraw. In all, there are forty Oz books known by Baum scholars as "The Famous Forty."

After this series ended, other authors turned to Oz to tell additional tales. The most popular are the works of Gregory Maguire, such as *Wicked: The Life and Times of the Wicked Witch of the West*, *Son of a Witch*, and *A Lion Among Men*. Maguire, a revisionist, uses the fantasy world of Oz to tell more adult stories that parallel what has already happened in the previous Oz books. Like *The Wonderful Wizard of Oz*, *Wicked* was also turned into a popular musical for the stage. Maguire is not alone in revising Oz. Stephen King uses the setting of Oz, specifically the Emerald City, in his *The Dark Tower IV: Wizard and Glass*, and in 2007, the Sci Fi Channel aired *Tin Man*, a six-hour miniseries that updates the classic *Wizard of Oz* tale for a twenty-first century adult audience by turning Baum's colorful and fantastic Oz into the O.Z. (Outer Zone), a bleak, dark, and immoral place.

The popularity of *The Wonderful Wizard of Oz* has not only created a cottage industry, but it also has given rise to academic curiosity. Could L. Frank Baum's modern fairy tale be something greater than wholesome entertainment? Over the past half century many cultural, social, economic, and political historians have suggested that Baum's 1900 tale most definitely is. Much of the debate has revolved around whether *The Wonderful Wizard of Oz* is a populist allegory that could help explain monetary issues of the 1890s or a subversive text that advocates consumer capitalism and tries to appease people's anxieties concerning the modern city. Neither explanation fits with Baum's explanation for writing *The Wonderful Wizard of Oz*; thus, a better explanation is needed to explain this modern fairy tale's significance to American history. Rather than focus on consumer capitalism, 1890s populism, or the Gold Standard, critics would come closer to the true intent of the tale by starting from Baum's own suggestion in the introduction to *The Wonderful Wizard of* Oz: "Modern education includes morality; therefore the modern child seeks only entertainment in its wonder-tales and gladly dispenses with all disagreeable incident. Having this thought in mind, the story of 'the Wonderful Wizard of Oz' was written solely for the amusement of children today. It aspires to being a modernized fairy tale, in which the "wonderment and joy are retained and the heart-aches and nightmares are left out."[1] If Baum wanted readers to interpret his story as a fairy tale, a far-fetched story, that keeps "the wonderment and joy" but leaves out "the heart-aches and night-mares" of religious morality education, then the story does hold some hidden agenda. Examining *The Wonderful Wizard of Oz* through a religious lens, rather than a social, political, or economic lens, shows that Baum uses Theosophy, especially its reliance on spiritualism, to get rid of "the heart-aches and nightmares" raised by fundamental Christianity's reliance on "hellfire and brimstone." If read as a religious allegory, Baum's fairy tale reveals the conflict in American religion at the turn of the twentieth century and remains a subversive religious populist text that advocates spiritual consumerism.

Populist Allegory or Consumer Capitalism

For some cultural historians, *The Wonderful Wizard of Oz* is more than a fairy tale to amuse children because it seems to encapsulate American politics, culture, and society of the 1890s. The historical debate over the significance of *The Wonderful Wizard of Oz* began in 1964 with Henry M. Littlefield's "The Wizard of Oz: Parable on Populism." In this article, the Mount Vernon High School teacher argues that *The Wonderful Wizard of Oz* is a populist parable where the Cowardly Lion represents William Jennings Bryan, the Tin Man symbolizes the industrialized worker, and the Scarecrow stands for the uneducated farmer. These three accompany Dorothy on her adventure to the Emerald City to find the Wizard of Oz, who supposedly has the power to grant them their wishes to find courage, receive a heart, obtain a brain, and go home. For Littlefield, this band traveling to see the Wizard is "Coxey's Army of tramps and indigents, marching to ask President Cleveland for work in 1894." Not only that, this journey down the yellow brick road is also a metaphor representing the conflict over bimetallism — Dorothy's silver slippers supposedly represent the free silver issue, which was the position that the People's Party and then William Jennings Bryan took during the 1890s, while the yellow brick road represents the dangerous gold standard.[2]

Littlefield's contention that "*The Wonderful Wizard of Oz* has provided unknowing generations with a gentle and friendly Midwestern critique of the Populist rationale" quickly became a popular interpretation.[3] Over the next several decades, historians and cultural critics such as Richard Jenson, Brian Attebery, Hugh Rockoff, and Gene Clanton added to this populist impulse, even though they remained partially skeptical of Littlefield's interpretation. Jenson, for instance, is hesitant to label Baum a populist, but he suggests that Baum could have been a liberal Democrat. He offers that Oz, which is the abbreviation of ounce, means that at least Baum's fairy tale is most definitely a commentary on bimetallism. He also suggests that Toto could be short for teetotaling Prohibitionists. Like Peterson, Attebery warns against viewing *The Wonderful Wizard of Oz* as a populist allegory, but he also cannot help comparing Dorothy to Mary Lease, the Kansas born suffragist and populist "who told her neighbors to raise less corn and more hell." Rockoff, who cares less about the social and political aspects of Littlefield's arguments, advances Littlefield's bimetallism argument by insisting that *The Wonderful Wizard of Oz* is a monetary allegory that should be used as a pedagogic device to better explain the economic battle between free silver and the gold standard. Clanton suggests that Littlefield's interpretation is slightly off. Rather than being a populist allegory, *The Wonderful Wizard of Oz* should be viewed as a progressive allegory; for Clanton, the Wicked Witch of the West was actually the evil of radical populism.[4]

Beginning in the early 1990s, Littlefield's populist argument began to lose its appeal. William R. Leach became its biggest critic when he contended that this fairy tale is not a subversive populist text; instead, Leach argues that the fairy tale used Theosophy, a mind-cure philosophy based on spiritualism, to advocate consumer capitalism.[5] Leach emphasizes the magical, colorful world of the make-believe Oz, especially the Emerald City, and suggests that Baum's fairytale provides "an optimistic, affirmative vision of America that reinforced the priorities and values of the new industrial order."[6] Leach argues that since Oz is more-or-less a benevolent place derived from Baum's careers as an actor, playwright, merchant, and editor of *The Show Window*, a journal instructing merchants how to display goods in their store window, then *The Wonderful Wizard of Oz* is a feel good story that reveals "the rewards of America's new culture and economy of consumption."[7] Since Leach concentrated on Baum's life as a businessman and later as a salesman, he argues that *The Wonderful Wizard of Oz* signifies urban abundance; unfortunately, this is probably the weakest part of his consumer capitalist argument because only a small part of *The Wonderful Wizard of Oz* takes place in the Emerald City, and it is not clear if Baum enjoyed living in urban Chicago over his rural childhood home, Rose Lawn, or his Hollywood home, Ozcot. Even though the Emerald City rests at the center of Oz, the novel's four main characters are all rural, and in many ways, the Emerald City is the Wizard of Oz's prison. The Wizard hides in his throne room in fear that the Wicked Witches will discover that he has no magical powers. The colors of the book might reveal, as Leach contends, the significance of advertising the modern city's cornucopia of material wealth. The decade of the 1890s is known not only as the "Gay Nineties" but also the "Mauve Decade," the purple dye founded by William Henry Perkins that became fashionable.[8] However, Leach's emphasis on color possibly undermines his consumer capitalism argument because Baum's interest in colors could come from his interest in the spiritual world. Baum's use of colors is similar to those of the Apostle John's in Revelations, and the use of different colored pages resembles the Wordless Bible employed by Charles Haddon Spurgeons, an English preacher, to evangelize illiterate orphans before being brought to America by Dwight Moody in 1875.[9] Also, it must not be overlooked that Baum was writing a fairytale to inspire the dreams of children, so color would be one key to stimulating the imagination.

Leach is not alone in dismantling the assumption that *The Wonderful Wizard of Oz* is a parable on populism. Others have examined the economic, social, and political aspects and have come to the conclusion that *The Wonderful Wizard of Oz* has little to do with William Jennings Bryan, the debate over bimetallism, and the opposition to capitalism. Today, there is nearly a consensus that *The Wonderful Wizard of Oz* is not a populist allegory. Scholars such as Katharine Rogers, Nancy Tystad Koupal, Bradley A. Hansen and Fred Erisman, to name only a few, have argued that Baum was likely a Republican progressive rather than a populist Democrat.[10] Their basic argument is that if Baum was not a populist, then he probably did not intend *The Wonderful Wizard of Oz* to be a populist allegory.

Even though he intended *The Wonderful Wizard of Oz* to be a modern American fairytale, Baum was not an overtly political man; thus, it is hard to argue that the story could be a political allegory about 1890s populism, especially since the Land of Oz is ruled by monarchs. Royalty and monarchs rule over the people and animals in Oz, and with Baum setting the story in the traditional medieval setting of most fairytales, it is hard to contend that the story implies much about the late nineteenth or early twentieth century American city. Also, it seems a stretch to argue that the story advocates capitalism because the journey, or pilgrimage, across Oz has nothing to do with money or riches — Dorothy wants to go home to poverty, the Lion wants courage, the Scarecrow a brain, and the Woodman a heart. None of them wants Aladdin's Cave of Treasures. Even though the Emerald City is full of jewels, the Wizard confesses to Dorothy that the Emerald City is no more luxurious or green than any other city "but when you wear green spectacles, why of course everything you see looks green to you."[11] In fact, the story focuses mostly on the destruction of the tyrannical, evil witches who had enslaved their subjects and on turning the Lion, Tin Woodman, and the Scarecrow into monarchs, suggesting that a proper leader has courage, compassion, and commonsense.

Baum's Spiritual Journey

In many respects, it is hard to see *The Wonderful Wizard of Oz* as anything more than a bedtime story, much less a book advocating either the Populist Movement or consumer capitalism. However, Littlefield's analysis still holds some significant insights that go beyond being a didactic device to help people understand populism or bring interest to the debate over bimetallism.

Because his interpretation rests on interpreting Oz as a rural story, *The Wonderful Wizard of Oz*'s significance could still rest on a spiritual populist interpretation because the story emphasizes not the city itself but Dorothy's pilgrimage to the Emerald City. Baum's own childhood at Rose Lawn suggests that he preferred the countryside over the city and probably is as important to explaining his fantasy books as his life as a businessman and salesman in the mid-west. His father thought that Baum was going to take over the family's agricultural ventures, and it was during his childhood that Baum became interested in raising poultry as well as beginning his initial forays into writing and acting.

It also needs to be remembered that Baum was raised by orthodox Methodists in Central New York. His mother, Cynthia Baum, was a strict Methodist who readily scolded him for ungentlemanly behavior. His father, Benjamin War Baum, attended Cazenovia Seminary, a Methodist school, and was an active member at his local Methodist Church as well as trustee of the Centenary M.E. Church Society.[12] Lyman's grandfather, John Baum, was a Methodist lay minister.[13] Before the American Civil War, this area was known as the "Burned-Over District" because of all the religious fervor. It was the place where Rev. Charles G. Finney held his greatest revivals, where Joseph Smith started Mormonism, where Millerites believed that the millennium was at hand, where the Fox sisters practiced spiritualism, and where abolitionists and woman's rights advocates liberalized Christianity to attack slavery and paternalism.[14] If *The Wonderful Wizard of Oz* holds a populist critique, then it does so by attacking fundamentalist Christianity. In many respects, it is much easier to argue that *The Wonderful Wizard of Oz* is much more a critique of America's religious orthodoxy than it is a story about political populism and consumerism. If read through a cultural rather than a social or political lens, then the novel's historical significance rests more as a religious commentary of the 1890s that validates spiritualism and rejects the hellfire and damnation of orthodox Christianity.

Though he was raised by Methodists, Baum, as a spiritual man, seemed to have been more influenced by his wife and mother-in-law who believed in spiritualism. His mother-in-law, Matilda Gage, was a renowned woman's suffragist from Fayetteville, New York. She spent the last years of her life writing *Woman, Church, and State*, an attack on Orthodox Christianity, which she believed kept women in bondage because it supported paternalism. Her opposition to orthodox Christianity was very much an anti-clerical attack; thus, her rejection of the male-dominated religious hierarchy led her down the path toward spiritualism. Gage frequently went to séances, believed in reincarnation, and even believed that the house at Campbell Park was haunted. During the 1890s, Matilda Gage spent a great deal of time with the Baums.

Her daughter Maud considered her mother her best friend; thus, it comes as no surprise that Maud was quickly influenced by her mother's spiritualism. Maud quit the Episcopal Church, and when the Baums lived in Chicago, she began to send her older sons to the West Side Ethical Culture Sunday School that taught ethics rather than doxology. On September 4, 1892, Maud and Frank Baum joined the Chicago's Ramayana Theosophical Society. It is not clear whether L. Frank Baum believed deeply in spiritualism or merely adhered to it to please his wife and mother-in-law. In any case, Baum scholar Katherine Rogers contends: "Frank found in theosophy a system of belief that satisfied his reason and at the same time fulfilled his strong spiritual needs." Theosophy is a religious philosophy originating with Helena Petrovna Blavatsky that advocates perfectionism by adhering to Asian religions, supports interreligious accord, and advances spiritualism "to investigate the hidden mysteries of nature." According to Rogers, theosophy helped L. Frank Baum develop his fantasy worlds by giving him spiritual laws that helped reveal spiritual truths much like science has done for earthly truths.[15]

In this respect, it seems that *The Wonderful Wizard of Oz* could possibly be a spiritual text. Katharine M. Rogers writes: "According to a clergy friend, 'He had a gospel of his own and he preached it through his books, although you certainly could not call them religious.'"[16] It does not take too much convincing to see that Oz is very much like heaven. Michael O. Riley, author of *Oz and Beyond*, contends that Oz is "Arcadia" or a "good place." It seems to be very much like heaven with a yellow brick road leading to a celestial city.[17] The Guardian of the Gates tells Dorothy and her friends that "if you did not wear spectacles the brightness and glory of the Emerald city would blind you."[18] Many aspects of *The Wonderful Wizard of Oz* imply spiritual twists to common Christian imagery.

The Evangelical and Her Christ-Like Companions

Although Leach's consumer capitalism argument seems flawed with his contention that Baum's "*The Wizard of Oz* has no connection to conventional Christianity as the Lion accidentally smashing the china church ... so amply testifies,"[19] Leach does admit that theosophy probably influenced Baum. He is correct in seeing *The Wonderful Wizard of Oz* as a trickster's tale. Like a trickster or a court jester, Baum likes witty remarks, and his witticism is often the most noticeable when he uses Christian symbolism. A short examination of *The Wonderful Wizard of Oz* reveals many traditional Christian symbols. In fact, the five main characters — Dorothy, the Scarecrow, the Tin Man, the Lion, and the Wizard of Oz — all appear to be variations of traditional Christian archetypes. Dorothy is the evangelical little girl, the Scarecrow is Christ as man, the Tin Man is Christ as servant, the Lion is Christ as king, and Oz is Christ as Lord or High Priest.

Leach, himself, alludes to Dorothy representing evangelicalism when he comments that Dorothy's silver shoes possibly come from John Bunyan's *Pilgrim's Progress.* Leach recalls that in Bunyan's tale, "By-ends," who cares much about worldly wealth, tells Christian: "We are always most zealous when religion goes in silver slippers."[20] In response, Christian says: "You must also own religion in his rags as well as when in silver slippers." Baum, of course, fuses these together by having the orphan Dorothy begin her journey to the Emerald City in her only dress, a gingham dress "with checks of white and blue," which was "somewhat faded with many washings" along with the silver slippers with pointed toes because her shoes were "old and worn."[21] In her rags and silver slippers, Dorothy is very much the 19th century evangelical girl like little Eva in *Uncle Tom's Cabin* or Helen Burns in *Jane Eyre.* The name *Dorothy* is derived from Greek meaning "the gift from god" (it is the combination of *doron* meaning "gift" and *theos* meaning "God") and is taken from St. Dorothea the virgin martyr killed under Diocletian. If one even misses these subtle religious clues, Baum makes it very clear after he has Dorothy leave the Emerald City on her adventure to kill the evil Witch of the West by having her wear a white dress, which she originally thought was green because of the green glasses she was forced to wear while in the city. In addition, she kills the witch by baptizing her with a bucket of water, and since the witch is pure evil, the water causes her to melt away. On a more personal level to Baum, Dorothy was more than a character; the name was passed down in the Gage family. Thomas Clarkson Gage, Maud's brother, had a baby girl named Dorothy, who lived only five months in 1898. Her death greatly agitated Maud, who possibly believed that Dorothy was the reincarnation of her recently departed mother.[22] This possibly explains why Baum has Dorothy wanting to leave the mystical Oz for grey Kansas. As the good evangelical orphan, Dorothy knows how much pain and suffering Aunt Em and Uncle Henry were experiencing with her loss, and she wants to return home and bring her spirit of joy back to them.

At first, it seems highly unlikely that the Scarecrow, the Tin Man, the Lion, and Wizard of Oz are all variations of Christ characters but, in many ways, these four characters resemble the four gospel depictions of Jesus Christ as Man in Luke, as Suffering Servant in Mark, as King in Matthew, and as God in John.[23] The first companion Dorothy "saves" is the Scarecrow from the wooden pole stuck up his back. Upon getting down, he announces: "Thank you very much. I feel like a new man."[24] According to orthodox Christian faith, once one repents his sin and accepts Christ as his savior, then his sinful burdens are forgiven because of Christ's sacrifice at Calvary, and he becomes, according to nineteenth-century evangelicals like Charles G. Finney, a "new man." Since a scarecrow is a straw man, he lacks confidence, and Baum signifies this by having him claim that he has no brain. In many ways, it seems that Baum is being a jokester because his new man is a straw man argument or misrepresentation of Christ as Man. Since he is made from straw, he tells Dorothy not to worry about hurting him because he cannot feel even a "pin," and the only thing he worries about is a "lighted match." The pin suggests crucifixion, and the lighted match suggests hell. Of course, Christ as Man did feel pain, hunger, fatigue, loneliness, and temptation, but the Scarecrow never experiences pain, nor does he eat or sleep. His great failure is that he is not scary enough to frighten crows. As the Scarecrow retells his creation to Dorothy, we discover that he "was only made day before yesterday." In other words, the Scarecrow came down from his pole only on the third day, and Christ rose from the dead on the third day. Of course, this resurrection moment is clarified by W. W. Denslow's picture of the Scarecrow on his pole looking very much like the crucified Christ on the cross. By stressing that Scarecrow is not scary — he failed to frighten away crows from the farmer's field — Baum stresses Christ's pacifism and benevolence. By having him desire knowledge of the world around him, Baum reveals that the Scarecrow has the commonsense and intelligence to be a good leader and teacher who knows the spirit of the law, even if he does not necessarily know the law.

The Scarecrow as the symbol of Christ as Man becomes clearer after we meet the Tin Woodman, who represents Christ as the Suffering Servant. Dorothy and the Scarecrow rescue the Tin Woodman as they travel on the yellow brick road through the forest. They discover the Tin Woodman rusted, and after a quick oiling of the joints that allow him to lower his ax, the Tin Man tells them his tragic tale. Like the Scarecrow, it becomes obvious that the Tin Man is a Christ figure. His history is one of obedience and love. Instead of a carpenter (as was Joseph, the earthly father of Jesus), the Tin Man's father was a woodman, so the Tin Man grew up and "became a wood-chopper." After his father's death, he took care of his mother and fell in love with a beautiful Munchkin girl, who lived with a hateful old woman who paid the "Witch of the East" to curse his axe. Over time, the axe cuts off all his limbs, torso, and head, and this former Munchkin had each appendage replaced by the work of a tinsmith, and over time, he was slowly transformed into a tin man. Even as a tin man, the Woodman remains a good servant who is now protected by his cursed axe.

The Woodman resembles Christ as the sacrificial lamb and brings to mind the Gospel of Mark, when Christ tells his disciples that "And whoever of you will be the chiefest, shall be servant to all. For even the Son of Man came not to be ministered unto, but to minister, and to give his life a ransom for many" (10:44–45 KJV). The Tin Woodman fits this criterion for a good leader perfectly; his understanding of pain and suffering make him the perfect ruler for the Winkies. However, before he replaces the Wicked Witch of the West, he has to wrestle with the many definitions of love — affection (*storge*), friendship (*philia*), eros, and *agapé*. At first, the Tin Man is concerned with affection and *eros* because the only people who matter to him are his family and sweetheart. He tells Dorothy and the Scarecrow, "But alas! I had now no heart, so that I lost all my love for the Munchkin girl, and did not care whether I married or not."[25] After being caught in a rainstorm and being rusted for a year, he came to realize that he needed a heart to learn how to love again because he still desired to marry his Munchkin maiden. So, he decides to join the pilgrimage to the Emerald City and ask Oz for a heart, and on this spiritual journey, he learns about *agape*, the unconditional love shown to others, as well as the friendship of his companions. By the end of novel, he has all but forgotten his Munchkin maiden.

During the Tin Man's discourse about a heart, he and the Scarecrow have a little debate about which is more important: the head or the heart. In many respects, this conversation was a very common discussion for nineteenth-century Christians. For orthodox Calvinists, one had to focus on one's head and follow the religious law of the Old Testament to prevent sin. For more liberal Christians, the emphasis was on the heart because salvation did not come from following the law but through God's saving grace. This was a common debate between divine law and saving grace in the annals of Christian literature, and Baum to a degree summarizes it by writing:

> "All the same," said the Scarecrow, "I shall ask for brains instead of a heart; for a fool would not know what to do with a heart if he had one."

> "I shall take a heart," returned the Tin Woodman; "for brains do not make one happy, and happiness is the best thing in the world."[26]

Of course, the happiness that the Tin Man talks about is not the hedonistic pleasures of wealth and riches in a consumerist society but of true love, the kind that Christ died for on Calvary.

The third Christ-like character is the Cowardly Lion, who represents Christ as King. The Lion is a common Christian symbol of Christ which has been used since the first Christians, and in Revelation, John gives Christ the title "the Lion of the Tribe of Judah" (Rev. 5:5). Of the four apostles, Matthew emphasizes Christ as king by stressing Jesus' lineage from David, but to the surprise of all, Christ was not the warrior god of old but a new merciful god who came to persuade rather than kill and destroy. Instead, Christ proclaimed when the high priest came to arrest him: "Put up again thy sword into its place: for all they that take the sword shall perish with the sword. Thinkest thou that I cannot now pray to my Father, and he shall presently give me more than twelve legions of angels?" (Matthew 26:52–53 KJV). So, it should come as no surprise that a jokester like Baum would make his kingly Lion cowardly. Baum introduces the Cowardly Lion by having him roar and leap at Dorothy, Toto, the Scarecrow, and the Tin Man as they continue their journey through the forest. After striking the Scarecrow and the Woodman who cannot feel pain, the Lion confronts Toto and Dorothy, and as he attempts to bite Toto, who is barking at him, he receives a slap from Dorothy. The Lion quickly whimpers and confesses that he is truly a coward and that his roar is bigger than his bite. In fact, he roars louder the more terrified he is of others. In addition, Baum writes:

> "It's a mystery," replied the Lion. "I suppose I was born that way. All the other animals in the forest naturally expect me to be brave, for the Lion is everywhere thought to be the King of Beasts. I learned that if I roared very loudly every living thing was frightened and got out of my way. Whenever I've met a man I've been awfully scared; but I just roared at him, and he has always run away as fast as he could go. If the elephants and the tigers and the bears had ever tried to fight me, I should have run myself—I'm such a coward, but just as soon as they hear me roar they all try to get away from me, and of course I let them go."[27]

Thus, the Cowardly Lion decides to join the quest to the Emerald City for a meeting with the Wizard of Oz in order to ask the great wizard for Courage.

The last of the main characters in *The Wonderful Wizard of Oz* is the Wizard himself. According to his son Frank Joslyn Baum and biographer Russell P. MacFall, L. Frank Baum got the name Oz from a filing drawer title O-Z.[28] This story seems very convenient, but L. Frank Baum was probably once again playing the trickster by naming his wizard Oz. If God is the Alpha and the Omega or A-O, Baum's God is the O-Z or Oz — the last letters in both the Greek and Latin alphabets. When Dorothy and company finally reach the Emerald City, they are informed by the "Guardian of the Gates" that few people ever ask to see the Wizard, who is sequestered in his palace-like temple, and claims that the Wizard "is powerful and terrible, and if you come on an idle and foolish errand to bother the wise reflections of the Great Wizard, he might be angry and destroy you all in an instant."[29] Further, when the four finally get their individual meetings with Oz in the throne room, they hear the Wizard proclaim: "I am Oz, the Great and Terrible" (66). This idea that Oz is both great and terrible seems to recall Apostle John's vision in Revelation where the Lord descends from the clouds and announces in a great voice of a trumpet: "I am Alpha and Omega, the beginning and the end" (Rev. 1:8 KJV). The Lord is great in the beginning because he made the world, but he is also terrible in that He holds the final judgment and can punish sinful souls by casting them into hell. If that is not proof enough, it also recalls Nehemiah's prayer: "I beseech thee, O Lord of heaven, the great and terrible God, that keepeth the covenant and mercy for them that love him and observe his commandments" (Nehemiah 1:5 KJV). Of course, the Wizard is the "Wonderful" Wizard of Oz, and Isaiah proclaims that the future Messiah "shall be called Wonderful, Counselor, The Mighty God, The Everlasting Father, The Prince of Peace" (Isaiah 9:6 KJV).

For Baum, the Wizard is God, especially dealing with priestly matters. One of the scariest moments of the novel is when Dorothy first sees what she believes to be the Wizard. Baum writes: "In the center of the chair was an enormous Head, without body to support it or any arms or legs whatever. There was no hair upon its head, but it had eyes and nose and mouth, and was bigger than the head of the biggest giant."[30] Dorothy's response is one of both wonder and fear. Then, the Wizard as this fearful Head orders Dorothy and her companions to kill the Witch of the West. To receive the Wizard's mercy and the fulfillment of their wildest prayers, they are instructed to present to the Wizard a sacrifice, the Witch of the West, to show that the four companions have to worship Oz and become his trusted and obedient servants. This also foreshadows that the Wizard is a false god, or as Dorothy will call him "the Great humbug," because the sacrifice is impure since Oz has no magical powers. He cannot grant Dorothy's wish to go home because he is an old man and former circus barker.

Oz as Religious Allegory

If the Wizard of Oz is indeed Christ as High Priest, then *The Wonderful Wizard of Oz* must surely be a Christian allegory. The debunking of the Wizard by Dorothy is central to the story. In fact, if Oz is indeed a priestly character, then it seems most definite that Baum is attacking orthodox Christianity. Christianity was undergoing great changes in America by the end of the nineteenth century. One change came from the shift in demographics. Many of the nation's new immigrants were Catholics; thus, many Protestants saw themselves under siege by the masses of foreigners coming to America to find jobs in factories across the nation. For rural and small town Protestants, these new Americans threatened the American way of life because they became the face of urban America. Another major force was that of secularization. Industrialization not only needed workers, but its innovations freed people from the farm and rural traditions and suggested that science was superior to religion in explaining how things occurred in the world.

American Protestantism reacted by splintering into two large groups — the Modernists and Fundamentalists. Modernists accepted the more secularized world and suggested that religion might not explain everything in the world, but the Bible revealed spiritual truths that science and technology could not disprove. Influenced by German Idealism, especially as presented by the German theologians Friedrich Schleiermacher and Alberecht Ritschl, Modernists saw religion as a purely spiritual matter of the heart rather than an intellectual matter. Fundamentalists rejected this notion. Science, especially Darwinism, threatened the Bible as God's Word, and secularization meant little more than the acceptance of man's sinful ways. Fundamentalists reacted to these attacks very much like their evangelical predecessors reacted to Unitarianism, deism, and the American Enlightenment. They denounced it and insisted that the Bible was without error or contradiction. Biblical inerrancy became the bedrock of American evangelicalism preached by revivalists such as Dwight Moody and Billy Sunday. In the spiritual market of the 1890s, revivalists fought for evangelical supremacy and attempted to turn back the tidal wave of -isms.[31]

Though Baum was raised a Methodist, his religious views by the time he wrote *The Wonderful Wizard of Oz* were greatly influenced by his wife's free thinking and belief in theosophy. Though theosophy was highly influenced by Asian religions and philosophies that appealed to intellects, reformers, and the genteel, it did have one thing in common with Fundamentalists — spiritual populism. In America, theosophy evolved from nineteenth-century spiritualism, a belief that people can communicate with the dead, popularized by Margaret and Katherine Fox. Beginning in the late 1840s, the Fox sisters helped eastern reformers, such as Horace Greeley, William Lloyd Garrison, Lydia Maria Child, and Elizabeth Cady Stanton (who resided in the same reform circles as Baum's mother-in-law Matilda Gage), communicate with departed souls. Greeley along with P.T. Barnum turned the sisters into mid–nineteenth century celebrities. Spiritualism, like evangelicalism, was a democratic or populist religious force that appealed to the unlearned masses and attacked the learned clergy.[32]

The Wonderful Wizard of Oz seems to be a spiritualist text that uses many evangelical and Christian symbols to critique what was going to be labeled as Fundamentalism. The story begins on the Kansas prairie among unlearned farmers: Dorothy, an orphan, living with her Uncle Henry, a farmer, and Aunt Em, a farmer's wife. Baum uses realism — he describes everything but Dorothy and her dog Toto as gray — in the first chapter to foreshadow that something bad is going to happen to Dorothy, who is going to die by a tornado. Baum's cyclone is the first religious symbol and resembles Elijah ascending to heaven in a whirlwind (2 Kings 2:11). When the tornado hits, Dorothy goes to retrieve Toto hiding under the bed rather than descend into the safety of storm cellar. As the house floats away, two very important things happen. The first is that Dorothy's dog Toto goes with her, and in the passage to Oz,

Toto actually falls through the house's trap door, and Dorothy grabs him by the ear. Of course, *toto* is Latin meaning "completely or in its entirety." This seems to be a playful disclaimer that one should not believe the rest of the story in its entirety because it is a fairytale.

The second important event is that "Dorothy closed her eyes and fell fast asleep."[33] This suggests that Dorothy actually died a proper physical death from the tornado because when she awakes from this sleep she finds herself

> in midst of a country of marvelous beauty. There were lovely patches of green sward all about, with stately trees bearing rich and luscious fruits. Banks of gorgeous flowers were on every hand, and birds with rare and brilliant plumage sang and fluttered in the trees and bushes. A Little way off was a small brook, rushing and sparkling along between to green banks, and murmuring in a voice grateful to a little girl who had lived on the dry and gray prairies.

In other words, this is the picture of Eden or the Paradise that John writes of in Revelation, and this heaven is protected by a great desert on all sides much like the Garden of Eden after Adam's fall.

She soon encounters three Munchkins and the Good Witch of the North. During this conversation she discovers that there is real magic in Oz, and there are two forms: good and evil. For orthodox Christians, there are only two spiritual forces: God's force to do good and Satan's force to do evil. The Munchkins and the Good Witch tell her she has just done a great good. Like Moses or Christ, she enters a strange land and frees bondsmen. Dorothy quickly realizes that all she really wants to do is return home to her Aunt Em. If Dorothy is truly dead, this is a spiritualist comment that departed souls want to return to those still on Earth, or at least in Kansas. So, the Good Witch advises Dorothy to follow the yellow brick road, wear the silver slippers, and go to Oz, the great and powerful wizard. The Good Witch's gentle kiss on the forehead is to protect Dorothy from any harm and suggests God's seal. In Revelation 7:2 and 9:4, John tells of how God will protect all those with "the seal of God" written on their "foreheads."

Dorothy begins her pilgrimage down the yellow brick road to the Emerald City, and on this pilgrimage, she meets her Christ-like companions the Scarecrow, the Tin Woodman, and the Cowardly Lion. On the way they meet challenges such as jumping over the abysses, fighting the wild beasts known as the Kalidahs, which have heads of tigers and bodies of bears, crossing the river of death symbolized by the Scarecrow getting stuck on the pole in the middle of the river, and finally surviving the deadly poppy field. Many of these obstacles are very similar to the obstacles that Christian had to deal with in *Pilgrim's Progress*. Christian also had to cross a river of death, and the Enchanted Ground in *Pilgrim's Progress* is very similar to the poppy field as it causes the traveler to become sleepy. Christian passes the challenge along

King's Highway from the City of Destruction to the Celestial City; Dorothy leaves grey Kansas, travels along the yellow brick road, and finally arrives at the Emerald City. Dorothy's spiritual journey to Oz teaches her confidence, benevolence, and courage.

Upon reaching the Emerald City's gate, Dorothy, the Scarecrow, the Tin Woodman, and the Lion are warned by the Keeper of the Gate not to bother the Wizard because he is "Terrible and Great" and could severely punish them. However, this humbug wizard, fearing Dorothy's power (her silver shoes), grants a meeting; however, before he will help Dorothy and her friends, Oz wants Dorothy to kill the Wicked Witch of the West. In other words, the false high priest wants a human sacrifice. On the way out of the city and after giving the green glasses back to the Keeper of the Gates, Dorothy's spiritual journey is revealed. The young evangelist learns that the new green dress she was given to wear to see the Wizard is in fact white. The trip to the Emerald City has purified her soul and turned her into a holy warrior whose mission is to kill the Wicked Witch of the West.

On their journey to kill the Wicked Witch, the Scarecrow, the Woodman, and the Lion show how their pilgrimages to the Emerald City have transformed them. Without hesitation, these three Christ-like characters reveal their true power and virtue by saving Dorothy from the Wicked Witch. The Tin Man, who cried earlier in the novel for stepping on an insect, protects Dorothy from a pack of wolves by chopping off their heads. The Scarecrow actually kills the crows sent by the Wicked Witch by breaking their necks. The Scarecrow also uses his own straw to cover Dorothy and the Lion while the black bees attack the Tin Man and die from broken stingers. The Lion uses his powerful roar to frighten the Winkies. Unfortunately, the Scarecrow's brain, the Tin Man's heart, and the Lion's courage were no match for the Winged Monkeys. The Wicked Witch uses her third and last wish of the Golden Cap to call the Winged Monkeys, who capture Dorothy, scatter the Scarecrow's straw, drop the Tin Man into a ravine, and jail the Lion. The Wicked Witch wants the Lion to become submissive as a horse and forces Dorothy to momentarily become a scullery maid like Cinderella. On this second journey, Dorothy plays a peripheral role. At first, she is protected by her friends and later by the mark on her forehead and does nothing until she gets angry at the Wicked Witch for trying to steal her silver shoes. In anger, Dorothy throws cleaning water onto the Witch and watches in awe at how the Witch melts before cleaning up the brown mess. Thus, the evangelical girl has cleansed evil from Oz, and she and the Lion "were no longer prisoners in a strange land."[34]

This part of the novel resembles Revelation. Baum depicts a cosmic war between good and evil, and then he reveals the shocking truth about the Wizard of Oz. After Dorothy kills the Witch by dissolving her with water, the adventurers return to the Emerald City and discover that the Wizard is merely "a little, old man, with a bald head and a wrinkled face" who has "been making believe."[35] This discovery comes when the Lion roars, which in return causes Toto to knock over the screen that the Wizard is hiding behind. Of course, at Christ's death, his soul went to heaven: "The veil of the temple was rent in twain from the top to the bottom; and the earth did quake, and the rocks rent" (Matthew 27:51 KJV). Many Christians believe that this breaking of the temple veil signified that all, and not only the temple priests, were invited into the presence of God, showing Christ's displeasure with the temple priests for falsely enforcing the law.

This scene suggests the same. For Baum, this humbug wizard was born in Omaha and was a balloonist promoting a circus until his balloon got caught in a jet stream that took him to Oz. In fact, he has no magical powers at all; instead, he is a confidence man who confesses: "'How can I help being a humbug,' he said, 'when all these people make me do things that everybody knows can't be done?'"[36] By revealing that Oz is a humbug, Baum leaves wonder and joy in the Land of Oz but has gotten rid of the "heart-aches" and "nightmares." The scariest person in Oz was the great Wizard; thus, turning him into a charlatan, Baum only leaves the best parts of Christianity represented by the Scarecrow, the Tin Man, and the Lion in Oz.

This revelation that the Wizard is merely a circus barker also suggests a subtle attack on revivalism. The Wizard has the appearance of a Mid-Western revivalist holding tent meetings. The most famous minister at the turn of the century was Billy Sunday, who was a former baseball player of the Chicago White Stockings before being converted. In the 1890s, Sunday traveled the Kerosene Circuit — traveling from small town to small town in Illinois and Iowa which normally lacked electricity, thus the revivals were lit by kerosene lanterns. Sunday would go from town to town using his celebrity as a former ballplayer to attract crowds. Known as a former ballplayer rather than a great theologian, Sunday's sermons stressed fire and brimstone as he ran, gyrated, and slid across the tent's stage. Sunday's well-rehearsed performance earned him little respect from more conservative ministers, but it won over followers and propelled Sunday to the evangelical forefront, becoming the most popular minister during the early decades of the twentieth century. Baum's revelation that the Wizard is not "Great and terrible" undermines the revivalist "hellfire and brimstone" sermons depicting God's wrath toward sinners.[37] Instead, the revivalist was much like a circus barker, and the Great Humbug was partially inspired by Washington Donaldson, a Barnum and Bailey magician and ventriloquist who was lost in a balloon over Lake Michigan in 1875.[38]

Of course, Dorothy does not believe in the Wizard of Oz's make believe — like the Wizard she knows reality outside of Oz and wants a real solution. For Dorothy, a brain made out of pins, needles, and bran, a silk heart stuffed with sawdust, or liquid courage could not return her to Kansas. The Wizard decides to solve her problem by making a hot air balloon, which he thinks will return both of them to civilized America. Fortunately, the balloon accidentally takes off without Dorothy, who is once again chasing after Toto. Baum seems to suggest that the Wizard is not only full of hot air, but his views are dangerous. If Dorothy had gone up in the hot air balloon, she too would have been lost and never have gotten home. Instead of following the Wizard's patriarchal views, Dorothy turns to the matriarchal views of Glinda, the good witch who resides in the Land of the South.

The four companions go on one last adventure to visit Glinda. During this adventure, they visit the "Dainty China Country," where everything is made out of delicate china. During their visit, the Lion accidentally breaks the china church, the only church mentioned in the Land of Oz. Baum writes: "Then the Lion gathered his legs under him and jumped on the wall; but just as he jumped he upset a china church with his tail and smashed it all to pieces."[39] This fragile Land of China in many respects represents the fragile orthodox world that Baum visited as a salesman selling china. Dorothy and her companions now represent a more liberated Christianity, without the male-dominated hierarchy, searching for a powerful woman who could grant Dorothy her greatest desire. In many respects, they are representing modernist Christian views not dependent on the Bible; thus, it is not surprising that the people of the "Dainty China Country" feared Dorothy and her friends. Baum writes: "'That was too bad,' said Dorothy, 'but really I think we were lucky in not doing these little people more harm than breaking a cow's leg and a church. They are all so brittle."[40] Baum seems to be giving a cautious warning to fundamentalist and orthodox religions, which are too brittle and inflexible to adapt to the changing modern world and would not survive because of it.

Dorothy and her companions finally reach Glinda, who is sitting on her ruby throne. This good witch tells Dorothy that she already has the means to get home, the silver slippers she has been wearing throughout all of Oz — the same slippers she got from killing the Witch of the East and defended by throwing water on the Witch of the West. All she has to do is click her heels three times and say, "Take me home to Aunt Em!" Dorothy whirls through the air and back to Kansas. As she magically travels back to Kansas, she loses the silver slippers. When she arrives back home, she runs up to Aunt Em, who is outside watering cabbages. Baum writes: "'My darling child!' she cried, folding the little girl in her arms and covering her face with kisses; 'where in the world did you come from?'" For Aunt Em, who made it to the safety of the storm cellar, Dorothy was literally gone — dead! Thus, Dorothy's coming back must have been a great surprise and relief. However, Baum does not go into great detail about this spectacular reunion. In fact, the chapter is the shortest in the whole book. In many respects, Dorothy's reunion with her aunt suggests the type of reunion that Maud probably believed that she could have with her dead niece. In this respect, Aunt Em is in many respects just like Maud, who believed that spirits could come back to Earth and seek out loved ones through visions. Aunt Em is the only one in Kansas who we know sees and speaks to Dorothy, whom she loved — the girl who brought color to the grey, harsh world of Kansas. In this respect, Dorothy's spirit coming back from Oz was "glad to be at home again!"[41] Dorothy once again will bring joy and hope to Aunt Em.

Conclusion

The Wonderful Wizard of Oz represents Dorothy's spiritual journey from the plains of Kansas where a tornado kills her through the Land of Oz, where she frees the Munchkins and Winkies by killing evil witches, and back to Kansas reuniting her with Aunt Em. On this journey, Dorothy and her companions, the Scarecrow, the Tin Woodman, and the Cowardly Lion, expose "Oz, the Great and Terrible" for what he truly is — a circus barker and a "great humbug." By suggesting that the Wizard represents the wrathful Old Testament God, the debunking of him suggests that *The Wonderful Wizard of Oz* is anticlerical. This becomes even more obvious when the Lion accidentally breaks the church in the dainty country of China. By advocating spiritualism and anti-clericalism, Baum advocates a spiritual populism; thus, *The Wonderful Wizard of Oz* is a populist text, but not a political populist text promoting the People's Party. Baum's use of traditional Christian imagery also suggests that *The Wonderful Wizard of Oz* was greatly influenced by America's spiritual capitalism. Baum grew up a Methodist, became an Episcopalian in South Dakota, and by the time be wrote *The Wonderful Wizard of Oz,* he and his wife had joined the Ramayana Theosophical Society in Chicago. Baum's own spiritualist journey suggests that the killing of the evil witches and the debunking of the Wizard removed the "heart-aches" and "nightmares" found in orthodox Christianity which had haunted children for the past two millennia.

Notes

1. L. Frank Baum, *The Wonderful Wizard of Oz*, ed. Michael Patrick Hearn (New York: Schocken Books, 1983), xvi.

2. Henry M. Littlefield, "Parable on Populism," *American Quarterly* 16:1 (spring 1964): 47–58.

3. Ibid., 57.

4. Richard Jensen, *The Winning of the Midwest: Social and Political Conflict, 1888–1896* (Chicago: University of Chicago Press, 1971), 282–283; Brian, Attebery, *The Fantasy Tradition in American Literature: From Irving to Le Guin* (Bloomington: Indiana University Press, 1980) 86–87; Hugh Rockoff, "The 'Wizard of Oz' as a Monetary Allegory," *Journal of Political Economy* 98:4 (August 1990), 739–760. For a precise historiography of *The Wonderful Wizard of Oz* as political allegory see David B. Parker, "The Rise and Fall of *The Wonderful Wizard of Oz* as a 'Parable on Populism,'" *Journal of the Georgia Association of Historians* 15 (1994), 49–63. To read the most comprehensive populist interpretation see *The Historian's Wizard of Oz: Reading L. Frank Baum's Classic as a Political and Monetary Allegory*, ed. Ranjit S. Dighe (Westport, CT: Praeger, 2002).

5. William R. Leach, "The Clown from Syracuse: The Life and Times of L. Frank Baum," in L. Frank Baum, *The Wonderful Wizard of Oz* (Belmont, CA: Wadsworth Publishing Company, 1991), 1–34; Leach, "A Trickster's Tale: L. Frank Baum's *The Wonderful Wizard of Oz*," in L. Frank Baum, *The Wonderful Wizard of Oz* (Belmont, CA: Wadsworth Publishing Company, 1991), 157–188; Leach, *Land of Desire: Merchants, Power, and the Rise of a New American Culture* (New York: Pantheon Books, 1993), 55–61 and 246–260.

6. Leach, "A Trickster's Tale," 161.

7. Ibid., 162.

8. Thomas Beer, *The Mauve Decade; American Life at the End of the Nineteenth Century* (New York: A. A. Knopf, 1926).

9. Austin Alvyn, *China's Millions: The China Inland Mission and Late Qing Society* (Grand Rapids, MI: Eerdmans, 2007), 1–10.

10. Katharine Rogers, *L. Frank Baum: Creator of Oz* (New York: St. Martin Press, 2002); Bradley A. Hansen, "The Fable of the Allegory: The Wizard of Oz in Economics," *The Journal of Economic Education* 33 (Summer 2002): 254–264; and Fred Erisman, "L. Frank Baum and the Progressive Dilemma," *American Quarterly* 20 (Autumn 1968): 616–623.

11. Baum, *The Wonderful Wizard of Oz*, 100.

12. Benjamin War Baum Obituary: "The Dark Messenger," *Syracuse Courier*, Feb. 15, 1887, and Bulletin Onondaga Historical Association, April 12, 1957, located in the Syracuse University Library.

13. Letter Bertha F. Ratliff to Russell MacFall, Oct. 30, 1960, located in the Syracuse University Library.

14. Whitney R. Cross, *The Burned-Over District: The Social and Intellectual History of Enthusiastic Religion in Western New York, 1800–1850* (Ithaca, NY: Cornell University Press, 1950).

15. Rogers, *L. Frank Baum: Creator of Oz*, 50–51.

16. Ibid.

17. Michael O. Riley, *Oz and Beyond: The Fantasy World of L. Frank Baum* (Lawrence, KS: University Press of Kansas, 1997).

18. Baum, *The Wonderful Wizard of Oz*, 62.

19. Leach, "Trickster's tale," 169.

20. Ibid., 161.

21. Baum, *The Wonderful Wizard of Oz*, 18

22. Rogers, *L. Frank Baum*, 89.

23. *The Scofield Study Bible*, ed. Rev. C. I. Scofield (New York: Oxford University Press, 1996), 990.

24. Baum, *The Wonderful Wizard of Oz*, 23

25. Ibid., 34.

26. Ibid., 35.

27. Ibid., 38.

28. Frank Joslyn Baum and Russell P. MacFall, *To Please a Child: A Biography of L. Frank Baum Royal Historian of Oz* (Chicago: Reilly & Lee, 1961), 110.

29. L. Frank Baum, *The Wonderful Wizard of Oz*, 61.
30. Ibid., 65–66.
31. For more on the conflict between Fundamentalists and Modernists see George M. Marsden, *Fundamentalism and American Culture: The Shaping of Twentieth-Century Evangelicalism, 1870–1925*(New York: Oxford University Press, 1980) and William R. Hutchison, *The Modernist Impulse in American Protestantism* (Durham, N.C.: Duke University Pres, 1992).
32. Stephen Prothero, "From Spiritualism to Theosophy: 'Uplifting' a Democratic Tradition," *Religion and American Culture* 3 (Summer 1993): 197–216.
33. Baum, *The Wonderful Wizard of Oz*, 10.
34. Ibid., 84.
35. Ibid., 96.
36. Ibid., 105.
37. Roger A. Bruns, *Preacher: Billy Sunday and Big-Time American Evangelism* (Chicago: University of Illinois Press, 2002).
38. Ibid., 83.
39. Ibid., 121.
40. Ibid., 121–122.
41. Ibid., 132.

Works Cited

Alvyn, Austin. *China's Millions: The China Inland Mission and Late Qing Society*. Grand Rapids, MI: Eerdmans, 2007.

Attebery, Brian. *The Fantasy Tradition in American Literature: From Irving to Le Guin*. Bloomington, IN: Indiana University Press, 1980.

Baum, Frank Joslyn, and Russell P. MacFall. *To Please a Child: A Biography of L. Frank Baum Royal Historian of Oz*. Chicago: Reilly & Lee, 1961.

Beer, Thomas. *The Mauve Decade; American Life at the End of the Nineteenth Century*. New York: A. A. Knopf, 1926.

Bruns, Roger A. *Preacher: Billy Sunday and Big-Time American Evangelism*. Chicago, IL: University of Illinois Press, 2002.

Cross, Whitney R. *The Burned-Over District: The Social and Intellectual History of Enthusiastic Religion in Western New York, 1800–1850*. Ithaca, NY: Cornell University Press, 1950.

Dighe, Ranjit S., ed. *The Historian's Wizard of Oz: Reading L. Frank Baum's Classic as a Political and Monetary Allegory*. Westport, CT: Praeger, 2002.

Erisman, Fred. "L. Frank Baum and the Progressive Dilemma." *American Quarterly* 20 (Autumn 1968), 616–623.

Hansen, Bradley A. "The Fable of the Allegory: The Wizard of Oz in Economics." *The Journal of Economic Education* 33 (Summer 2002): 254–264.

Hutchison, William R. *The Modernist Impulse in American Protestantism*. Durham, NC: Duke University Press. 1992

Jensen, Richard. *The Winning of the Midwest: Social and Political Conflict, 1888–1896*. Chicago, IL: University of Chicago Press, 1971.

Leach, William R. "The Clown from Syracuse: The Life and Times of L. Frank Baum." L. Frank Baum, *The Wonderful Wizard of Oz*. Belmont, CA: Wadsworth Publishing Company, 1991.

_____. *Land of Desire: Merchants, Power, and the Rise of a New American Culture*. New York: Pantheon Books, 1993.

_____. "A Trickster's Tale: L. Frank Baum's *The Wonderful Wizard of Oz*." L. Frank Baum, *The Wonderful Wizard of Oz*. Belmont, CA: Wadsworth Publishing Company, 1991.

Littlefield, Henry M. "Parable on Populism." *American Quarterly* 16:1 (Spring 1964): 47–58.

Marsden, George M. *Fundamentalism and American Culture: The Shaping of Twentieth-Century Evangelicalism, 1870–1925*. New York: Oxford University Press, 1980.

Parker, David B. "The Rise and Fall of *The Wonderful Wizard of Oz* as a 'Parable on Populism.'" *Journal of the Georgia Association of Historians* 15 (1994), 49–63.

Prothero, Stephen. "From Spiritualism to Theosophy: 'Uplifting' a Democratic Tradition." *Religion and American Culture* 3 (Summer 1993): 197–216.

Riley, Michael O. *Oz and Beyond: The Fantasy World of L. Frank Baum.* Lawrence, KS: University Press of Kansas, 1997.

Rockoff, Hugh. "The 'Wizard of Oz' as a Monetary Allegory." *Journal of Political Economy* 98:4 (August 1990), 739–760.

Rogers, Katharine. *L. Frank Baum: Creator of Oz.* New York: St. Martin Press, 2002.

The Scofield Study Bible, ed. Rev. C. I. Scofield. New York: Oxford University Press, 1996.

War, Benjamin. "Baum Obituary: 'The Dark Messenger.'" *Syracuse Courier,* Feb. 15, 1887.

CHAPTER 17

The Ethics and Epistemology of Emancipation in *Oz*

JASON M. BELL AND JESSICA BELL

Whether in economic debates about gold and silver standards or in political debates about populism, L. Frank Baum's modern commentators have often sought for the motivations of the Wizard of Oz stories in his adult social context. Perhaps there are traces of such themes, but these hardly seem symbolically important enough to inspire a timeless tale; moreover, they are accidental rather than essential, as they are certainly not to be found systematically throughout all the books of Baum's Oz series.

As Baum's Oz stories were meant for the young (including, as he makes clear in an introduction to one of the books of the series, for the young at heart), we may do better to look at the social contexture of Baum's youth, an age overshadowed by the great and bloody struggle that resulted in the abolition of slavery in the United States. In this, we find a theme that is prevalent throughout the entire history of Oz. The effort to abolish slavery and establish diversity is essential to its heroes; the effort to institute slavery and race superiority is essential to its villains, and the strife between the two sides is a theme whose intensity and scale may serve to inspire a story for all ages.

Who is this abolitionist, Dorothy? A little girl from Kansas, whose humble house crushes a powerful slave owner, the Wicked Witch of the East. Before turning to dust, the Witch held the Munchkins in bondage, "making them slave for her night and day."[1] The end of this oppression, of course, explains the great rejoicing of the Munchkins when their tormenter is finally defeated. Though at first Dorothy is an abolitionist only accidentally, her role as intentional emancipator is quickly established: she frees the Scarecrow from his servitude to the Munchkins, the Tin Woodman from his rusty bonds imposed by the curse of the Wicked Witch of the East, and later, she frees

225

herself, the Cowardly Lion and the Winkies from their enslavement to the Wicked Witch of the West. In later Oz stories, Dorothy continues as the champion of abolition, although with ever increasing numbers of allies.

And what was Kansas during the period of Baum's youth? It was the place of the beginning of the end of slavery. In the years surrounding Baum's birth, Kansas was "Bleeding Kansas," the state that witnessed what might truly be called the opening shots of the Civil War. Thousands of abolitionists sold all that they had in order to move there and cast their vote against slavery, while violent pro-slavery Border Ruffians marched in from Missouri to stop them. It was in Kansas where John Brown and a few armed allies, along with pacifistic abolitionists, struggled for freedom against the much larger pro-slavery forces to determine whether Kansas would thereafter be free or slave. The intensity of the battles in Kansas reflected the broader scope of the question — at stake was not merely whether Kansas would be free or slave, but whether the United States would be free or slave, as everything hinged on the tie-breaking votes of the future senators from that state. This was the question of 1856, the year of Baum's birth, and it became the national question during the period of Baum's childhood, in the Civil War of 1861–1865.

Surely it was no more obvious in 1856 that Kansas would become the lightning bolt that would burn down the institution of slavery in the United States, than that a little girl from Kansas would free all of Oz from its many powerful slave owners. And yet Kansas and its humble citizens played precisely this crucial, but frequently overlooked, role in world history.

Having more extensively considered Dorothy's first abolitionist efforts in *The Wonderful Wizard of Oz* in a recent article,[2] we here turn to consider this theme in subsequent books of Baum's Oz series, to show that the struggle against slavery is as important to the abolitionist heroes of Oz as it was to the abolitionist heroes of Kansas. We will conclude with a reflection on what may be termed Baum's pluralistic epistemology and ethics, in his arguments for the superiority of the quality of knowledge enabled by an inclusive and respectful society, as contrasted with the ignorance, brutality, and weakness that follows from imperialistic conquest, slavery, and from gender and race discrimination.

And Dorothy Goes Marching On: Abolition in Oz

Baum's second Oz story, *The Marvelous Land of Oz* (1904), commences with the account of the boy Tip, enslaved by the witch Mombi, who has tired of his insubordination and decides to destroy him. Mombi, by means of her magic, brings Jack Pumpkinhead to life, intending to turn him into the obedient slave whose labor will justify her dispensing with the boy. Tip, however, decides to run away and to take the new slave with him, saying to himself, "I don't like to leave Jack Pumpkinhead to the tender mercies of old Mombi."[3]

Joined by Professor Wogglebug, and soon others, the riders on this Underground Railroad practice the traditional philosophical disciplines of the Academy to reach safety; for instance, they use mathematics to solve a tricky problem, which is contrasted with Mombi's lack of abilities in this area. The point here is, of course, that their problem-solving requires cooperation, whereas Mombi's attempt to establish her own superiority has in fact made her lonely and unable to solve any problems at all. Jack Pumpkinhead, meanwhile, learns to overcome his terror of his own mortality, for philosophy is, as Socrates puts it, practicing for death. The group likewise learns the classical philosophical notions that wisdom, intelligence and contentedness are far superior to monetary wealth and greed. In this and the other Oz stories, Baum makes explicit reference to the worth of the discipline of philosophy, a discipline which, above all, requires a free community of inquiry.

The most significant plot point of this book for the future history of Oz is that the boy slave Tip is revealed to be the princess Ozma, the legitimate ruler of Oz, whose true appearance had been concealed by Mombi's magic. The former slave becomes the beloved ruler of the land, and her servants gratefully and willingly choose to serve her because she is fair and wise. Thenceforth, Ozma will tolerate no enslaving magic in her realm, and her domains become the last stop on the Underground Railroad for many later freedom-seekers, just as her rule becomes, subsequently, the target of numerous plots and attacks by the remaining slave owners, huddled in various lairs and underground caverns at and beyond the borders of Oz, forever plotting to regain ownership of their human chattel.

Upon being delivered to Oz once again in the next book, *Ozma of Oz* (1907), Dorothy quickly finds she has another mission of abolition, and she is joined by Ozma and her tiny army to accomplish it. This small band, numbering under 50, faces off against the well-trained 50,000-member army of the Nome King Roquat to free his slaves, the Royal Family of Ev; the odds here are like those faced by John Brown's seriously outnumbered forces in his battles in Kansas, Missouri, and Harpers Ferry. In a scene reminiscent of the legal wrangling between pro-slavery and pro-abolition forces in the decades preceding the Civil War, Roquat insists that he bought the slaves fairly and in obedience to the laws of the place, while Ozma and Dorothy appeal to a higher law and announce that they are willing to fight for freedom despite the overwhelming odds arrayed against them. Baum, perhaps thinking of his mother-in-law Matilda Gage's public opposition to slavery and to the political oppression of women, uses a character who embodies the feminine principle, Billina the chicken, to outsmart and humiliate the chauvinistic Roquat. The hyper–male Nomes are terrified, above all, of eggs. And for good reason: Roquat is outwitted, with egg literally on his face, as his slaves escape to safety.

The fourth and fifth books of the Oz histories, *Dorothy and the Wizard in Oz* (1908) and *The Road to Oz* (1909), are less concerned with a direct study of slavery, and more with a philosophical study of the strength of the dutiful, loyal community of freely participating individuals, in contrast to the weakness of the estranged, appetitive individual, who looks at neighbors as mere resources to be exploited.

Dorothy and the Wizard in Oz is the story of the Wizard of Oz's redemption from his earlier tyranny, as he learns to dutifully walk the path of loyalty. In this story, Eureka the cat exemplifies the appetitive life, her "depraved appetite for pork"[4] bringing a moment of disharmony to the typically vegetarian Utopia of the Emerald City. The positive moral message is taught by the now-reformed Wizard, that it is better to fight, even at risk of death, for the noble cause of the beloved community, than to sell duty to purchase one's own life in a debased survival.

In *The Road to Oz*, the appearance of the enslaving peoples is brief, and they are quickly and handily defeated. The main story here is of the redemption of the Shaggy Man, an erstwhile lonely thief who is put on the path to community and salvation by his displays of loyal friendship, a process finally brought to completion by his dip in the Truth Pond, after which he cannot tell a lie. Along the way, we learn from such characters like Johnny Dooit that the only path to happiness is a cheerful devotion to one's work and camaraderie with other workers. A theme emerges in this book that is frequently repeated through the rest of the Oz books, that the happy community is one that turns to art criticism, and away from criticism of intrinsic traits, like skin color. In this case, we meet the Musicker, whom the majority of the traveling party vote to leave behind, with all arguments based solely on the quality and loudness of the music. Scenes like this are repeated numerous times throughout the Oz books, with good music portrayed as beneficial to thinking, and bad music as injurious to it. For Baum, art criticism comes to take the legitimate place of illegitimate claims of race and gender superiority. The final party scene of this book, in all its joy, does not include the Musicker, but it does include those former slaves of previous books: the Winkies, the Munchkins, and the Royal Family of Ev.

The next books of Baum's Oz series return to consider the plots of rich and powerful tyrants who aspire to add humans to their possessions. These stories are especially concerned with the sociological and psychological character of these tyrants and with their inability to achieve the social cooperation, or even the coherence of memory within individual selves, that they need in order to succeed in their plans. We meet again, in the sixth book of the series, *The Emerald City of Oz* (1910), the Nome King Roquat, who is portrayed as a classic tyrant — his paranoia is such that he tortures and destroys his best generals and is obsessed with building and training his army so that he can destroy the happiness of his peaceful neighbors. No matter the cost, he wants to enslave Dorothy, Ozma, and the other citizens of Oz to revenge his earlier defeat. His advisor Guph realizes that the Nomes will need allies, so he promises the most nefarious gangs beyond Oz's borders that they may have a share of the captured slaves.

In this book, Baum broadens his critique of slavery to a critique of the more heartless aspects of capitalism, the bondage of farmers to the onerous burdens of unpayable mortgages. Back in Kansas, Dorothy's Uncle Henry and Auntie Em are about to lose their farm to a mortgage that is impossible to pay. Thus, they happily take Dorothy's offer to join her in Oz. At first shocked by their strange new home, they eventually come to love Oz and its inhabitants. Even when it appears inevitable that they will become the actual slaves of Roquat, as his seemingly invincible army advances on the Emerald City, Dorothy's relatives turn down the option of escaping back to Kansas and its own version of slavery: Auntie Em says cheerfully, "I've been a slave all my life, ... and so has Henry.... I'd rather take my chances with the rest of you."[5]

It's no wonder they would want to stay, as we learn something of the fairness of Oz's economy under Ozma's rule: everything is owned by the monarch, but she and the people share freely; the happy citizens divide their time evenly between work and play, and "there were no cruel overseers set to watch them, and no one to rebuke them or to find fault with them. So each one was proud to do all he could for his friends and neighbors, and was glad when they would accept the things he produced."[6]

Two epic journeys are paralleled in this text. The first is that of Dorothy and a small group of friends from the Emerald City who travel through Oz to introduce Uncle Henry and Auntie Em to its diverse and colorful peoples. The second is that of the Nome King's General Guph, who looks to secure the aid of the "evil creatures who have magic powers sufficient to destroy and conquer the Land of Oz."[7] He seeks out such vicious characters as the Growleywogs and Whimsies and, in return for their pledges of support, promises them a cut of the profits in the form of thousands of Ozite slaves.

The journey of Dorothy's party is an educational one, beginning with a visit to the Royal Athletic College of Oz, after which they meet curious and interesting people among the Cuttenclips, the Fuddles, and the residents of Utensia, Bunbury and Bunnybury. They also meet the tiresome but harmless

Flutterbudgets and Rigmaroles, and they solve some disputes, such as the geographical argument of the Zebra and the Soft-Shelled Crab. Each encounter teaches something new, even when, as in the lands of the Rigmaroles and the Flutterbudgets, the residents provide demonstrations of how not to act. In each visit, Dorothy and her companions learn the importance of diplomacy and cooperation.

Guph's journey, on the other hand, is marked by hostility and deception, with increasing discord growing among the would-be conquerors. The Growleywogs, not content with their promised 20,000 Ozite slaves, intend, after their conquest, to "rob the Nome King and make him our slave"; their Grand Gallipoot announces, "I'd like King Roquat for my own slave. He could black my boots and bring me my porridge every morning while I am in bed."[8] The Nome King and Guph, meanwhile, plot their own betrayals of their allies, and Guph lies to and plots a betrayal of his own King. The banquet of the malicious tyrants, prior to their invasion, is not a happy occasion:

> The Nome King and his terrible allies sat at the banquet table until midnight. There was much quarreling between the Growleywogs and Phanfasms, and one of the wee-headed Whimsies got angry at General Guph and choked him until he nearly stopped breathing. Yet no one was seriously hurt, and the Nome King felt much relieved when the clock struck twelve and they all sprang up and seized their weapons.[9]

Contrasted with the disharmony and disloyalty of the evil allies, the Oz people are marked by loyalty and intelligence. As the massive army approaches the Emerald City to conquer them, Dorothy suggests to her friends that they use her Magic Belt to escape to Kansas, but Ozma refuses to desert her people. In the end, no one is willing to desert Oz and Ozma to save themselves. What these allies lack in force of arms, they make up in solidarity and in their ability to create an intelligent plan of counterattack. Ozma, after rejecting calls for violence against the invaders, agrees with the Scarecrow on a plan to trick the invaders into drinking from the fountain of forgetfulness: the invaders, like the Wicked Witch of the first Oz story, are ruined by water. Only this time they are not destroyed but redeemed; drinking the water, they forget their evil ways. The forgetfulness induced by the water symbolizes what had all along been their central failing, their inability to form and abide by a coherent plan, as such a plan would have required a coherent community to support memory. The tyrants, as Baum and Plato understand, most need precisely the thing that they can never possess — a genuine community, in which individuals may overcome their limitations by cooperation.

The themes of slavery and racism, and their negative epistemological consequences, are especially apparent in Baum's seventh Oz book, *The Patchwork Girl of Oz* (1913). Here we meet the character of Dr. Pipt, the crooked magician who gave Old Mombi the Powder of Life with which she brought Jack Pumpkinhead to life to make him her slave. Dr. Pipt is making another batch of the powder, which his wife Margolotte intends to use to bring to life a patchwork girl she has made so that she may have a servant to help her do housework. "What is a servant?" The Patchwork Girl asks, after being created. Dr. Pipt tells her she is "...a sort of slave," one who has "no right to leave."[10]

Margolotte explains that the patchwork construction of the girl is meant to keep her in her station, for "Munchkins do not care for any color other than blue." Therefore, a patchwork quilt, being "such a dreadful mixture of colors would discourage her from trying to be as dignified as the blue Munchkins are."[11] She explains that her patchwork girl will "find herself to be of so many unpopular colors that she'll never dare be rebellious or impudent, as servants are sometimes liable to be when they are made the same way their mistresses are."[12] Margolotte is obsessed with keeping her slave in a subjugated position and plans to give her only enough brains to do her work properly, since "a servant with too much brains is sure to become independent and high-and-mighty and feel above her work."[13]

The slave owners' plans go quickly awry. Ojo, a boy who plays a role something like that of Huckleberry Finn — agreeing in theory with slavery even as he does not let the theory effect his own friendships — surreptitiously interferes with the magical formula that is to bring the Patchwork Girl to life and gives her brains in abundance, with such qualities as poesy, courage, cleverness, judgment, ingenuity, learning, and self–reliance, "thinking it both unfair and unkind to deprive her of any good qualities...."[14] Thus, the brought-to-life Patchwork Girl is a free spirit, proud of her multicolored hue, and the smartest person in the room. The moment of her creation is marked by a fortunate disaster: her sudden movements startle Margolotte and Ojo's uncle, Unc Nunkie, causing them to knock over a magical bottle that turns them both into statues.

Rejecting the slave name Margolotte has chosen for her, the Patchwork Girl calls herself Scraps and feels no obligation to remain with Dr. Pipt as a household servant. However, Scraps does volunteer to help her creators in a way of her own choosing and announces that she will make the journey with Ojo to find the magic ingredients necessary to bring the two petrified unfortunates back to life.

Baum's overarching epistemological question in this story concerns how Ojo is to progress from his unfortunate condition and nickname, "Ojo the Unlucky," to become "Ojo the Lucky." Even Margolotte knows that "knowledge is the greatest gift in life"[15] and that knowledge will prove the key to finding Ojo's luck. But how is he to find knowledge? This is a lesson that he must learn from Scraps, who repeatedly proves herself in the course of their journey to be the most intelligent, creative, and brave of the group. Above all, Ojo must learn, from a lesson that Scraps announces at the outset, that a lucky person is one "who has the intelligence to direct his own actions."[16] Ojo's unlucky biases, however, make him at first blind to the importance of self–direction. For instance, he denies Ozma's legitimacy as ruler of Oz, because she is "only a girl,"[17] and after Scraps announces her intention to be free of her owner, Ojo rebukes her: "Why, you belong to Dr. Pipt.... You were made for a servant, Scraps, so you are personal property and not your own mistress."[18]

The anti–racist and anti–slavery symbolism in this text is thickly layered. Scraps, the intended slave, is made of cotton, a fact which Baum repeatedly stresses, and her hairstyle evokes cornrows (her hair was "of brown yarn and hung down on her neck in several neat braids").[19] We meet a character named Diksey (i.e., Dixie) whose decrepit city is marked by foolish wars over wounded honor and by anti–female legislation written by an old bachelor who, as Scraps puts it, "ought to be skinned alive!"[20] Finally, Ojo receives a humiliating punishment in the Emerald City: he is made to wear a white prisoner's robe, with a "peaked top,"[21] which "covered him from head to foot, but had two holes just in front of his eyes,"[22] plainly evoking the garb of the Ku Klux Klan. Though the punishment is actually for breaking a law about picking clover, Ojo receives it immediately after having declared his support for the institution of slavery and his opposition to rule by women. Ojo, as was proper, "felt very miserable and greatly ashamed of himself," as his robe "told all he met of his deep disgrace."[23] As penance, straight from the Socratic/Platonic doctrine, he must learn more so that he can become brave and strong; his criminal weakness is attributed, like his unluck, to ignorance. In the end, the Wonderful Wizard of Oz declares Ojo redeemed by his loyal and generous nature. He frees Margolotte and Unk Nunkie from the slavery of petrifaction and declares that Scraps is to be "nobody's servant but her own."[24]

The eighth in the series of Baum's Oz books is a collection of short stories called *Little Wizard Stories of Oz* (1913). In one of these, "Little Dorothy and Toto," Dorothy is again made a slave while she and Toto are out exploring the "queer nooks and corners"[25] of Oz. They are captured by the cruel giant Crinklink. When Dorothy asks his other captives, "What will Crinklink do with me?" a field-mouse gives a litany of the dreadful fates of the giant's captives, concluding with, "Some he makes his slaves — even as we are — and that is the most dreadful fate of all." Sure enough, Crinklink's castle is full of a year's worth of soiled dishes, and he tells Dorothy, "You are young and strong, and will make a good dishwasher ... you're going to make 'em clean or get trounced." His punishment for broken dishes is "one lash from my dreadful cat-o'-nine-tails for every piece the dish breaks into...." Dorothy refuses an easy opportunity to kill Crinklink in his sleep, stating "I couldn't poss'bly kill anything—even to save my life." Toto is less merciful, but Dorothy and the readers of the Oz histories again are reminded that the primary dangers remaining in Oz are those inhabitants who wish to make others their slaves.

The ninth Oz book, *Tik-Tok of Oz* (1914), parallels the themes of overcoming slavery and tyranny with the themes of attaining gender equity and diversity. Betsy Bobbin and the Shaggy Man are indignant that the inhabitants of the Rose Kingdom refuse to be ruled by a female, preferring to wait for a King Rose to ripen rather than pick the beautifully ripe Rose Princess. As the Kingdom's ignorant denizens put it: "We won't have her! We want a King! ... No girl shall rule over us!"[26] When Betsy and Shaggy pick her anyway, they and the Princess and Betsy's mule Hank are banished from the Rose Kingdom, but Shaggy is on an important mission to free his enslaved brother, and the girls and Hank, soon joined by Polychrome and Tik-Tok, accompany him to help.

Baum has repeatedly shown his understanding that women can be excellent leaders. However, he parallels the story of the Rose Princess, and its call for gender equity and female empowerment, with an illustration that female leaders are equally as capable of being tyrants. In this book's parallel story, the power-hungry Queen Ann Soforth seeks to conquer, plunder, and enslave her neighbors, and, indeed, the world. Ruler of the tiny kingdom of Oogaboo in a far corner of Oz, Queen Ann has "a warlike spirit that preferred trouble to idleness."[27] She has grown bored of ruling her tiny kingdom, and so decides to form an army (of 16 officers and one private) to conquer the inhabitants of the world and "inform them that they are our slaves."[28]

Queen Ann is a somewhat more comic manifestation of the power-hungry tyrant than are, for instance, the Nome King and his allies. Ann's tiny army is rather cowardly and hopes to avoid conflict. Only the lone private, Files, is interested in fighting. The rest remain on their mission with Queen Ann not out of loyalty to her or the cause, but out of fear of her temper and of Private Files's gun. They quickly get lost, find no one to conquer, and wish they were home.

Betsy Bobbin's and Queen Ann's parties eventually meet. Private Files sticks Queen Ann's banner in the ground with the declaration, "I hereby conquer this territory in the name of Queen Ann Soforth of Oogaboo, and all the inhabitants of the land I proclaim her slaves!"[29] However, the rest of the army trembles in fear at the sight of the Shaggy Man and Tik-Tok, and offer themselves up as slaves in exchange for being spared. The exasperated Queen Ann orders Private Files to capture Betsy, who declares, "we won't be anybody's slaves,"[30] while Files decides it is impolite to bind innocent girls and resigns. The officers are finally spurred into action by their queen's threat that if they do not recapture their gun–toting private, they are "liable to be captured and made slaves"[31] by a more powerful foe. The conflict is solved when the Shaggy Man produces his Love Magnet, and all present agree to band together to march upon the Nome King Ruggedo (the former King Roquat, who forgot his own name after drinking the water of forgetfulness) so that Shaggy can free his brother from slavery and Queen Ann can conquer a deserving foe.

Observing their approach, the Nome King constructs a trap to send them through a tube to the other side of the world, thinking that the group will be destroyed by the most powerful people in the world, the residents of Tititi-Hoochoo. But those people, we learn, are so strong because they are self–directed and equal; they are not kings or tyrants, but they are powerful because they are "private citizens." Being as wise as they are powerful, they recognize that the intruders did not disturb them voluntarily, and so they send a Dragon to join in the effort to conquer Ruggedo.

The battle, then, is set, with a willing and cooperative band of allies on one side and Ruggedo and his troops on the other. But Ruggedo's army is hardly motivated to any loyal self–sacrifice on his behalf. Ruggedo uses his Nomes cruelly, and they refuse to do any work when their master is not around, even though he whips them when he is present.[32]

When the party of abolitionists arrives, Ruggedo falls in love with Polychrome and tries to seize her. He also tries to make Tik-Tok a slave, but Tik-Tok, now in possession of the group's only gun, raises it, and the Nomes retreat in fear. Reminiscent of John Brown's practice of using violence only in self–defense, Queen Ann tells Tik-Tok not to use his gun unless it is necessary, and Tik-Tok announces to the Nomes that he will fire only if they try to capture him.

Ruggedo is handily defeated and replaced by the kinder, gentler Kaliko, who, as his name (i.e., Calico) suggests, seems to be the most feminine character we meet among the hyper–masculine Nomes. Afterward, young Betsy wonders why, after all, the Shaggy Man's brother needed to be freed at such trouble, for they discovered him living in a forest in an underground cavern so large "it is almost like being out of doors."[33] He eats "the best food in the world"[34] and is not required to do any work. Betsy comments, "Why, it's more like visiting than being a prisoner."[35] But Ruggedo had made him the Ugly One by altering his appearance, a form of enslavement that appears frequently throughout Baum's Oz series. And, as Kaliko explains the problem, the slave "cannot go where or when he pleases, and is not his own master."[36]

The tenth Oz book, *The Scarecrow of Oz*, contains a story similar to that of the Rose Princess: a rightful female ruler is being denied her position as Queen, and worse still, the ruling powers try to force her into marital slavery against her will. The false King Krewl is not only keeping his niece Gloria from assuming her rightful place on the throne, but he is trying to make her wed the wealthy Googly-goo, wanting to sell Gloria into marriage for a bunch of jewels. But Gloria loves Pon, the gardener's boy, a common servant, who later proves to have his own possible claim on the throne. King Krewl hires witches to freeze Gloria's heart so that she will not love Pon, thinking this will force her to marry Googly-goo.

Again, a diverse array of forces, this time led by the Scarecrow, Cap'n Bill, Trot, and a flying Ork, unite to defeat the tyrants; and again, we learn that cooperation and negotiation prove far more durable than coercion. For instance, Cap'n Bill, desperate for transportation, temporarily captures some birds but then offers them a deal: he will use a magical formula to greatly increase the size of volunteers, if they are willing to carry him and his friends to their destination, and afterwards the birds will keep their new powers. A number of the birds volunteer for the service. There are several instances like this one in the Oz books — the heroes might engage in tricks for a moment, but any transformation or service must be done with free consent.

And again, we learn that the tyrannical rulers are essentially cowards who flee at the first sign of real danger. The people, freed from their wicked rule, are offered the choice between the two royal claimants, Gloria and Pon, and by a comfortable majority, they vote for the female leader (who has indeed proved rather more durable and intelligent), demonstrating that the inhabitants of that land were far wiser than the inhabitants of the Rose Kingdom in the previous book.

Baum's next tale, *Rinkitink in Oz,* was published in 1916, at the height of World War I, and symbolically appropriates themes from that conflict. The boy prince Inga and the people of Pingaree, living a peaceful seafaring existence on an island in the Nonestic Ocean, are attacked by warriors from Regos and Coregos, islands to the north. Surprised by the attack, nearly all the inhabitants of Pingaree are captured and enslaved, with the males sent to work in one of the conquering kingdoms and the women in the other. The only ones left are Inga, the visiting king Rinkitink, and his talking goat Bilbil. This story is especially concerned with the rights of seafaring peoples, appropriate for an American public troubled by the sinking of the Lusitania and by advertisements published in American newspapers by the German powers, forbidding Americans the right to travel by boat to trade or visit with Germany's adversaries.

Inga, like Dorothy, discovers a potent type of magic that will aid him in his quest to free the slaves — a set of pink, white and blue pearls (likely symbolizing the colors of the American flag) that give him strength, wisdom, and protection from harm. The pearl of wisdom advises Inga to make a journey to free the slaves and leads him to a "lustrous" black boat — whose color we may compare with Toto's — that will lead him directly to the heart of the slave owning states.

Much of this tale is concerned with the comic bickering between Rinkitink and Bilbil. Although jolly Rinkitink is ostensibly King and surly Bilbil is ostensibly his servant, Bilbil is obstreperous, working only on his own terms and after having sardonically lambasted the fat king Rinkitink along the way. This interaction, full of humor and compromise, contrasts with the humorless and severe slave owners of Regos and Coregos, who are willing to engage in negotiation only when it becomes clear that they have no power to conquer by force of arms, and even then, they negotiate without any spirit of honesty.

Just as Dorothy loses one of her silver shoes but still manages to defeat the Wicked Witch, so too Inga loses two of his pearls and is left, for a time, with only the white pearl of wisdom, which continues to counsel him that patience, bravery, and determination will lead him to emancipate the slaves. And, indeed, by his own persistent efforts and by the cooperation of an ever-widening circle of friends, Inga recovers the lost magic, sets the slave owners to flight, frees the slaves, and becomes reunited with his family and people. After a celebratory visit to Oz, Bilbil is revealed to have formerly been the Prince Bobo, who was placed under an evil transforming charm, and he is returned by Glinda's magic to his former status.

We may do well to compare the 1916 adventure of Bilbil/Bobo and Rinkitink with J.R.R. Tolkien's story of Bilbo and the history of the freeing of the slaves in Middle Earth, published starting two decades later. The Hobbit Bilbo, like Rinkitink, is a short, fat, humorous homebody who is coerced to embark on an adventure against his initial will, but who proves rather good at it. Bilbo, like Rinkitink, is the very epitome of avuncular, whose main function is to aid his nephew in battling against Sauron, the slave owning Wicked Wizard of the East. For in both Baum's Oz and Tolkien's Middle Earth, it is merely a halfling, a youth, who will strike the death blow against the immensely powerful slave owners.

The Lost Princess of Oz (1917) opens with the discovery that several powerful magic items of Oz have disappeared, and Ozma herself has gone missing. Ozma's friends quickly join together to plan her rescue. Loyal Dorothy is willing to face risks to save her friend: "'We'll not get into danger if we can poss'bly help it,' promised Dorothy, 'but we shall do anything to find Ozma, danger or no danger.'"[37] They are even willing to face the dreaded Herkus, who are so powerful that they "are waited upon by giants whom they have conquered and made their slaves."[38] The rescuers soon learn that the likely suspect in Ozma's kidnapping is a former Herku citizen and magician called Ugu the Shoemaker who is "very ambitious to become the most powerful magician in the world."[39]

On the way to his castle, they meet another band of travelers in search of the same magician, for he has also stolen the magic diamond-studded gold dishpan from Cayke the Cookie Cook. The Wizard proposes the two groups of travelers team up to get back what has been stolen, for "We must go to the Shoemaker in one mighty band, for only in union is there strength."[40]

These allies have again found the power of cooperative work and of utilizing the strengths and skills of the various members of the group. Ugu, by contrast, works alone, convinced that his intelligence and power is superior to anyone else's and, thus, that he is worthy of ruling over others. The path to wickedness indeed takes this indirect route, for Ugu did not regard himself as evil, but "wanted to be powerful and great, and he hoped to make himself master of all the Land of Oz that he might compel everyone in that fair country to obey him. His ambition blinded him to the rights of others, and he imagined anyone else would act just as he did if anyone else happened to be as clever as himself."[41] It is clear that his ambitions involve subjugation and enslavement, as he hoped that with his theft of powerful magical equipment, and elimination of his rivals, he "could force all the inhabitants of that fairyland to do as he willed."[42]

But as we have learned from previous lessons of the Oz series, when comrades band together loyally to serve a cause, their power increases exponentially to defeat seemingly insurmountable dangers. Though certainly less powerful in physical strength and magical ability than the magician, the allies of Dorothy's party use their various intelligences and skills to overcome the barriers that Ugu has set for them: a ring of fire, a wall of steel, and a well-trained army.

Ugu, transformed into a dove after his defeat, sulks for a while before realizing that his powerless and benign condition is indeed superior to being a powerful but lonely magician. He flies to Dorothy to apologize, saying "I'm surprised that I was such a wicked man and had so little regard for the rights of others. I am now convinced that even had I succeeded in making myself ruler of all Oz, I should not have been happy, for many days of quiet thought have shown me that only those things one acquires honestly are able to render one content."[43] And Dorothy forgives him.

At the beginning of *The Tin Woodman of Oz* (1918), we meet the free-spirited Woot the Wanderer, master of his own decisions, who sets the stage for the contrast of the various forms of enslavement found throughout the remainder of the work. In the previous book, the Cowardly Lion encourages his comrades to appreciate the diversity of the group and take pride in their own unique forms. In this book, being unwillingly given another form is likened to slavery.

This story gives the account of the Tin Woodman's early love of the Munchkin girl Nimmie Amee, the personal slave of the Wicked Witch of the East (the Witch crushed by Dorothy's house in *The Wonderful Wizard of Oz*). His plans to marry Nimmie Amee were interrupted when he rusted in the forest and, unable to move, missed their wedding. The Tin Man is reminded of his marital promise by Woot, and they go on a journey, accompanied by the Scarecrow, to find out whether she is still interested in marrying him. Along the way, the three are trapped by the Giantess Mrs. Yoop, who enslaves people by transforming them into other creatures for her own amusement. In fact, they discover that she has already caught Polychrome and transformed her into a canary. Soon Woot, the Scarecrow, and the Tin Man are turned into unnatural shapes — a green monkey, a straw bear, and a tin owl.

Mrs. Yoop displays perhaps the most terrifying face of slave ownership from all the Oz books, as she is not ugly or laughable, but rather is as cultured, well-mannered, and witty as she is evil. The group hatches a plan of escape, and the boy Woot, despite his terror of capture, risks being caught to rescue Polychrome, even though he has not yet had the chance to befriend her.

The first major point of this book is that mere freedom from imprisonment is not sufficient to attain happiness; the form of a worthwhile life is also needed. Thus the party of four, though freed from Mrs. Yoop's castle, is still quite miserable, unable to regain their natural shapes that would allow them to live as they choose. They meet another character in a similar plight, Tommy Kwikstep, who has been transformed from a happy and fast runner to a tortured soul with twenty legs, now unable to perform his chosen work of quickly running errands for anyone who needed his services. Similarly, the American slaves, granted freedom from slavery but without political or economic autonomy, still remained far from the condition of true self-direction that would have allowed for individual and social harmony. As Polychrome puts it: "It is much nicer to be free, even though I still bear the enchanted form..." and as Woot agrees, "Neither of us can be happy again unless we recover our rightful forms."[44]

The second major point of this book is that true freedom involves the freedom to make one's own decisions. Freed from the enslavement of the Wicked Witch of the East, Nimmie Amee has achieved her measure of happiness with her chosen husband, and her decision is not at all the one that the Tin Woodman assumed all along she would make; it is decidedly her own.

The theme of the power of enslaving transformations is again central in the next book, *The Magic of Oz*. Kiki Aru, an unpleasant boy who is dissatisfied with his life, discovers a magic word that can transform himself and others into whatever he wishes. He uses his newfound power to escape his confining mountaintop life and soon meets the dispossessed Nome King, Ruggedo. Ruggedo wants to use Kiki's power to form an army and enslave the Oz people by trapping them in the forms of animals, while giving the animals of the forests, drafted into an army, the forms of the Oz people. The two conspirators secretly plan to double cross each other: Kiki does not trust Ruggedo and "promised himself that as soon as they had conquered Oz, he would transform the old Nome into a marble statue and keep him in that form forever,"[45] and Ruggedo plans to learn the boy's secret, then turn him into firewood and burn him up "and so be rid of him."[46] And this, Baum concludes, "is always the way with wicked people. They cannot be trusted even by one another."[47]

As Kiki and Ruggedo are scheming to secure the help of the most ferocious beasts of the wild forest of Gugu, Dorothy and the Wizard make their own plans to journey to the forest. Dorothy, trying to come up with an original birthday present for Ozma, wants tiny monkeys to jump out of her birthday cake and perform tricks. In clear opposition to the wickedness of Kiki Aru and Ruggedo, the Wizard stresses the importance of attaining consent to shrink and train the monkeys. He says, "I see no reason why we can't do it, just the way you say, if only we can get the wild monkeys to agree to it."[48]

Both parties head for the same forest with plans to convince the animals to agree to having their forms altered to serve someone else's purpose. The difference is that Dorothy and the Wizard plan on being honest with the animals, to convince them to adopt the foreign purpose as their own, and afterward be returned to their proper sizes and homes. Kiki and Ruggedo, whose plan would not otherwise appeal to the beasts, appear to them in the made-up forms of lion-monkey-eagle combinations, Li-Mon-Eags, and falsely claim that they are there "to warn the forest beasts that the people of Oz are about to make war upon them and enslave them, so that they will become beasts of burden forever after and obey only the will of their two-legged masters."[49]

The Leopard King objects in defense of the Oz people: "They have let us alone, and we have let them alone. There is no reason for war between us. They have no slaves. They could not use us as slaves if they should conquer us. I think you are telling us lies, you strange Li-Mon-Eag...."[50] Ruggedo then tries to appeal to avarice:

> The people of Oz have many good things — houses with soft beds, all sorts of nice-tasting food, pretty clothes, lovely jewels, and many other things that beasts know nothing of.... So I propose that before the Oz people have the time to make all those ropes to snare you with, that all we beasts get together and march against the Oz people and capture them. Then the beasts will become the masters and the people their slaves.[51]

Before the smooth-talking Ruggedo can convince the animals to attack the Oz people, Dorothy and the Wizard, riding on the Cowardly Lion and the Hungry Tiger, show up. When it becomes clear that the two big cats are respected by even the Leopard King and that these friends of the Oz people "would probably try to prevent war between the beasts of the forests and the people of Oz,"[52] Kiki decides he needs to act quickly before their plot is revealed and their plans foiled. He also decides to act without consulting Ruggedo, who up to this point had "wanted to do everything his own way, and made the boy, who alone possessed the power of transformations, obey his orders as if he were a slave."[53] Kiki quickly transforms Dorothy, the Wizard, the Cowardly Lion, the Hungry Tiger, the Leopard King, and even Ruggedo into different shapes and scrambles away as all the other forest animals disperse in panic.

Ruggedo and Kiki decide to try to salvage their plan by transforming some monkeys into giant soldiers and inducing them to fight the Oz people. Their plan backfires when the transformed monkeys are so big they are trapped by the trees, and the Wizard, transformed into the nimble form of a fox, overhears the magic word as Kiki is performing the transformations. The Wizard disables Kiki and Ruggedo by turning them into nuts, and after he transforms the giants back into monkeys, they are so grateful that when the Wizard asks for a dozen volunteers for Ozma's birthday party, a hundred offer their services.

Toward the end of the book, Baum gives a description of the ideal ruler in the personage of the former slave, Ozma of Oz. Kind, gentle, and just, Ozma understands that her position obliges her to solve her people's problems, ensuring that they are content and well cared for. Her character stands in stark contrast to some of the other rulers we have met in the series, those tyrants who use their position and power to exploit and oppress for their own gain. In her fairness, she does not discriminate against others, and is "the friend of the most humble person in her dominions."[54] Indeed, "Ozma was more interested in unusual people than in ordinary ones — just as you and I are."[55] She even gives old Ruggedo, his memory once again wiped clean by the fountain of oblivion, a place to live in the Land of Oz.

The last of Baum's Oz histories, *Glinda of Oz* (1920), is certainly the most modern of his tales. It has been said that with Tik-Tok Baum invented the first fictional robot, and in this last book, we find Baum giving, nearly three decades before George Orwell's *1984* and well prior to the formation of the East German Stasi, a portrayal of the total information awareness of universal surveillance as conducted by "democratic" dictatorships, which enslave and torture their peoples just as surely as did the old-fashioned type of dictatorship. Against this stand the efforts of Glinda — not as a solitary sorceress, but as one of the many famous people of Oz who have assembled, in a kind of "League of Nations" effort, to rescue Ozma and Dorothy from captivity and to bring an end to war and slavery in their fairy land.

Some commentators have called this the darkest of the Oz books. Perhaps this is because Baum removes slavery from the 1800's and its comfortably antique associations and reimagines it in the modern global and technological age. Still, this book is far brighter than Orwell's *1984* because Baum teaches that it is still the traditional philosophical disciplines — courage, loyalty, work, respect and care for others, and devoted openness to learning from others — that announce final emancipation, bringing to completion the process started in Oz by Dorothy and in Kansas by her immediate predecessors.

In *Glinda of Oz,* Baum quickly recalls us to the theme of slavery. Ozma and Dorothy, immediately after having set out on a journey to bring peace to the warring Skeezers and Flatheads, whose peoples are enslaved under cruel dictators, are surrounded and trapped by giant spiders. The spiders are hungry not for food, but for slaves; as the Spider King explains, "We need someone to keep house for us. There is sweeping and dusting to be done, and polishing and washing of dishes, and that is work my people dislike to do. So we decided that if any strangers came our way we should capture them and make them our servants."[56]

Forming an alliance with a crab, Ozma grants it protection from the spiders, and in exchange the crab cuts a hole in the powerful web that entraps them. After escaping, Dorothy wonders why magic cannot legitimately do the work that slavery illegitimately seeks to do — to make life easy for those in control. Ozma gives the lesson, in common with the teachings of Socrates and Hegel, that work itself is empowering:

> If every one could wave a wand and have his wants fulfilled there would be little to wish for. There would be no eager striving to obtain the difficult, for nothing would then be difficult, and the pleasure of earning something longed for, and only to be secured by hard work and careful thought, would be utterly lost. There would be nothing to do you see, and no interest in life and in our fellow creatures. That is all that makes life worth our while — to do good deeds and to help those less fortunate than ourselves.[57]

Further testifying to Oz's advanced political state, its wise leaders practice a post–war policy that sought to replace illegitimate leaders, rather than to punish their vanquished peoples as well. As Ozma puts it, "I do not think the Flathead people are as much to blame as their Supreme Dictator. If he is removed from power and his unlawful magic taken from him, the people will probably be good and respect the laws of the Land of Oz, and live at peace with all their neighbors in the future."[58] Had Ozma or Dorothy been in charge of implementing justice in post–World War I Europe, there likely would not have been a World War II. As Dorothy similarly puts the case to Ozma, in favor of replacing the corrupted leadership of the two parties warring at the edge of Oz: "My idea is that neither of them is fit to rule anybody, 'cause they're cruel and hateful. So you'll have to give the Skeezers and Flatheads new rulers and teach all their people that they're part of the Land of Oz...."[59]

Victory is achieved just as surely for the Skeezers and the Flatheads as it was for Ojo, precisely by their defeats — to be defeated by justice is to commence with an empowering education. And to make the case for America's wars more plausible, whether in Iraq, Afghanistan, Vietnam, or Grenada, might not the invading heroes say with Glinda and Ozma, in addition to "Nation X is ruled by cruel and corrupt dictators who ought to be overthrown," that "Victory in Nation X shall be achieved when an excellent Academy has been established there"? This practically successful idea was understood both by Baum and some of the wiser overseers of reconstruction on post–World War II West Germany. Baum knew, following Socrates's lesson, that the world improves not by causing pain to adversaries, but by increasing the number of smart, dutiful people and widening the field on which those individuals can visit one another.

This is Baum's case for the modern manifestation of the classical ideal; it is not "dark," but light. And its hope is not a naïve one, as Baum's childhood witnessed the coming of national unity after America broke many of the bonds of its self–imposed slavery. This renewed hope was purchased at a tremendous price — it would take *six million* war deaths in America today to proportionally approximate the death toll from its Civil War.

What then shall be the new ideal? It is Oz's governing principle, embodied in its sole legal dictum under the rulership of Ozma: "Behave yourself." It is, in other words, philosophy's principle of Rational Autonomy. This means to work, to play, to help the needy, and to serve a culture comprising many colors and both genders. Sometimes, by necessity, it also means to struggle to overcome those whose growing appetites cause them to fail to behave themselves and who seek to own or control others.

The last words Baum grants of the occurrences of Oz are his farewell gift to his readers. It is Scraps, the runaway slave, who proposes the solution to free Ozma and Dorothy from their imprisonment, and it takes the collaboration of many of their friends — some born free, some born slaves, and one among them even a former tyrant — to implement the rescue. It is Glinda who conceives of the plan to provide the former slave owners with the education and intelligence that will allow them to overcome their selfish ways, and it is Ozma — herself a runaway slave — who approves the plan and advises that it is our duty not merely to free the slaves, but also to free the slave owners, even if such a duty is not a pleasant one.

The Metaphysics of Equality in Oz

Baum has been accused, by some critics, of a racist disregard of the rights or opinions of certain groups. These critics typically cite some of Baum's journalistic editorials from his Dakota days or his early poetry to justify these claims, and several recent republishers of the Oz books, instead of criticizing, have simply excised passages so as to protect their sensitive readers' eyes from sentences that might make fun of whatever group is to be considered especially under that publisher's protectorate.

As for the newspaper editorials, we have read them and were struck not by their racism, but by Baum's loud and bitterly ironic denunciation of the racist genocide of the Native peoples that was occurring at the time of their publication. In these editorials, Baum mocks those who destroy the Native peoples using so many jokes, so tightly packed together, that one comes to realize that he needed to write the Oz books in part so that he could retell the jokes, but with some plot in between them — a plot in which the laughable oppressors, instead of losing by "winning," are saved from their folly by being defeated by a dangerous gang of polite girls.

One can only forgive the honest comedian for gallows humor, and not condemn him. Genocide was being committed, and in his journalism, Baum hollered as a witness at the scene of the crime. It is not to discredit the other American critics of genocide of that day, but it is indeed the case that most of them wrote from comfortably distant East Coast cities while Baum did it from near the front lines of battle.

As for the passages stricken from the Oz pages by morally zealous, humorless republishers — we can justify their survival and continued inclusion in reprintings of the Oz stories with two reasons. First, Baum jokes at everyone's expense, and this may be the reason why his mother-in-law, Matilda Gage, the well-known abolitionist, first encouraged him to publish his poetry. A Jew who tells Jew jokes and Nazi jokes and Irish jokes and Black jokes and Polish jokes is plainly of a different ethical stature than a Nazi who tells only Jewish and Polish jokes. There is moral discernment involved in making the distinction, but once the labor of this discernment is conducted, the judgment should be obvious. But the publisher who excises precisely one category of jokes told "at the expense of" one particular group, while leaving all the others in place, has clearly not done the work of making this distinction, and certainly is not doing anyone any favors.

Second, all the winning epistemological and ethical arguments of Oz point to a committed pluralistic theory. In *The Patchwork Girl of Oz*, Scraps is merely the first character to truly appreciate her own racial beauty; the Glass Cat and the Woozy later revel in their own — the Woozy in a fully sympathetic manner, and the Glass Cat in an obnoxiously superior, racist manner. But the cat is at least not aggressively racist; it is simply an arrogant cat.

Just as most of the good people of Oz turn away from socializing with the Glass Cat, the Tin Woodman turns away from socializing with himself— upon meeting the head of his former Munchkin body (who lives on even after the Tin Woodman receives his new tin head), he hears his old self say, "It would be unnatural for me to have any interest in a man made of tin. Please close the door and leave me alone." The unflappably dapper Woodman stutters, perhaps the only time he ever does: "'I did not think that my old Head could be so disagreeable,' said the Emperor. 'I — I'm quite ashamed of myself; meaning you.'"[60] Perhaps Baum did indeed harbor some secret racism in his youth; perhaps we all do. But even if Baum held such a secret, he at least had the dignity to become educated until he knew to be ashamed of it, to close the door, and to walk away.

In *The Lost Princess of Oz*, Toto, the Cowardly Lion, Hank the Mule, the Woozy, and the Sawhorse argue over which of them is the most beautiful. The Lion finally resolves the argument by explaining,

> Were we all like the Sawhorse, we would all be Sawhorses, which would be too many of the kind ... were you all like me, I would consider you so common that I would not care to associate with you. To be individual, my friends, to be different from others, is the only way to become distinguished from the common herd. Let us be glad, therefore, that we differ from one another in form and in disposition. Variety is the spice of life, and we are various enough to enjoy one another's society; so let us be content.[61]

In Oz, those who do well are those who appreciate both diversity and humor. All are to be loved and appreciated, and all can be teased, while imperialism and tyranny are temptations for all those who take themselves entirely too seriously while not taking others seriously at all.

Perhaps we of the ever-rising new day, with all the comfortable support of our global politics and the blanket of our national power, have taken to thinking that we are innately superior, that our neighbors are weak because they are destined to do our bidding, and that the weak at home and abroad should be consumed to satisfy our proliferating desires or to cure whatever ails or annoys us. Perhaps we have forgotten to laugh in the appropriate way. Such a landscape would be a dreary one, like Ruggedo's underground kingdom.

So too, things were dreary in the enslaved America of Baum's youth. And Dorothy comes from a gray, gray, dreary place, the parched plains of Kansas.

Yet, she can laugh and make loyal friends no matter their color: blue, black, yellow, tin, patchwork. And, thus, she proves that she has learned, from her Free State Kansas predecessors, the ethical, epistemological and indeed metaphysical secret of success — we overcome our limitations as merely finite individuals, just as our communities overcome their limitations as finite communities, by philosophical cooperation with neighbors. Two little abolitionists, Dorothy and Toto, just crash landed in the big, mean slave state of Oz — they're going to need all the help they can get.

Notes

1. Baum, L. Frank. *The Wonderful Wizard of Oz.* Project Gutenberg EBook, Chapter 2. All references of Baum's books in this article will be to the Project Gutenberg Ebook versions of those texts, which can be found at http://www.gutenberg.org. Since these versions of his work contain no page numbers, we will reference the individual book and chapter.

2. Jason Bell and Jessica Bell, "Freeing the Slaves in Oz," in *The Wizard of Oz and Philosophy*, edited by Randall E. Auxier and Phillip S. Seng (Chicago: Open Court, 2008), 49–62.

3. *The Marvelous Land of Oz*, Chapter 3.

4. *Dorothy and the Wizard in Oz*, Chapter 19.

5. *The Emerald City of Oz*, Chapter 26.

6. Ibid., Chapter 3.

7. Ibid., Chapter 4.

8. Ibid., Chapter 8.

9. Ibid., Chapter 27.

10. *The Patchwork Girl of Oz*, Chapter 5.

11. Ibid., Chapter 2.

12. Ibid.

13. Ibid., Chapter 3.

14. Ibid.

15. Ibid., Chapter 2.

16. Ibid., Chapter 5.

17. Ibid., Chapter 13.

18. Ibid., Chapter 14.

19. Ibid., Chapter 3.

20. Ibid., Chapter 23.

21. Ibid., Chapter 18.

22. Ibid., Chapter 15.

23. Ibid.

24. Ibid., Chapter 28.

25. *Little Wizard Stories of Oz*, "Little Dorothy and Toto."

26. *Tik-Tok of Oz*, Chapter 6.

27. Ibid., Chapter 1.

28. Ibid., Chapter 3.

29. Ibid., 8.

30. Ibid.

31. Ibid.

32. Ibid., Chapter 14.

33. Ibid., Chapter 19.

34. Ibid., Chapter 22.

35. Ibid., Chapter 19.

36. Ibid.

37. *The Lost Princess of Oz,* Chapter 6.
38. Ibid.
39. Ibid., Chapter 12.
40. Ibid.
41. Ibid., Chapter 19.
42. Ibid.
43. Ibid., Chapter 26.
44. *The Tin Woodman of Oz,* Chapter 11.
45. *The Magic of Oz,* Chapter 4.
46. Ibid.
47. Ibid.
48. Ibid., Chapter 6.
49. Ibid., Chapter 8.
50. Ibid., Chapter 8.
51. Ibid.
52. Ibid., Chapter 12.
53. Ibid.
54. Ibid.
55. Ibid., Chapter 22.
56. *Glinda of Oz,* Chapter 2.
57. Ibid.
58. Ibid., Chapter 7.
59. Ibid., Chapter 9.
60. *The Tin Woodman of Oz,* Chapter 18.
61. *The Lost Princess of Oz* Chapter 10.

Works Cited

Baum, L. Frank. *Dorothy and the Wizard in Oz.* New York: Rand McNally, 1971.
_____. *The Emerald City of Oz.* New York: HarperCollins, 1993.
_____. *Glinda of Oz.* New York: HarperCollins, 2000.
_____. *Little Wizard Stories of Oz.* New York: HarperCollins, 1994.
_____. *The Lost Princess of Oz.* New York: HarperCollins, 1998.
_____. *The Magic of Oz.* New York: HarperCollins, 1999.
_____. *The Marvelous Land of Oz.* New York: HarperCollins, 1985.
_____. *The Patchwork Girl of Oz.* New York: HarperCollins, 1995.
_____. *Tik-Tok of Oz.* New York: HarperCollins, 1996.
_____. *The Tin Woodman of Oz.,* New York: HarperCollins, 1998.
Bell, Jason, and Jessica Bell. "Freeing the Slaves in Oz." In *The Wizard of Oz and Philosophy.* Eds. R. Auxier and P. Seng. Chicago: Open Court, 2008.

About the Contributors

Randall Auxier was the keynote speaker at OZ 2009: The Yellow Brick Road in the 21st century. His lecture there continued his fascination with all things Oz. He is the editor of works on Oz and the Grateful Dead. In his non–pop culture life, he directs the Library of Living Philosophers and teaches philosophy at Southern Illinois, Carbondale. He and Kevin Durand are constantly amazed that they moved in the same circles for years at Emory, only to finally meet each other in Oklahoma.

Claudia A. Beach serves as director of theatre at Henderson State University (Arkansas), where she teaches classes in acting, directing, theatre history and playwriting. She earned degrees from Stephen F. Austin State University and a Ph.D. from Texas Tech. She has directed more than sixty theatrical productions and acted in Shakespeare festivals, summer stock, dinner theatres, and television commercials. She has been named College Teacher of the Year by the Arkansas State Communication Association, is a past board member of the Southwest Theatre and Film Association, and past editor of *Southwest Theatre Journal*.

Jessica and Jason Bell are very grateful to Randall Auxier for giving them the idea to write about Oz. Their children are a constant reminder of the joy and wisdom one encounters in Oz. They try to recall that youthful wisdom for their older students. Jessica teaches science and social studies at the Casady School in Oklahoma City; Jason teaches philosophy at the University of Central Oklahoma in Edmond.

Agnes B. Curry spent her high school and college years in Atchison and has thus been subject to every possible joke about not being in Kansas anymore. Her initial acquaintance with *The Wizard of Oz* was with the movie at about age 5, and she still harbors a fear of trees. At Saint Joseph College in West Hartford, Connecticut, she teaches philosophy and directs the Honors Program. One of her mantras to students is that "philosophy is everywhere" and to demonstrate that point, she talks a lot about television programs and popular culture.

Kevin K. Durand came to Baum's Oz in an odd way — in the middle of a hurricane in Louisiana. *The Wonderful Wizard of Oz* was tucked alongside *Gone with the Wind* on his grandparents' bookshelf. He teaches philosophy at Henderson State University, where his department colleagues range from amused to enthusiastic about Oz. He continues to point out that Plato and Aristotle both thought the theatre of the day worthwhile grist for the philosophical mill.

Charity Gibson became interested in *The Wizard of Oz* during the time of her graduate studies while taking a children's literature course. She graduated from the College of the Ozarks with a degree in English education and completed her master's degree from Missouri State University where she focused on English literature. She currently teaches and resides with her husband in southern Missouri.

Jené Gutierrez is a graduate student at Texas State University, pursuing a master's degree in literature. Like many others, she has cherished the story of Dorothy's journey since her first encounter with the film version, enhanced by her study of Joseph Campbell. She has no doubt that *The Wizard of Oz* will endure many years as one of the most beloved tales of all time.

Paula R. Kent has enjoyed *The Wizard of Oz* ever since her parents first suggested she see the movie and she witnessed her twin sister roll under the family coffee table in fear of the Wicked Witch of the West and her flying monkeys. She is completing work on her doctorate while teaching composition at Texas Woman's University.

Mary K. Leigh is completing a master's degree at Henderson State University in Arkadelphia, Arkansas. With combined areas of study in literature and philosophy, she often finds herself demonstrating to her students the relevance of popular culture to just about everything. Seeing *Wicked: A New Musical* in London opened her eyes to the many facets of the Land of Oz. Her current project concerns Aristotelian virtue ethics and *The Dark Knight*.

Gail Linsenbard teaches social and political philosophy in the Liberal Studies Program at New York University. In addition to her published papers on Sartre, Simone de Beauvoir, and William James, her book *Starting with Sartre* will appear in 2010.

Emily A. Mattingly is a Ph.D. student at the University of California, Riverside. She specializes in modern American literature and culture, children's and adolescent literature, and gender and sexuality studies. Her recent research focuses mainly on girlhood, feminist and queer theories, intertextuality, performativity, and gendered violence. A recent Kansas transplant who now lives among Southern California's orange groves, she frequently visits the Land of Oz with her little dog, too.

Kristin Noone is a Ph.D. student at the University of California, Riverside, where she is studying the intersections of medieval literature, fantasy literature, and popular culture. Her academic writing has covered such topics as Welsh mythology and popular culture, ghosts in medieval romance, unicorns and Robin Hood, Beowulf on film, and grotesque heroes in the land of Oz, and her short fantasy fiction has appeared in anthologies such as *Marion Zimmer Bradley's Sword & Sorceress 23* and *Strange Worlds of Lunacy*, and (forthcoming) the magazine *Aoife's Kiss*.

Anne Collins Smith read many fantasy works as a child and her interest has never abated. She counts herself lucky to be not only permitted but encouraged to teach courses and write articles on philosophical topics in *Star Trek* and *Harry Potter*. Viewing *Tin Man* reminded her of her early love of the Oz series and she has returned to it with enthusiasm.

Kevin P. S. Tanner, Jr., came to know Oz by being raised in Chittenango, New York, the birthplace of L. Frank Baum. He lived in a hometown with yellow brick sidewalks and shops named after various Oz characters and places and witnessed its annual parade celebrating Baum's birthday several times over the years. He teaches American history at Austin Peay State University.

Josef Velazquez teaches philosophy at Stonehill College in Easton, Massachusetts. He wishes to thank his friend Agnes Curry for letting him get involved in her projects on philosophy and popular culture. He also wishes to thank his friend John Golden for turning him on to Russian Formalism.

Ronald J. Zank watched the film *The Wizard of Oz* throughout his childhood and was shocked to discover there was a book at his local library. Despite more than 25 years working in theatre, his only Oz-related production has been *Scraps! The Ragtime Girl of Oz*. He is lucky to have faculty at the University of Missouri encourage him to write about adaptations of Oz for his dissertation. When not Oz-ifying, his research includes musical theatre, the Federal Theatre Project, gay and lesbian playwrights, *Buffy the Vampire Slayer* and early to mid–20th century drama.

Index